PRAYING UNTO SALVATION

A *Study of Righteousness*

Patricia Nordean

May 2021

To my dear friends
Steve and Cathy Corcoran
and their wonderful family of
seven children!
God bless you abundantly

Patricia Susan Nordean

DEDICATION

To my loving husband

Carroll Russell

*without whom this book would truly not have been possible.
Thank you, Sweetheart, for your support, encouragement,
and technical help during the fifteen years of spiritual
growth which developed this reference work. Your faithful
prayers have covered me.*

To our children:
Honey Amber and John Elijah
Joshua Carroll and Afton Janelle
Jeremiah Taft
Elijah Vincent
Bear John Carroll
Boss Ryan
Boone Ransom

To my mother, Judith Evelyn, who led me to the Lord.

I love you all forever.

ACKNOWLEDGEMENTS

I wish to thank those whose ministry I greatly
appreciate:

Rev. Kenneth Wayne Hagin and Rev. Lynette Rooker Hagin
Rhema Bible Church and Training Center

Rev. Pat Robertson
Christian Broadcasting Network

Revs. Richard and Lindsay Roberts
Oral Roberts University

Pastors Billy Joe and Sharon Daugherty
Victory Christian Center and Bible Institute

Pastors David and Judith Curry
Liberty Christian Fellowship, Belfast, Ireland

Pastors Rodney and Adonica Howard-Browne
River Revival Church .and Bible Training Center

As my first teachers of the things of God:

Mary Taulbert
Jeanne Wilkerson
Sister Gwen Shaw
Rev. Clara Parfitt

With special thanks and appreciation for their
lives of faith:

Rev. and Mrs. Tim Stemple – Family Prayer Center
Rev. Gary Carpenter–Family Prayer Center
Rev. Douglas Jones—Rhema Bible Church
Rev. Anthony Cook—Rhema Bible Church
Rev. Brian McCallum—Rhema Bible Church
Rev. Ron McIntosh–Victory Bible Institute

For the eternal impartations of God's glory
special appreciation to:

REV. KENNETH E. HAGIN

REV. ELSIE JUSTUS

PASTOR BENNY HINN

PASTOR DAVE ROBERSON

PRAYING UNTO SALVATION

FOREWORD

**Acts 13:26 Brethren, sons of the family of Abraham, and all those
others among you who reverence and fear God, to us has been sent
the message of this salvation [the salvation obtained
through Jesus Christ]. AMP**

*J*ust as there exist a myriad of denominational,
non-denominational, interdenominational and
other churches that profess a saving knowledge of
the Lord Jesus Christ, so there are many and varied
ways, methods and techniques to pray for the lost
of humanity that have resulted in varying degrees of
success. Throughout the Church Age those given to
prayer, the Hidden Stones, as intercessors have been
called by missionaries, have had experience with the
supernatural power of God flowing through them that
resulted in the salvation of an individual, people
group or nation. Christian martyrs—the hidden stones
of our foundation—are those who choose to suffer
death rather than to deny Christ or His work. Hidden
stones sacrifice something very important to further
the Kingdom of God. They endure great suffering for
Christian witness. As the Ruwach, the wind of the
Holy Spirit or the breath of God, has blown upon the
dust of this earth's humanity through the centuries,
life has resulted in this group and that group, each

ix

receiving the strength and faith to understand and believe some part of the Sozo (salvation) of the Almighty. Jesus has the key of David and the keys of hell and death, Peter was given the keys of the Kingdom of heaven, the Mosaic Law contains the key of knowledge, Scripture mentions the key to doors of the upper room and as the Father grants us revelation knowledge, understanding and wisdom in His ways; we are able to appropriate more and more of what Jesus died to obtain for His body. It is the understanding of these ways and the use of these keys, the knowledge of His truths and the operation of His laws that enable us to set the captives free. Faith will prove a key to unlock every mystery of the truth; obedience will secure our entrance through the door thus opened. Jesus has the key of David — He opens the doors no man can shut and shuts the doors no man can open. He has the keys of hell and of death. All power is given unto Him in heaven and in earth. Jesus Christ is God. Jesus is the Holy One, the True One, and the Faithful and True Witness. He is the Authorized One. How does this concern us? When we are born again, we are seated at the right hand of God <u>in Christ Jesus,</u> far above all principalities, powers, rulers of darkness, thrones, dominions, and every name that can be named in heaven and in earth. Scripture mentions the way of peace, the way of truth, the way of righteousness, and the way of salvation. *Acts 16:17 …These men are the servants of the most high God, which shew unto us the way of salvation.* This book is concerned with the way of salvation.

Brother Kenneth E. Hagin often said that we Christians who hear prophetic utterances of the Holy Spirit understand what has been spoken, but 97% of the time our interpretation of God's purpose through the prophetic utterance is skewed. I believe the focus of the Church, especially in Pentecostal/ Charismatic circles, with regard to salvation, is skewed. Rather than focusing on Christ's victory at Calvary we have skipped over it. We are to focus on

Christ at Calvary and on the salvation of lost souls. This is why God filled us with His Holy Spirit. The resurrection power of Jesus Christ is for the purpose of seeing the lost saved. This is God's purpose for the Age of Grace. Having understanding of the following chapters that results in affirmative action will produce righteousness. Instead of this, one portion of the Body of Christ has focused on the world as a source and turned inward to look at the Church. Another group in the Body of Christ has merely paused at the Cross of Christ and instead focuses on the resurrection power of Christ and the portions of Scripture found in the Epistles to the Church. Almost every believer I have come in contact with is a member of a particular "camp" or belief system within the Body of Christ. When Israel returned from Babylon there were no longer tribes or camps within that nation. Let's let go of religion and come up higher in God! The blessings of God are only able to come upon the Body of Christ when we are unified. From the Body of Christ God's blessings will spread to all Mankind. *Psalm 133. Behold, how good and how pleasant it is for brethren to dwell together in unity! It is like the precious ointment upon the head, that ran down upon the beard, even Aaron's beard: that went down to the skirts of his garments; as the dew of Hermon, and as the dew that descended upon the mountains of Zion: for there the LORD commanded the blessing, even life for evermore. KJV* I believe our vision of Jesus Christ and His so great salvation needs to be bigger and more unified. The day that is coming is a Day of Reformation for God shall bring the Church back to center. The Hand of the Lord is bringing this to pass. God is One. He desires oneness with the Body of Christ. Satan divides and fractures. Rather than using the information in this book to start a new denomination, let us eliminate fifty or so denominations and come into unity in the Body of Christ with the Oneness only found in God.

This reference work has been written to point its
readers to the Lord Jesus Christ. He is our Way, our
Truth, and our Life. This is not a new creed given
to foster belief in what is believed **about** Christ.
Rather it is given to point the way to spontaneous
joy and freedom **in** Christ Jesus. It is given to help
readers understand God's will and do it. I wrote
this book because I wanted to be sure that I understood what the Bible teaches about salvation. I am
going to heaven. I desire an abundant entrance to
heaven. I desire to understand the will of God and
to DO it properly according to God's revealed Word.
I want to obey God! However, I can't obey Him if I
haven't studied to show myself approved unto Him. We
have all our existence in God. He is great and vast
and, frankly, beyond our comprehension. Therefore,
although Jesus Christ is the only Door into God,
once we have entered Him, the room we enter is so
vastly enormous that we cannot see the walls! He is
our only way to find pasture. He is our only way to
enter in and out. God Himself is so wonderful, with
so many glories, that our entire life must be spent
discovering Him. I began this study when I encoun-
tered a crisis in my life. It began as an endeavor
to understand and document the truth of Scripture
with regard to salvation. I am sure that the salvation of the lost is the will of God. Therefore I have
proceeded from this point forth to understand God's
will so that I might do it. Because of the weakness
and futility of my personal humanity I would ask you,
the reader, not to speak against the truths contained herein. I am not God! I am endeavoring, just
as you are, to know Him. Jesus said, *"Whoever says
a word against the Son of man will be forgiven, but
whoever speaks against the holy Spirit will never
be forgiven, neither in this world nor in the world
to come." Matthew 12:32.* Rather, ASK GOD! Ask Him to
reveal the truth of the matter to you, personally.
I do not want your blood on my hands. It has been
well said that he who knows only his own position
does not know even that. It is good to widen our

outlook even if we do not change our position; for, as Dorothy Sayers wrote: "There's nothing you can't prove if your outlook is only sufficiently limited."

Many Christians in today's world perceive salvation as an accomplished fact, which it is, but they are proceeding forward from their knowledge of salvation into that new thing or the next step for mankind, etc. For example read Jesus' post resurrection discussion with the disciples in *Acts 1:6-8*. However, I believe that the times and the seasons are in God's Hands and only He can move us forward past this Age of Grace. He has given us a job to do, which we have not completed, and nothing is happening or will happen until we get the job done. God clearly told us through Jesus Christ that the end of the Age would not come until the gospel of the Kingdom is preached "in the whole world as a testimony to all nations." I really don't think very many "Christians" know what the gospel of the Kingdom is. The Gospel of the Kingdom is JESUS! He is our righteousness, peace and joy. The King rules His Kingdom and there is much to learn of Him. ALL His enemies shall be put beneath His Feet!

So many people want to question the Word of God, add to the Word of God, weaken the Word of God, lie against the Word of God, or misinterpret the Word of God. These attitudes are what caused the Fall of man in the Garden of Eden. God's realities are subtle. Rather I believe all of our answers to all of our problems lie within what the Father God accomplished through Jesus Christ on the Cross of Calvary and in His Resurrection. We must study and delve into that salvation that He has provided. All the answers lie within that act and we must search them out as though searching for gold and precious gems. *Proverbs 25:2 It is the glory of God to conceal a thing: but the honour of kings is to search out a matter.* Salvation has become almost passé among Christians — a three sentence prayer accompanied by a public appearance. Then the only obligation is to tithe, volunteer in your local church and forever sit as a spectator.

Yet the Fall of mankind in the Garden of Eden occasioned a visitation of Almighty God, the Creator of the Universe, to our planet. He has been here once and everything He did was done then. He is coming again. Therefore we should pay close attention and learn what He requires of us individually and corporately, growing in the grace and the knowledge of the Lord Jesus Christ until we accomplish His purposes and fulfill His plan. There are still provinces of the enemy that must be conquered!

Salvation occurs instantly and spiritual growth is a process. When conceived, a child is not immediately born. It requires nine months of formation or gestation. Converts are born. Disciples are made. It can be easy to get converts and very difficult to disciple them when they are converted. In today's society the process of spiritual formation has been skipped. On the whole, the Church has become fragmented, legalistic, and divisive or is no longer considered relevant. The same is true of spiritual formation. There is so much confusion in the world with regard to truth because Christian doctrine has been taught from different sources other than Jesus Christ. Doctrine has been and is being taught from a Pharisaical source, an Christological source, an Apostolical source and an Ecclesiastical source. I believe the true truths are hidden in the Person of Jesus Christ and His accomplished work at Calvary. *Colossians 2:2, 3 [For my concern is] that their hearts may be braced (comforted, cheered, and encouraged) as they are knit together in love, that they may come to have all the abounding wealth and blessings of assured conviction of understanding, and that they may become progressively more intimately acquainted with and may know more definitely and accurately and thoroughly that mystic secret of God, [which is] Christ (the Anointed one). In Him all the treasures of [divine] wisdom (comprehensive insight into the ways and purposes of God) and [all the riches of spiritual] knowledge and enlightenment are stored up and lie hidden. AMP* In the book of Daniel we are told that these hidden mysteries have been stored up until the time of the end. It is now time for them to be revealed.

Salvation is a progressively upward spiral toward God. In the Way of Salvation man is conformed to the image of God in Christ Jesus. Jesus Christ is our Promised Land. He is our Starry Night! In Ezekiel 20:33-44 the process of the Way of Salvation is delineated by the Holy Spirit of God through Ezekiel. In *Isaiah 60:18* it is written, *"Violence will not be heard again in your land, nor devastation or destruction within your borders; but you will call your walls salvation and your gates praise."* Isaiah 26:1-4 *"We have a strong city; He sets up walls and ramparts for security (salvation), open the gates, that the righteous nation may enter, the one that* <u>*remains faithful, the steadfast of mind*</u> *Thou wilt keep in perfect peace, because he trusts in Thee. Trust in the Lord forever, for in God the Lord, we have an everlasting Rock."* How is this accomplished? What is a steadfast mind? Mere intellectual knowledge or only visions makes one arrogant, but love builds a person up and makes them bold in character. Truth and love together bring humility and responsibility. Therefore we must set our mind on things above for our life is hidden in God. God's salvation is a protection to us — a hiding place. We enter into the Secret Place, the Shadow of the Almighty, because we died with Christ, and now we no longer live, but only Christ Jesus lives His life through us.

Jesus Christ had a program for training disciples. It still works today. He imparted into the lives of the 500, but He discipled the twelve. He had three who were closest to Him. He invested Himself in the twelve. We can't give other people something we ourselves don't have. We have to have God's vision and His plan. We have to have the grace of God in our lives to give it to somebody else. We must invest ourselves in other people. We must have genuine concern, care and love for those God brings to us. If not now, when? If not the person standing in front of you, then who? People are not paper towels—you don't throw them away. We have a responsibility to those given us of God to make them into vessels of honor, meet for the Master's use. Exponential growth of the gospel comes from mentoring disciples properly. First our own family members must be led to the Lord and discipled in the grace of God.

The salvation that the Heavenly Father provided before the beginning of the foundation of the earth in the shed blood of Jesus Christ belongs to all men now. The appropriation of that work which Christ accomplished must be realized in each individual's life. God made the way for every fiber of each person's being to be so flooded with His light and glory and liberty and love that heaven on earth may be realized now. The Apostle Paul prayed that those who were chosen would receive salvation with eternal glory. This is called the glorification of God. It is God's unmerited favor and blessing. It is available to each person on earth, but not all understand what it is or its value. They do not understand why it is important to appropriate the grace of God, or how to appropriate it. God working through redeemed mankind desires to establish the Kingdom of God upon the earth. God desires the Oneness of relationship with Mankind. The Good Samaritan, seeing the wounds and cruel blows the man had received, had compassion on him and went to him, bound up his wounds, poured in oil and wine, set him on his own beast, brought him to an inn, and took care of him. Is not this the example our Lord has set before us?

Therefore, at the end of this age we must gather together all the understanding and revelation knowledge we can corporately obtain to secure the Harvest. This book has been written for that purpose. Jeanne Wilkerson said: "If the universal church of the living God focused all the tributaries of prayer that flow from the main stream of God into the world today, we could turn the world right side up in no time. That is the truth! There is unfathomable power in prayer… Through the powerful release of prayer, we can influence the world's system and bring to pass the multitudinous promises and blessings of God." We need to correct our focus.

This last, huge end-time thrust of the Body of Christ during the Church Age will be accomplished by the whole body. Revival is needed that is permeated with a depth of repentance and a depth of discipleship, both personal and corporate. We each must have the Lord's vision, personally and for our own city, state and nation. We are not waiting for the Harvest, for the fields all around us are white unto Harvest. We must pray for laborers. Laborers must be prepared to abide in Christ and bring forth fruit that will remain throughout eternity. Each and every member of the Body, each and every organization and ministry, and each and every church and denomination, needs to receive and flow in the life of God. Each needs to repent of that thing that stands between them and God. Each must let go of fear. Each must do its part and move forward in the unity for which Jesus prayed in John 17. (*Joel 2*) Each of us must bring the will, plan and purpose of the Father to pass in love. Individuals will not predominate, churches will not predominate, ministries and organizations will not predominate, but all will have their part. The baton has passed from our fathers to us. It is time for our sons and daughters to go forth as laborers into the world system, doing signs, wonders, and miracles, and offering the salvation which Christ Jesus died to purchase for our planet. It is time for the miraculous! We must be able to dispense the true knowledge of salvation to them, that what they offer the lost will have the unlimited power of God. We want what is true, whole and complete, not a fragmented derivation of one group's revelation. Let every knee bow and every tongue confess that Jesus Christ is Lord! To the glory of the Father in heaven! Let us worship Him and obey Him in spirit and in truth.

Only God is omniscient, yet we must endeavor to the best of our ability to grasp the essentials and get as full an understanding of the big picture as possible. That is why we discuss many aspects and perspectives of the subject. Like the light that is spread out in a spectrum as it passes through a diamond, different perspectives yield different colors, and each has its own unique beauty and worth. Each is true, and yet each truth yields to the higher and greater revelation of the full knowledge that the life of Christ depicts. We must explore and seek the revelation of the whole, even as we seek to understand the wheel within the wheel—each individual part. All true facts are superseded by The Truth. God is One.

It is important to realize that God is not limited to an order or progression, and neither must we endeavor to limit Him because of the feebleness of our human understanding. However, we, as human beings, learn most efficiently in a building-block progression and that is why the information in this book has been presented in this style. Holy wars have been waged over our ability to understand or perceive "how God does it" and to assert that He only "does it" that way. It is my earnest prayer that this reference work will not inspire such debate, but rather that it will be a springboard for those called to witness to the lost, and for those called to intercede to touch the heart of God, realizing that He has absolutely no limitations of any kind and that people have been saved in all manner of ways. The important thing is to stay on the cutting edge of the wind of the Holy Spirit as He ministers the Word of God and brings life. It is my hope that this reference work will impart a clearer insight into the Big Picture of Christ's salvation.

The extensive "Intercessors Scripture Reference for the Salvation of The Lost" is in no way organized in a definitive manner. It is hoped, however, that the organization that is provided will be helpful and will enable the intercessor to focus on certain goals and give a progression of purpose. I have purposefully omitted as much commentary as possible because it is the Word of God that is quick, powerful

and sharper than a two-edged sword, not my understanding and commentary. I do not believe that the
way I study the Bible is necessarily the best way or
the only way to study the Bible. Yet I have found
life through these ways of study. We need fullness of
understanding, not glimmers of light here and there.
We must not only understand the Scriptures, but we
and those we pray for must be brought to the point
of action and change in order that true spiritual
growth is achieved. This cannot be accomplished by
man's opinion. As we are led by the Holy Spirit to
pray a specific portion of the Word for the individual, God, in all of His power, is released to
minister life to those for whom we pray. We must
wait upon God and only act in His timing. Space at
the end of each section is provided to give each
intercessor the ability to add their own revelatory
understanding of the subject and the Scriptures the
Holy Spirit leads them to.

God's Love and God's power are the bottom line.
*1 Corinthians 2:4-6 And my speech and my preaching
was not with enticing words of man's wisdom, but in
demonstration of the Spirit and of power: That your
faith should not stand in the wisdom of men, but in
the power of God. Howbeit we speak wisdom among them
that are perfect: yet not the wisdom of this world,
nor of the princes of this world, that come to naught:
KJV* The last books of the New Testament before the
Revelation of Jesus Christ are about the Love of God.
If you do not see the value and the importance of the
Love of God then you have missed the whole point of
the Bible. God is Love! The Christian Bible has been
organized in such a way that it ministers spiritual
growth. The Bible must be read over and over again
while praying in tongues. This is the traditional
way to gain understanding, revelation and the love
and power of God.

It is also crucial to understand that salvation is
a supernatural occurrence that takes place between
the Creator of the universe and the spirit of man
and it is only due to His choice that we, the body

xix

of Christ, become involved. The Body of Christ is not God. I am not God. You are not God. This collection of scriptures has been organized to enable the intercessor to pray accurately the will of the Father, realizing that all control and manipulation are not His way but stem from the enemy of all mankind through unredeemed flesh. Control and manipulation using the Word of God is evil! Always remember that God is the Living God and His will **shall** prevail. According to Scripture, God, Himself, deals in powerful judgment with those who control and manipulate using His Word. We must be led by God to speak forth His will. Therefore, let us press forward in that spirit of revelation knowledge of the Lord Jesus Christ that illumines our hearts and minds with His love and truth, and set the captives free! Our humanity and the smallness of our minds, emotions and wills sometime make it difficult for us to perceive, much less walk in, any portion of the greatness of Almighty God. Many are found either to the far right in religious order, form and control that is excessive, or to the far left in error and heresy that is an abomination to God. (If you find yourself to be such a one—repent and change!) God Almighty has given us this life as a transition of our soul from carnality to spirituality. However, I believe that there is a remnant in the middle, those who love God, love people and remain balanced, joyful and happy. Jesus Christ came that we might have life and have it more abundantly!

WORD OF THE LORD

*T*wo long days have I waited for you to come forth!
Two long days. Many generations have passed as
I have waited for you to come forth but now, for
such a time as this, are you come forth! You are
come to bring forth My signs and wonders and miracles and healings and all the gifts of My Holy Spirit
to meet the need of a fallen and sinful humanity at
the brink of eternal damnation. For such a time as
this have I brought you forth! To do My will. In the
volume of the Book is it written of you, O precious
one! Bring forth My salvation to a hurting and des-
perate mankind. Show forth My love! Watch and see as
I work through you. I shall be highly glorified and
lifted up as you obey Me! Finally, My power shall be
unleashed upon this earth in an unprecedented manner
as I have longed to do, saith the Lord Jesus Christ!
The fulness of times is come! My glory shall cover
the earth as the waters cover the sea!

JULY 5, 1976

God needs <u>you!!</u> He needs you to fulfill your place in His Body. He needs you to be so filled with His love—first for yourself, then for the Body of Christ and then for the spiritually dead of this world—that you will be an avenue for His power to flow through. God will do a work in this earth and He must do that work through you. When you are in right relation to self and fellow man then you are a proper channel of God's love.

God wants you to have the right attitude and vision, the right perspective of your place in Him and His plan for you. How can He do this though when every man looks upon himself as an island and seeks his own glory, rather than the glory of God?

We must be unified in God's love! How can we do this if we are unable to hear the Voice of God's Spirit? How can we do this if we don't walk in the spirit, operating in the spirit realm rather than this fleshly realm?

We must come together in God's love! The command of God is that we love one another; as Jesus Christ loved us, that we also love one another.

God has a plan for your life. Yes, you, in particular! He knows everything about you, including the number of the hairs on your head. He loves you. Jesus Christ loves you. That's why He died for you and you alone and all of mankind together. God will work through you as you allow Him to—as you lay down your self life and allow the life of Christ to be lived through you. Don't allow yourself to be given over to acts of lawlessness.

TABLE OF CONTENTS

Foreword. ix
Chapter One 25
Who Is God?
Chapter Two 59
What is Man?
Chapter Three 79
What is Religion?
Chapter Four. 108
Religion: Then and Now
Chapter Five. 133
What Did Jesus Christ Accomplish?
Chapter Six 159
Who Are We When We Are *In Christ*?
Chapter Seven 182
What Happens As Salvation Occurs?
Chapter Eight 216
What Is The Work Of The Trinity In Salvation?
Chapter Nine. 237
How Does The Intercessor Conform To God's Ways?
Chapter Ten 269
What Is The Work Of The Intercessor?
Chapter Eleven. 290
The Armor Of God
Chapter Twelve. 309
How Do We Worship God?
1. Prayer For A Share In The Work Of Redemption
   by Walter Rauchenbush. 331
2. Prayer For The Lost by Patricia Nordean. . .333
3. The Prayer of Salvation by Patricia Nordean. .339

CHAPTER I

WHO IS GOD?

Look to Me and be saved, all the ends of the earth!
For I am God, and there is no other.
Isaiah 45:22 AMP

*G*OD: He is the All-Powerful (**OMNIPOTENT**), All-Knowing (**OMNISCIENT**) and Ever-Present (**OMNIPRESENT**) **ONE.** Who is He? What is He like? Why are things the way they are? Most of us feel that God is just like us—that His motives, aims and goals are like our own, or rather, that our motives, aims and goals reflect His. This is called anthropomorphism = applying human attributes to God. However, God is so far removed from the nature of man and so entirely above us that we, only after allowing the work of the cross free reign in our hearts, can hope to begin to understand the smallest, tiniest bit of Him. What has He said about Himself in His Word? *Exodus 3:14 And God said unto Moses, I AM THAT I AM: and he said, Thus shalt thou say unto the children of Israel, I AM hath sent me unto you. Isaiah 43:10b-13 "I am He: before Me there was no GOD formed, neither shall there be after Me. I, even I, am the Lord; and beside Me there is no saviour. I have declared, and have saved, and I have shewed, when there was no strange* *god among you: therefore ye are My witnesses, saith the Lord, that I am GOD. Yea, before the day was I am He; and there is none that can deliver out of My hand: I will work, and who shall let it?"*

Observing the effects of sin on the earth, many generations of our forefathers have concluded that God is an angry God and that judgment of man is His highest goal. Yet this conclusion is also the result of sense observation and not spiritual truth. It comes as a result of observing the Law of the Old Testament seen through the nature of mankind itself, rather than the grace which comes by faith in the New Testament. In the Old Testament God's judgment did fall on various nations — the Amelakites, the Hittites, and the Girgashites, etc. — and they were removed as nations and people groups in the earth. Their own evil came back upon them. But 2000+ years ago God gave His only begotten Son, His dearly beloved Son, to remit the sins of all mankind. God had spoken forth His coming in the Garden of Eden at the occurrence of the Fall of Man. This is when religion came to be. He referred to His Son as The Seed, sent to redeem mankind from their sin of disobedience which took place in the Garden of Eden. Jesus is pure Love itself. It was God's very own blood that flowed through the body of His Son to redeem mankind. Life is in blood. He has never harmed mankind. He ceased from judgment for the Bible says that He gave all judgment into the hands of the Son. *John 5:22 For the Father judgeth no man, but hath committed all judgment unto the Son: KJV* Jesus said He did not come to destroy men's lives but to save them. God sends no one to hell. People send themselves to hell when they reject God's plan of salvation. People judge themselves when they choose the darkness instead of the light. There is only one plan of salvation. What will you do with Jesus Christ? *John 3:18-21 He that believeth on him is not condemned: but he that believeth not is condemned already, because he hath not believed in the name of the only begotten Son of God. And this is the condemnation, that light is come into the world, and men loved darkness rather than light, because their deeds were evil. For every one that doeth evil hateth the light, neither cometh to the light, lest his deeds should be reproved. But he that doeth truth cometh to the light, that his deeds may be made manifest, that they are wrought in God. KJV*

Judgment is not about using the power of God to kill people and put infirmity upon them. We are all guilty and filthy in sin because of the Fall of Man in the garden of Eden. Judgment's true goal is to bring justice and righteousness to pass in the earth. God loves and desires true justice for every man. Justice embodies the idea of moral equity. Judgment is the application of equity to moral situations and may be favorable or unfavorable according to whether the one under examination has been equitable or inequitable in heart and conduct. It is not about being the toughest, meanest dog in the pack. God desires life—true eternal life—on this earth. He desires restoration of all people. God is neither male nor female. He Is. God is One. God is Love. God is Light. There is nothing in God's justice which forbids the exercise of His mercy. It is God's good pleasure to give His children the keys of the kingdom. God is never at cross-purposes with Himself. No attribute of God is in conflict with another. For several thousand years people have equated God with the angry judgment of mankind that resulted in severe calamities for the individual and all related to them. This is Old Testament theology. Jesus Christ brought grace and truth and introduced us to God as Father. For although God is neither male nor female He has taught us about His own nature and character through typifying Himself as a Father so that we are able to understand Him. We must be taught to love. God created man in His image as male and female therefore we must be able to "see" what it is that God requires of us as human beings. I believe it is time for mankind, as a whole, to come up higher in the grace and mercy of God past the judgment of the Old

Testament Law into the true Light of Jesus Christ. God is a Good God.

Luke 11:13 If ye then, being evil, know how to give good gifts unto your children: how much more shall your heavenly Father give the Holy Spirit to them that ask him? Matthew 7:11 If ye then, being evil, know how to give good gifts unto your children, how much more shall your Father which is in heaven give good things to them that ask him? KJV The Holy Spirit of God is a "good thing" or "good gift"! Jesus said that judgment comes when we do not believe Him and in Him. Jesus is the Light of the world. We must believe in the light. When we choose to believe in and seek darkness instead of the Light then we are judged because we have not believed in the Light. This is a prerequisite for our covenant with God.

Jesus commended John the Baptist to us. John taught mankind to repent. Jesus came to restore all things that we might have the Promise of the Father—the Most Precious Holy Spirit—Who is Himself God. The nature, character and action of the Holy Spirit may be typified as that of a Mother, although the Holy Spirit, as God, is neither male nor female. In Scripture the Holy Spirit is addressed as "He". The Age of Grace was given to mankind that the ministry of the Holy Spirit might be realized. The idea of "Family" is God's idea. He promised and planted the Seed of His Son in this earth that He might reap a harvest of many sons and have a family. The Holy Spirit reveals the Father to us. He empowers us to do works of service. He teaches us the Word of God. Satan has no power over what God has already judged.

The most important knowledge attainable on earth is to know and understand **Who God Is?** Yet God, as God, is **INCOMPREHENSIBLE.** Then how are we as mere created beings to know Him? This knowledge is found in the Holy Bible—God's Word to mankind. Jesus Christ is the Living Word of God. When we look at Him through His Word we see God the Father. God has deigned that through His Holy Word we might search after Him and find Him when we seek Him in faith and in love. God is **HOLY**. What does the Holiness of God mean? It has to do with His Righteousness, His Truth and His Love. The knowledge of the holy is the most valuable eternal attainment one can ever hope to achieve after salvation. It is enduring truth. I don't know about you, but I desire to know God. It is my greatest and most passionate desire. I hunger and thirst to know Him more. God is **LIFE!**

God is **IMMENSE**! He is not confined by space or by time. God is **ETERNAL**. Time and space are aspects of the created world. God is not limited by our three-dimensional, naturalistic world, nor is He limited by what some call the fourth dimension of time. We do not know how many dimensions are in God. Pastor Paul Yongghi-Cho of Korea (pastor of the world's largest church) preaches that the fourth dimension is the dimension of the spiritual kingdom of faith. God spoke to Pastor Cho's heart, "Son, as the second dimension includes and controls the first dimension, and the third dimension includes and controls the second dimension, so the fourth dimension includes and controls the third dimension, producing a creation of order and beauty. The spirit is the fourth dimension. Every human being is a spiritual being as well as a physical being. They have the fourth dimension as well as the third dimension in their hearts." Pastor Cho teaches that "men, by exploring their spiritual sphere of the fourth dimension through the development of concentrated visions and dreams in their imaginations, can brood over and incubate the third dimension, influencing and changing it." God is supernatural, beyond our natural understanding. *Isaiah 55:9 says, "As the heavens are higher than the earth, so are my ways higher than your ways and my thoughts than your thoughts."*

Rev. Ron Carlson and Rev. Ed Decker have written about the immensity of God's creation in what we call outer space or the universe: "Have you ever truly thought about how great God is? Have you ever imagined what the magnitude of the cosmos really is? The speed of light is 186,000 miles per second. In

29

one second, light can travel around the earth at the equator 7 1/2 times! If you go outside on a clear night, you can see a band going across the sky which appears as dense clouds across the center of the sky. Actually that is the rim of what we earthlings call the Milky Way. What you are seeing are not clouds but stars, so many billions of stars that it appears to us to be clouds. *Psalms 147:4 He telleth the number of the stars; he calleth them all by their names. KJV* If you were traveling at the speed of light, it would take you 4 1/2 years just to reach the nearest star you can see at night! A light-year is how far light travels in one year. In one year light will travel 6 trillion miles. The nearest star is Alpha Centauri, 4 1/2 light-years away, which means that the nearest star that you can see at night is something like 27 trillion miles away! And that is just the *nearest* star in our galaxy. There are over 100 billion stars in our Milky Way galaxy! As huge as this sounds, ours is one of the *smallest* galaxies in the universe! In fact, astronomers with the 200-inch telescope at Mount Palomar in California estimate that as they look out through the cup of the Big Dipper constellation they can see over one million galaxies the size of our Milky Way or bigger. At the speed of light it would take us a hundred thousand light-years to cross the Milky Way galaxy. This means that our small galaxy is six hundred thousand trillion miles across. And astronomers can see over one million galaxies that size or bigger just in the cup of the *Big Dipper*. Think of the magnitude of what we are saying!" Our planet, Earth, compared in size to the Milky Way Galaxy is about the size of a quarter compared to the size of the nation of America. Does this help you understand the magnitude of God, Who formed the Universe by breathing it out of His Mouth? *Psalms 33:6 By the word of the LORD were the heavens made; and all the host of them by the breath of his mouth. Deuteronomy 8:3 ...by every word that proceedeth out of the mouth of the LORD doth man live.* (We usually use this Scripture for fasting. However, think about it in relation to the Universe.) *KJV* I love to look up into the sky at night to search for the Big Dipper. When I find it in the night sky I am reminded that this Age of Grace is about the outpouring of the Holy Spirit upon mankind. God isn't using the Little Dipper to pour out the Holy Spirit. He is using His Big Dipper!

Psalms 115:15 Ye are blessed of the LORD which made heaven and earth

Psalms 121:2 My help cometh from the LORD, which made heaven and earth.

Psalms 124:8 Our help is in the name of the LORD, who made heaven and earth.

Psalms 134:3 The LORD that made heaven and earth bless thee out of Zion.

Psalms 135:5-7 For I know that the LORD is great, and that our Lord is above all gods. Whatsoever the LORD pleased, that did he in heaven, and in earth, in the seas, and all deep places. He causeth the vapours to ascend from the ends of the earth; he maketh lightnings for the rain; he bringeth the wind out of his treasuries.

Psalms 146:5-6 Happy is he that hath the God of Jacob for his help, whose hope is in the LORD his God: Which made heaven, and earth, the sea, and all that therein is: which keepeth truth for ever: KJV

Carlson and Decker go on to say, "Leaving the Milky Way galaxy, the farthest thing that astronomers can see or hear with their most sophisticated equipment is a quasar, which is 15 billion light-years away, which means it is 90 billion trillion miles away. We have no idea what is beyond that, but

31

astronomers estimate that this quasar 90 billion trillion miles away emits enough energy in one second to supply all the electrical needs of the earth for one million years. That's just *one* quasar, and there are millions of quasars in the universe. Do you begin to get the picture? The Bible says that the God Who created all this holds it together *by the power of His Hand*. And some people wonder if God is really big enough to solve their problems? God is far bigger than our finite minds can hope to comprehend. Yet the God whose energy transcends all the energy in the universe by infinity nevertheless loves each one of us. That God is concerned about you personally. The Bible says God considers you more important than all those galaxies put together. What a tremendous truth! <u>As you begin to get a glimpse of what God is really like, it will change the way you pray</u>. When you come into the Presence of the Almighty Creator, it becomes an awe-inspiring thing. It becomes a thing of *wonderment."*

God was WITH Abraham, Moses, Joshua, Ruth, Esther, King David of Israel, etc. When God is with someone He manifests His Presence as His Hand being with them. When God speaks to an individual that He is with them He often says, "My Hand is with you." In the above paragraph we have seen that the immensity of the universe is held together by the power of the Hand of God. If you are God's child, God's Hand is with you. *Habakkuk 3:3-4 God came from Teman* (southward, which signifies blessing), *and the Holy One from mount Paran* (their beautifying). *Selah (*which in Hebrew means think about that one for awhile, Bubba). *His glory covered the heavens, and the earth was full of his praise. And his brightness was as the light; he had horns coming out of his hand: and there was the hiding of his power.KJV* God's Hand is His Holy Spirit. The Holy Spirit of God is **within** each individual Christian when they are born-again. The Holy Spirit comes **upon** the Christian to ready them for service unto God when they are baptized in and with the Holy Spirit. God's Hand is His Presence in the

Person of the Holy Spirit. This means that the power that holds the Universe together is with you, you little flesh creature, you. Does that just fry your brain, or what?!!! *Isaiah 45:11-12 Thus saith the LORD, the Holy One of Israel, and his Maker, Ask me of things to come concerning my sons, and concerning the work of my hands command ye me. I have made the earth, and created man upon it: I, even my hands, have stretched out the heavens, and all their host have I commanded. KJV*

Pastor Dave Roberson teaches there are nine attributes of God's nature expressed through the three Persons of the Trinity that are the essence of His Love:

Love	=	**God's Essential Nature** **Attitude of God Toward Men**
Truth	=	**Reality & Manifested Essence**
Omnipotence	=	**All Powerful**
Omnipresence	=	**Everywhere Present**
Omniscience	=	**All Knowing**
Righteousness	=	**Right Character & Action**
Sovereignty	=	**Supreme Authority**
Immutability	=	**Unchanging**
Eternal Life	=	**Alive Forever**

In the Old Testament God is known by the names Yahweh and Jehovah. The Hebrew people so honored God that even these names were not written or spoken. God's Names are represented in Hebrew Scriptures by the symbolic letters YHWH. Through many incidences and interactions with Old Testament saints He manifested His character and took upon Himself names describing His attributes and acts:

Jehovah = unoriginated, Immutable, Eternal and self-sustained Existent One

Jehovah Sabbaoth = Lord of Hosts
Jehovah Nissi = God our Victory, God our Banner
Jehovah-M'Kaddesh = the Lord our Righteousness, God that sanctifies us
Jehovah Jireh = God our Abundant Supply—God sees our needs and provides ahead for them
Jehovah Rophe = God our Healer
Jehovah Shalom = God our Peace
Jehovah Tsidkenu = God our right thoughts and right acts—our righteousness
Jehovah Rohi = the Lord our Shepherd
Jehovah Shammah = Jehovah is There—God's Presence is with us always—Emmanuel
Eloah or Elohim = Omnipotent and pre-eminent God Who is to be worshipped
El Shaddei = the many-breasted One Who sustains and provides, God Almighty
El Elyon = the Most High God
Adon, Adonai, Adonim = Ruler, Beloved Master, Owner and Proprietor, Blesser
Flowing Oil = Perfume poured forth, the Anointed One

God is ultimate and true reality. The God of all creation: He is our **CREATOR**. God is **SPIRIT**. He is **LIGHT**. He is **LIFE**. God is **HOLY**. God is **RIGHTEOUS**. God demands righteousness because His holiness is our standard for living. He is **LOVE**. He is **TRUTH** itself. He is **GOOD**. Morally, God is absolutely Pure, Perfect and Majestic. God **FORGIVES** man. He will not come to mankind with wrath but with righteous justice. He is **JEALOUS**. He is **FIRE**. He is an all consuming Fire. *Rom 4:17 God, who gives life to the dead and calls into being that which does not exist.* NAS His loving-kindness endures forever. Eternity lies in His Heart. God does not live in eternity; eternity lies in God in the sense that He created the Universe. Scripture states that He breathed out the stars from His Mouth. All His entire creation lies within His Heart. That means He is a very big God! Absolutely nothing is impossible to God!!! God bases everything on truth.

He doesn't have truth—He is Truth. He rules every-thing from the inside out. He is Sovereign. He is Immutable. He is what He does. God's most powerful weapon is His Word. He gave that to us. His compassion and gentle forbearance for mankind are without end. His mercy triumphs over judgment. God is balanced. He is both judgment and love but Scripture teaches us that His mercy triumphs over His judgment. At the end of holy canon the books of John teach us God is love. **GOD IS LOVE.**

The Bible does not teach us God is Judgment. Judgment is within God because God is Truth. Actually, each person's judgment lies within them. God does not send judgment upon a person. Rather, the truth of who they are spiritually comes upon them eternally unless they remain connected to God in relationship and allow the Holy Spirit to cleanse them of sin. When you are born your judgment lies within you and unless you find God and His way of salvation that judgment will ultimately consume you. You will bear the judgment of your own sin and the sin of the generations that came before you. Will your eternity be determined by the physical passions and desires within your body or by the Love of Almighty God? God has given each person this lifetime to put away sin and to rise higher in His Light. God's Word teaches us how to do this. We must receive the mercy and the grace of God and obey Him. REPENTANCE, CONFESSION of the Word of God, and CONFORMITY to the image of God in Christ Jesus will allow us to walk free of our sin nature and the judgment that lurks at the door of our heart. The glory of Almighty God in the Person of the Holy Spirit is the power that enables us to withstand the raging passions of our flesh nature as this process takes place. God's glory is manifest upon our flesh as we hear His Voice and obey Him.

Genesis 1:27 So God created man in his own image, in the image of God he created him; male and female he created them. NIV We have been created in the image of God as both male and female. Mankind has been given an organ called the brain which has two

35

lobes—one lobe governs the right side of the body and the other lobe governs the left side of the body. *Job 11:6 ...show you the secrets of wisdom! For sound wisdom has two sides. NASU* We are all familiar with the seemingly contradictory nature of God but Scripture clearly points out that there are <u>at least</u> two sides to God. God is much, much greater and more vast than our imaginations can hold. God is both **TRANSCENDENT** and **IMMINENT**. Transcendent = Very excellent, superior, to surpass, to excel, to exceed. Transcendence means that God is detached from all His creation as an independent, self-existing Being (Isaiah 40:12-17). This refutes the New Age teaching that God is Mother Earth. God is not the earth or the cosmos. He is the Creator, not the creation. Imminent = To hang over, to threaten, appearing as if about to fall on, impending judgments, evil or death. Imminence means God's all-pervading presence and power within His creation (Isaiah 57:15). God is actively concerned and involved with His creation. This attribute of God refutes the concept of Deism, which says God wound up the world like a watch and then left it to run down on its own. The Society of Spinoza believes, as do many scientists, that individuals are not free but causally bound in their thinking, feeling and acting. The belief that human actions are determined, beyond their control, by both physical and psychological laws, does not take into consideration the supernatural nature of Almighty God. God has given mankind free will. These beliefs ultimately emanate from viewing God through humanism. In other words God is seen from the perspective of Man as the center of the Universe. The Law of Christianity is imminently and transcendently called the Word of Truth. Therefore we must search both sides of God to even begin to understand His greatness:

Exodus 3:14, 6	Transcendent	Imminent
Joshua 2:11	power	love
John 1:1, 14, 17	truth	grace
Revelation 19:11-13	judgment	mercy
Isaiah 57:15	doing	being
	leadership	relationship
Job 11:6-9	holy	compassionate
	separate	belonging
	Father	Mother
	analytical	hemispheric
	assertive	responsive

In addition to this understanding, the New Testament presents the Trinity of God by describing their unique functions:

	Almighty God (Spirit) Operations	Holy Spirit (Soul) Gifts/Fruit		Jesus Christ (Body) Administrations
1 Corinthians 12:4-6	1. apostles	1. Word of Knowledge	1. love	1. Apostle
1 Corinthians 12:28	2. prophets	2. Word of Wisdom	2. joy	2. Prophet
Ephesians 4:11	3. teachers	3. Gift of Faith	3. peace	3. Evangelist
1 Corinthians 12:8-10	4. miracles	4. Gifts of Healings	4. longsuffering	4. Pastor
Galatians 5:22, 23	5. gifts of healings	5. Working of Miracles	5. gentleness	5. Teacher
	6. helps	6. Prophecy	6. goodness	
	7. governments	7. Discerning of Spirits	7. faith	
	8. diversities of tongues	8. Tongues	8. meekness	
		9. Interpretation of Tongues	9. temperance	

God has created all these offices and gifts for the perfecting of the saints, for the work of the ministry, that we might all be edified and come into unity and the fullness of His Love.

God is a Conqueror and He says in His Word that He makes us more than conquerors through Christ Jesus. There is a heavenly legality to God's ways of overcoming evil. These ways have nothing to do with earthly logic and understanding. They are of God. Life is different than they taught you in the world. *Ezekiel 1:16 The appearance of the wheels and their*

work was like unto the colour of a beryl: and they
four had one likeness: and their appearance and their
work was as it were a wheel in the middle of a wheel.
KJV The wheel within a wheel = time vs. eternity.
God cast light forth from Him. We must look at this
life from the perspective of God in eternity. Have
an eternal perspective. More than anything else an
eternal perspective will help you through this life.
When you face a problem ask God to show you what
He saw you do to get out of the fix. You can't call
things the way they are. You must call them the way
God sees them or else you don't need God.

God is All Powerful. Six Greek words describe His
power in the New Testament:

Dunamis = force (literally or figuratively); specially, miraculous power (usually by
implication, a miracle itself): ability,
abundance, meaning, might (-ily, -y, -y
deed), (worker of) miracle (-s), power,
strength, violence, mighty (wonderful)
work. **INHERENT POWER**

Kratos = perhaps a primary word; vigor ["great"]
(literally or figuratively): dominion, might
[-ily], power, strength. **RULING POWER**

Ischus = from a derivative of is (force; compare
eschon, a form of Strong's NT:2192);
forcefulness (literally or figuratively):
ability, might ([-ily]), power, strength.
ENDOWED POWER

Energeia = efficiency ("energy"): operation, strong,
(effectual) working. **DISPLAYED POWER**

Exousia = (in the sense of ability); privilege,
i.e. (subjectively) force, capacity, com-
petency, freedom, or (objectively) mastery (concretely, magistrate, superhuman,
potentate, token of control), delegated
influence: authority, jurisdiction, liberty, power, right, strength. **AUTHORITY**

Arche = beginning; then, the chief **RULE** or ruler

There is a demonic principality named origins.

In the Old Testament, God's power is given example in His bringing the Hebrew nation through the Red Sea in deliverance. In the New Testament, God's power is given example by raising Jesus Christ from the dead. These actions were performed by the Hand and Arm of God in physical manifestation of His power. The exercise of God's power is the Operations of the Father in 1 Corinthians 12:6. God gave His power to man in the Garden of Eden in the form of dominion. We did not lose power in the Fall, we lost authority. The Holy Spirit of God raised Christ from the dead. Jesus Christ returned the authority to us. You have to have power to exercise authority. We have the Exousia over satan's Dunamis. We exercise God's authority when we use the Name of Jesus Christ. As we obey God's Word to us the power is released through us. In the New Testament our first order of dominion is our own flesh nature or soul. God is in every way imaginable **ALL-POWERFUL**. His Presence should never be taken lightly. Scripture teaches us to reverence God and to fear God.

In addition to the above the Apostle Paul adjures us in Ephesians 3:14-21 to explore what the breadth, length, height and depth of love is, i.e. God's love in Christ, as He is our All in All. This is also contained in Job 11:6-9.

Depth—fathomless: He knows intimately the life of each universe of existence within each molecule in the universe throughout eternity. 2 Peter 1:12—His attitude toward men will be to always remind us of the Truth.

Breadth—boundless: the whole counsel of God contained in the Holy Bible, including the Mind of Christ.

Height—measureless: the entire Universe throughout all time exists within God. Luke 10:27; Leviticus 19:18; Deuteronomy 6:5—our attitude toward God can only be one of irrevocable and absolute love and obedience.

Length—endless: time orientation—darkness & destruction increase as one moves away from God Who Is the Light—time ceases in God—youth, health and life exist in God Who Is Life Eternal.

God's love will override the truth of our sin. Sin means separation from God. There are many true facts in this life but the Spirit of Truth supersedes true facts. For example: A doctor may diagnose a person with cancer, but God's Word teaches us that we were healed two thousand years ago on the Cross of Calvary by the stripes Jesus Christ bore in His Person. God's Truth supersedes the true facts given by the doctor. However, just as our born-again experience was received by faith we must receive our healing by faith. Jesus healed them all. God is good and His goodness will triumph over the evil of man's sin of separation from Him. As we come to God progressively, veils are removed from our understanding. Our minds receive greater and greater light and truth. We understand. We are enabled to rise up higher in life. The darkness, uncleanness and fear within us are given over to faith in the truth of Who God is. Error and darkness fall away. We act in faith with the strength and power of God enabling us to do more and to be more. As we learn God's Word the ignorance within us is replaced by the knowledge of the Word of Truth. Our ways change. Our youth is renewed. God has given us both grace and truth in Jesus Christ. He never gives up on us. God is **GOOD**. God is **PURE**. He is greater than evil. Love never fails. God is **KIND**. He is gentle. His gentleness secures His throne. Yet our vision is so marred and limited by sin that we, His own children and creation, have been unable to fathom the depths of His love. God is unchanging. God is **IMMUTABLE**. He is stable, fixed, and immovable. He is the same—yesterday, today and forever.

In the Old Testament there are seven Hebrew words defined as love:

'Ahab =   (aw-hab'); or 'aheb (aw-habe'); a primitive root; to have affection for)sexually or otherwise): KJV—(be-) love (-d, -ly, -r), like, friend. Spiritual affection for holy things which is opposed to all evil and only satisfied with a likeness to God. 'ahabah (a-hab-aw); feminine of 'ahab and meaning the same: KJV—love.

`Agab =   (aw-gab'); a primitive root; to breathe after, i.e. to love (sensually): KJV—dote, lover.

Racham =   (raw-kham'); a primitive root; to fondle; by implication, to love, especially to compassionate: KJV—have compassion (on, upon), love, (find, have, obtain, shew) mercy (-iful, on, upon), (have) pity, Ruhamah, X surely.

Chashaq =   (khaw-shak'); a primitive root; to cling, i.e. join, (figuratively) to love, delight in; elliptically to deliver: KJV—have a delight, (have a desire, fillet, long, set (in) love.

Dowd =   (dode); or (shortened) dod (dode); from an unused root meaning properly, to boil, i.e. (figuratively) to love; by implication, a lovetoken, lover, friend; specifically an uncle: KJV—(well-) beloved, father's brother, love, uncle.

**Rea` =**   (ray'-ah); or reya` (ray'-ah); an associate (more or less close): KJV—brother, companion, fellow, friend, husband, lover, neighbour, X (an-) other.

**Ra` yah =**   (rah-yaw'); feminine of reya`; a female associate: KJV—fellow, love.

In the New Testament there are three Greek words defined in the English language as love:

Agape = (ag-ah'-pay); love, i.e. affection or benevolence; specially (plural) a love-feast: KJV—(feast of) charity ([-ably]), dear, love. Agapao (ag-ap-ah'-o); perhaps from agan (much) to love (in a social or moral sense): KJV—(be-) love (-ed). Love which is a fruit of the Holy Spirit.

Phileo = (fil-eh'-o); to be a friend to (fond of [an individual or an object]), i.e. have affection for (denoting personal attachment, as a matter of sentiment or feeling; while agape is wider, embracing especially the judgment and the deliberate assent of the will as a matter of principle, duty and propriety: the former being chiefly of the heart and the latter of the head); specifically, to kiss (as a mark of tenderness): KJV—kiss, love. Philadelphia (fil-ad-el-fee'-ah); fraternal affection: KJV—brotherly love (kindness), love of the brethren.

Thelo = (thel'-o); or ethelo (eth-el'-o); in certain tenses theleo (thel-eh'-o); and etheleo (eth-el-eh'-o); which are otherwise obsolete; to determine (as an active option from subjective impulse; whereas to be willing properly denotes rather a passive acquiescence in objective considerations), i.e. choose or prefer (literally or figuratively); by implication, to wish, i.e. be inclined to (sometimes adverbially, gladly); impersonally for the future tense, to be about to; by Hebraism, to delight in: KJV—desire, be disposed (forward), intend, list, love, mean, please, have rather, (be) will (have, -ling, -ling [-ly]).

We have no concept of eternity, no comprehension of Life. That is what mankind cannot understand:

the **CONTINUING PRESENT** of God, i.e.

NOWNOWNOWNOWNOWNOWNOWONOWNOWNOWNOWNOW

Yet God <u>is</u> **LIFE**. God is **LIVING**. He is the continuing present **LIFE**. God has life and personality.
He is not merely an impersonal force. "Let the Force
be with you" is not an accurate description of Who
God is. God is not a giant computer in the sky. He is
not just "the Man upstairs". Please read Jeremiah 10.
God is **SPIRIT** with life and personality. He speaks,
He hears, He sees, He declares, He creates, He wills.
He expresses anger, remorse, joy. He loves, He adjudicates. God is personal; He is a personal Creator,
and He is personally concerned about each of us as
His personal creations. To say that God is devoid of
these attributes is to make Him far less than Who
He really is. Only a personality can love. God, who
created this world, can love because He is living
and personal. It isn't something He learned to do. He
always was God, and He always had this nature. The
tiniest glimmer of a reflection of His Light sustains
nations for centuries. God is **LIGHT**. Light is the
only unchangeable constant in the universe. Energy
can change, light cannot. God is the center of all
creation. *James 1:17 Every good gift and every per-*
fect gift is from above, and cometh down from the
Father of lights, with whom is no variableness, nei-
ther shadow of turning. KJV **God is GOOD. God is LOVE.**
There are no shadows of change in God. God dwells in
the unapproachable Light. God has called us to walk
in the Light as His children of Light. Walking in
the light is important because it serves as a connection between time and light. There is no time in
God. God is **ETERNAL**. Time exists when one moves away
from God. The farther one is from God the faster the
progression of time. Degeneration speeds up, the
aging process increases, as one moves away from God.
The closer one travels to the speed of light time
stretches and expands. When a Christian walks in

agreement with God, doing His will, he enters into the supernatural realm. Light travels at 186,000 miles per second. Light has a quantifiable speed. When one travels at the speed of light time ceases and one enters into eternity. The closer one is to God the more life one experiences. Youth, purity, energy, strength, innocence and life exist in God. Death, darkness, aging, destruction exist away from God. There is no distance in the spirit. Therefore, our closeness to God is not determined physically but spiritually because God is Spirit and those who worship Him, worship Him in spirit and in truth.

God brings provision through giving. He brings forgiveness through the midst of affront and scandal. God brings life from death and destruction. His ways are ways of peace but it is a peace that comes in the midst of chaos, confrontation and calamity. God is all powerful. God is **OMNIPOTENT**. His power is shown forth through weakness. His strength comes through joy. Scripture teaches there are many ways of God. We must study these ways and become proficient in our knowledge of them. The knowledge and understanding with insight into the ways of God are crucial for our success in this life and in eternity. They give us wisdom. Yet, at the same time, knowledge for knowledge's sake is a form of witchcraft. It is sin to idolize knowledge alone. We are responsible for what we know. We must "be" it and we must "do" it. This is an essential issue of each individual's life. Scripture also mentions many different <u>spirits</u>. These "spirits" also need to be studied and delved into. Understanding these attributes is essential in conforming one's ways to God. Scripture also mentions different <u>laws</u>. There are laws in the Old Testament. There are laws in the New Testament. We must understand God's intention in the creation of laws. What is their purpose? Are they relevant to me as a New Testament believer? How do they benefit me? (Is this just an Old Testament teaching?)

So, we say in our hearts, if He is so good and powerful why is He so stingy with Himself? Why is the Way so difficult? Actually, the Way has been exis- tent since the beginning. It is the same as it has always been. Nothing has changed. He has not changed. The door has always been open. The Father is always at home and is waiting for you! So then, why don't we get it? What is the missing link? "People aren't stupid," we say. "Why is everything in such a mess?"

Knowing God is a matter of the heart. God is **SPIRIT**. God is a **SPEAKING SPIRIT**. He has life and personality. God spoke to Moses out of the fire; Moses heard only a voice (Deuteronomy 4:33-37; 5:22-29; 14:12-19). There was no man standing there in the flames, but God, who says He is spirit, was there. There are fifty references to the voice of the Lord God in the Old Testament. The Kingdom of God is a spiritual Kingdom. Because of the work of Jesus Christ on the Cross of Calvary it lives within the human heart. The Presence of the Holy Ghost upon a person may cause them to speak as the oracles of God. For example, *Luke 1:41-42 "….and Elisabeth was filled with the Holy Ghost: And she spake out with a loud voice, and said…."* KJV It is up to each one of us, according to our own heart's desires, whether or not we know God; and if we do choose to know Him, how well we know Him, and for what purpose, and with what result. God's power flows at the speed of thought. God has freely given mankind all of Himself that is needed to be saved. God has given mankind free will to choose his destiny. We each choose our own eter- nity. Our right to our own free will is extremely important to God. Heaven will not override an indi- vidual's free will for any reason. No one can keep you from heaven if you desire to be there eternally. You, personally, have the free-will right to choose to obey God.

To find God we must find the entrance or door to Him. To find that door we must have certain attri- butes within ourselves. He does not change. We, on the other hand, might need to change. We must press in to the Father to obtain the grace to change. Jesus Christ is The Door God has chosen for mankind to enter in and to go out from His Presence. Jesus Christ is not spirit. Jesus Christ is both Man and God. Jesus has, in this Dispensation of Grace, both flesh and bones. *Luke 24:37-43 But they were terrified and affrighted, and supposed that they had seen a spirit. And he said unto them, Why are ye troubled? and why do thoughts arise in your hearts? Behold my hands and my feet, that it is I myself: handle me, and see; for a spirit hath not flesh and bones, as ye see me have. And when he had thus spoken, he shewed them his hands and his feet. And while they yet believed not for joy, and wondered, he said unto them, Have ye here any meat? And they gave him a piece of a broiled fish, and of an honeycomb. And he took it, and did eat before them. Jesus said in John 5:25 Verily, verily, I say unto you, The hour is coming, and now is, when the dead shall hear the voice of the Son of God: and they that hear shall live. KJV*

You see, **God hides Himself.** *Isaiah 45:15 "Verily thou art a God that hidest thyself, O God of Israel, the Saviour."* He works at it. Rich Mullins, the songwriter, describes God as "Hard to Get". He is very good at hiding Himself. Why does He do that? Because He is very Good. He is absolutely and totally good. God has His own ways of doing things and He keeps His ways secret, too. God, in His infinite wisdom, has secrets hidden before the foundation of the world. He has ways of mystery which are hidden for the good of all creation. In His Word He says that it is His glory to conceal a matter, but the glory of kings is to search out a matter. (*Proverbs 25:2*) Are we not created kings and priests unto Him? We must find out His mysteries and His secrets and bring them to pass in our reality by doing them in His timing. His ways are very, very different from our ways. Do you think that is a contradiction? Well then, I imagine you have not taken this into consideration: evil.

The power of evil is real. Do you think it is a problem for God? No, it is not a problem. God is all-powerful. However, God is absolute goodness. He is only good and there is no evil in Him at all, not even that that we would consider necessary as obvious for the good of all. It simply is not present in the Father. Most of God's own children have compromised this truth. James 1:12-17 KJV

So, if God is so Good and He hides Himself, then how are we to know Him? The Bible teaches us that the fear of the Lord is the beginning of wisdom. The fear of God is something to be sought after and to be learned for it brings success in this life. The reverential and worshipful fear of the Lord brings life and is a fountain of life. It is clean. In James 1:5 the Lord's half-brother adjures us to ask God for wisdom, for God does not rebuke those who ask for His wisdom. It is this wisdom from God that enables us to stand in life and having done all to stand. With wisdom the Holy Spirit will teach us prudence, discretion and will give us good counsel. This life is full of imperceptible spiritual land mines that can only be navigated by God Himself. He will make a way for us where there seems to be no way. It is futile and a trap to fear man or to fear a "prince". The Bible commands us to love our brethren but not to trust them. God commands us not to fear men whom we can see but only to fear Him, Who has the power of life and death. *Luke 12:4-7 And I say unto you my friends, Be not afraid of them that kill the body, and after that have no more that they can do. But I will forewarn you whom ye shall fear: Fear him, which after he hath killed hath power to cast into hell; yea, I say unto you, Fear him. Are not five sparrows sold for two farthings, and not one of them is forgotten before God? But even the very hairs of your head are all numbered. Fear not therefore: ye are of more value than many sparrows. KJV* Eternity is forever.

We have a new nature when we are born again. The Holy Spirit, Himself, is our Teacher and when we are baptized in the Holy Spirit, He will work through us to work the plan of God for each one individually and the Master Plan of the Father will be fulfilled. The Holy Spirit reveals the mysteries of God to us individually. God has a purpose for your life and for mine. God will order our life, bringing total fulfillment and success as we hear His Voice and obey Him.

Keep in mind that the Body of Christ is to be married to the Lord. The Body of Christ is the Army of the Lord. We are the virginal warrior Bride. It is an army that is constantly on the move. It is moving forward, taking ground, and redeeming the time. Mankind has sought freedom for millennia. Generation upon generation has fought war after war for freedom in one realm or another. Every institution has been challenged. Bondage after bondage has been overcome. God has been busy restoring mankind and raising him up in the fullness of His life. Freedom is essential for true life to occur. The love of and desire for freedom is key in the walk of the spirit. The nation of America is called with a redemptive purpose of spiritual freedom. It is here that spiritual freedom is to be realized for all mankind and the battles are fought to attain it. God brought peoples out of the nations to America to bring the nations of peoples in to God. From its inception until the current time more missionaries have gone into the nations from America than anywhere on earth. In recent elections our nation chose the charisma of personality rather the ideals of freedom. We have been defeated by the very system of government that was initially used to give us our freedom. Enemies have used our system of government to enslave us. Therefore, we may conclude that it is not government that brings freedom: It is God!

God gave the people of Israel the Law when they refused to come to Him at Mount Sinai, and God gave Jesus' disciples the Church in like manner. John the Baptist and Jesus Christ presented the Kingdom of God through their ministries but God's people did not receive His King or His Kingdom. Instead they crucified the King of Glory. These two institutions (the Law and the Church) were given to mankind by God to teach and train them to know Him and understand His ways. They were given as schoolmasters that we might

48

grow up in God and His King's dominion until everything that "offends" is taken out of the way and mankind willingly receives its King. God never intended
that we venerate or worship the institution or its
instruments or look to them to be saved. This is the
error that Israel fell into as a nation. They chose
to worship the system of religion rather than the
Person of God. The Person of Almighty God is to be
the object of our worship not the institution created by Him to school us in His ways. The definition
of minister is a servant, not a lord.

Without directly addressing it, the Bible has
much to say about the motives, ways and strategies
of both God and man. Everything in our Christian
life depends on the revelation we have of the Trinity
of God: the Heavenly Father, Jesus Christ, and the
Holy Spirit. The higher our revelation of Christ,
the higher our walk in the spirit. Yet no matter the
heights we attain to, if pride or any other wrong
motive enters in, we miss the mark. Megalomania is
defined as a mania for great or grandiose performance
and/or infantile feelings of omnipotence, especially
when retained in later life. Both integrity and
purity of heart are essential in our motives, ways
and strategies in life. The only correct way is to
be like Jesus. He is our pattern in every area of
life. He is our spiritual pioneer. He related to God
as His Father.

Another area of confusion and contention among
the leadership of the Body of Christ has to do with
understanding baptism and communion, both in definition and in purpose. Different parts of the Body of
Christ have different understandings of what Baptism
and Communion accomplish, both naturally and spiritually. However, mankind cannot determine what
Baptism and Communion are and what they accomplish.
Neither can man determine what his doctrine is and
what he believes. Doctrine that originates in man's
understanding can not be of value eternally and
spiritually. Only God, Himself, can determine what
is correct doctrine and what we, as mankind, must

believe. We must hear from God and corporately come to a unified understanding in these matters. We must believe God. Scripture delineates at least nine baptisms yet also says that there is one baptism and one Spirit.

The point of this earth and our lives upon it is Jesus Christ. Man has always feared the supernatural power of Almighty God. We must let go of that fear and learn to believe. We must trust God. We must know that He is Love. We must know that His supernatural, awesome power will bring us life and good and receive it. God set His love upon us when we were yet sinners. He made a decision to love us. It was not a feeling. We must receive God. Scripture does teach us repeatedly to reverence or fear God because of His greatness but it also teaches us to love Him for His goodness. It is our love and trust in God that will propel us onward and upward and forward. God desires to be One with His Bride. It is error to only equal the Church with the Bride of Christ. It is also error to only equal the Church with the Kingdom of God. We must change into the image of the Lord Jesus Christ and be filled with the Light of God. Jesus was a humble servant. Jesus died to make all things new. These matters are crucial to our existence. We should only follow the Trinity's example of walking in love.

The point of our life on this earth is Jesus Christ. It is the Kingdom of God that is to come upon this earth. For God's Kingdom to come we must love the truth and we must love freedom. Jesus taught His disciples to preach the Kingdom of Heaven. We must do likewise. Our job is to personally obey God—not to be a controlling god to our fellow man. We must find the call God has upon our life and we must fulfill that call. We must do it. We must stay in that call until God takes us home or moves us into another call. Many great ministers have missed God on this point. Satan uses this deception at the highest levels. Realizing that God is in control and that this is His earth and His ministry on the earth will help us. Ministry is just a job. It is not who we are. We cannot choose our job. Our jobs are assigned to us by the Father. He gives us the tools we need to do the job He assigns us. Spiritual truth and spiritual freedom cannot be compromised. If our eye is dark, how great is that darkness!

So Who is this Good God, you say, and why do so few know Him? Many have been called, but few chosen because few have believed and fewer still have obeyed. And yet, even so, God's good purposes continue to be fulfilled and carried out and Mankind, as a whole, continues to come higher and higher into God's perfect plan, as generation upon generation is purified in His image. God's relationship with Mankind, as a whole, has been one of progressive growth through the millennium. Ultimately there are those who are conformed to His image and being like Him, are one with Him. This group is called the Beloved in Scripture. Scripture also teaches about the Bride, the Manchild and the Remnant.

Well then, why is there suffering, you say? God regards it favorably when we endure the pain of unjust suffering. We are called to suffer for righteousness sake. Jesus did. Suffering comes because of our free will choice. The most costly thing heaven has ever sustained is your free will. This is what our fellowship with God is made of. God values our free will. This is what family and fellowship is made of. God values life. When we choose God and we choose to subject our free will to His will, God is extremely pleased. This is His goal. But doesn't God care that we suffer? Yes, He cares much more than we care, actually. But He knows secrets about our sufferings that even we don't know. One of them is eternity. Another is obedience. Jesus Christ learned obedience to God through His suffering. He trusted God and did not retaliate. Abraham learned obedience as he went. We are waiting for the Church to be obedient. God truly has created us in His image. He has given us the ability to create. Just as God spoke this universe into being so do we speak forth the parameters

51

of our own lives. God is a Speaking Spirit. We, created in His image, are speaking spirits. For millennia we have busy as bees—creating. God is merciful and He has given us a solution to the mess we've made. He gave us a baby and named Him, Jesus Christ.

Actually God is so good that He came here Himself to solve our problems. God the Father, God the Son and God the Spirit—the Three in One. He came and lived in skin and felt what it felt like to be poor, rejected, full of sorrows and acquainted with grief. He allowed us to kill Him at the pinnacle of success and during the prime of His manhood. He forgave us. Most of us haven't really decided whether or not we forgive Him for existing. NEVER, I say never, forget that ALL things are possible with God. There is absolutely nothing impossible to God! It doesn't matter what rat hole you crawl out of. It doesn't matter how ignorant or sick you are. It doesn't matter how twisted, warped or destroyed you are. God can overcome any oppression. God can break any bondage. He created your life in the first place. He can make you into anything He wants you to be. God raises the dead. God is the Creator of the entire Universe. Nothing is impossible to Him! When you come to God and give your life to Him, He can do absolutely anything with anyone! He can set you before kings! God is GOOD. God is LOVE. When God chose to love you He did not take into consideration your current condition. He searches and seeks for those who will give Him their whole hearts. He combs the earth looking for those who will listen to Him, those who will trust Him, those who will obey Him. Will you be one that God exalts? Will you be one who will obey Him?

"Tonight, as every night, I long for you and wait for you that I might reveal unto you some secret, some treasure of truth from My vast storehouse of wisdom. Rest in Me and wait upon Me for I shall surely reveal much unto you as you do.

Trust also in Me for I, the Lord your God, shall explain to you the very mysteries of God. Yes, the very mysteries of God.

Each and every day the depths of the oceans call forth to the heighths of eternity seeking My glory, seeking My love (favour). Each and every night the mountains do howl as they yearn for My presence—that Life would be theirs once again. Deep calleth unto deep. Heighth calleth unto heighth. All do seek My glory. All do seek My Face. All desire is toward Me.

Yet it is not so with My ultimate creation—My man. Man alone rejects Me in all My creation. Man alone refuses My love. Even those who are dedicated wholly unto Me, or so they suppose, do not know or understand Who I Am. I AM Life. I AM Love. I AM all joy and happiness, grief and sorrow. I truly AM ALL in ALL.

I shall reveal even more unto you. Before all creation existed—I AM. Before anything was—I AM. All proceeds from Me. All is contained within Me. Yet I am not some giant conglomeration of microcosims. I am all intelligence. I am all knowledge. I am all Beauty. I am all Skill and Craft. Nothing was made that is made that I did not make.

Everything shall ultimately return unto Me. Even man, himself, shall return unto Me. Death and hell shall return unto Me.

Satan shall return unto Me. Eternity shall return unto Me. I AM the ALL in ALL.

Yet My people do not know this. They know very little of Me, Myself. Yet all they pursue is within Me. If My people were to pursue Me they would be absolutely fulfilled, absolutely sustained, absolutely protected. I AM everything to them. Yet they do not know Me."

God gave us a book of instructions, much more than a manual and self-help guide. It is called the Bible. All the answers and all the solutions are in it. It is the self-defining revelation of Almighty God. What's more God, Himself, uses it for one-on-one conversations with us on a daily basis. It is a very handy book. Have you ever wondered why the Bible is arranged as it is? When we consider the revelations it contains we must think, not of building block progression, but rather of an elevator that ascends from level to level. Jewish people call the first five books of the Christian Bible The Torah. The Psalms are attributed to King David of Israel. The Psalms are divided into five books. These five books are each a commentary and accompaniment on the five books of The Torah. In the four Gospels of the New Testament Jesus Christ said He had much more to tell His disciples but that they could not then bear what He had to teach them. In the Epistles of the New Testament the Pauline Epistles reveal God's pattern and progression for spiritual growth unto Christian perfection. Many believe the Pauline revelations to be the "much more" that Jesus Christ desired to reveal to those who believe Him. The three epistles: Romans, Ephesians and Thessalonians, reveal Church doctrine and revelation. They are arranged canonically, not chronologically. Romans reveals justification. Ephesians reveals sanctification. Thessalonians reveals glorification. The books of 1 Timothy and 2 Timothy reveal consecration. Many believe that the

Old Testament Book of Daniel is completed by the New Testament Book of the Revelation of Jesus Christ. The Bible has many, many secrets and hidden things in it but there is, of course, a catch. All the goodies in it are hidden too. They can only be spiritually discerned and understood as the Holy Spirit reveals them to us according to our personal desires and the decisions of our hearts — not our intellects.

The Holy Spirit is our Teacher and our Guide. The Bible is written to the people of God. It is not written to unbelievers. When God writes to the wicked (twisted, warped) He has written to those who believe (who consider themselves Christians) but have not obeyed His Word properly. *2 Peter 1:19-21 We have also a more sure word of prophecy; whereunto ye do well that ye take heed, as unto a light that shineth in a dark place, until the day dawn, and the day star arise in your hearts: Knowing this first, that no prophecy of the scripture is of any private interpretation. For the prophecy came not in old time by the will of man: but holy men of God spake as they were moved by the Holy Ghost. KJV* Today many individuals feel that they have a God-ordained right to choose what they, themselves, believe. Still others with dogged resolution follow the leadership of men that they can "see" rather than God alone. Yet the Bible teaches us that God is One. God has presented one truth to us in His Holy Word. We must learn to understand and believe the truth of the Bible. Heads up, people! It is up to us to choose to <u>change</u> to conform to His will and ways and allow Him to bring about that change in us by His mighty power. We must press into the Father to obtain the grace to change. Our whole lifetime was given of God for the purpose of conformity to Jesus Christ. A three sentence prayer is not all there is! When we become still and enter into His rest He will guide each Christian from within their own heart. Prophecy from without us should confirm what we have already heard and known within. We can only truly know and understand what is within us when we seek the Heart of God in prayer.

Not every opportunity is from God. Isaiah 55:8, 9 Many people run off with just the thoughts of God but don't press in to get the ways of God to see how to carry out the thoughts of God. You must understand the ways of God. God has a timing for His will to come to pass properly. Moses cried for God's Presence—God's ways. The Presence of God has to do with His Heart, His ways, His attributes and His justice, i.e. His nature. It is the same as His shadow. Presence = Shadow. God's Presence cancels self. God's Presence brings heavens realities into your life. God's Presence will still you and quiet you. God's Presence and quietness is the result of abundance. True natural and earthly abundance is found in taking joy in the simple, everyday things of life. Spiritual abundance comes in God's Presence. The Hebrew children only knew God's acts. And finally, you must wait upon Him. When we take the first opportunity presented to us we might miss God's best. We must listen to Him. God's timing is always perfect. It has been said that it is better to go too slow when following God's leading than too fast. Are we willing to wait decades for the fulfillment of God's will in our lives? It has been said that life is what happens while we are waiting for the vision given us of Jesus Christ to come to pass. God wants to give exponential growth but often the Church isn't ready to receive it. Too often one runs without having gotten a really good look at the goal; i.e. we must receive the highest vision of Jesus Christ as is possible before we run. When something is really of God, He brings it to pass all by Himself. We must not get into error by trying to force the fulfillment of something God has said to us according to our will and understanding and in our own timing. Let go of the fear that your life is not going to count or that you won't be able to do anything for God. God will do what He said to you that He would do, **if** you follow His leading. God, the Father, spoke audibly and publicly to Jesus three times as recorded in the Scriptures. When we are in the will of God and are obedient to His will, God speaks to us. What has God said to you lately?

One of the very best things about God is that He is supernatural. Smith Wigglesworth said, "We can't know God by what we feel or see or hear. We can only know God by what is said about Him in His Word." We must not go to the world to form an understanding of Who God is. The prayer closet is not the place to get to know the Heavenly Father. The first thing God will reveal to us in the prayer closet is our own self. We must go to the Word of God to get to know the Heavenly Father. We can only know of God what the Holy Spirit tells us and confirms with the Word of God.

Remember when you were a kid and you wanted to fly and be able to disappear. You dreamed of so many exciting adventures? That is because God created us to be that way. Eternity is like that. One of His secrets is that we can begin to live like we will in eternity here on earth. The choice is ours. God is extremely exciting and does the neatest things. He uses His power in the most delightful and powerful ways imaginable. Think of mountains and the intricacies of an orchid. *Isaiah 55:12 For ye shall go out with joy, and be led forth with peace: the mountains and the hills shall break forth before you into singing all the trees of the field shall clap their hands."* Guess Who created them? My mother, Judith Gilchrist Hensley says, "God is the greatest Master of Art and Beauty. He is the greatest Musician of all. He created the notes! He is the original Horticulturist. Everything that lifts your soul, gives you joy and delight and causes you to perceive beauty is from the Creator God." God thought of the whole idea of flowers and sea shells, color and music. God is the One Who created language, the ability to communicate and thought itself. God is a Speaking Spirit. God created all that exists. God is Love.

God's compassion is truly amazing and awesome! God, Himself, is so Good! He is so rich in mercy, lovingkindness and compassion. His love is infinite.

God loves every believer as much as He loves Jesus. God loves and cares for the broken, the useless and the helpless. He cares for those who cannot help themselves—those who are of no apparent use to anyone. He restores that that is destroyed. Nothing is impossible to God! He takes care of every living thing, even the tiniest little birds and flowers. They are worlds within themselves and God is good to them. God is **WONDERFUL.** He is a Holy God. He is <u>so</u> very Good! The power of God is a holy fire! **There is always <u>more</u> of God!**

CHAPTER II

WHAT IS MAN?

**All that the Holy One, blessed be He, created in the world,
He also created in man.**
Babylonian Talmud Avot de Rabbi Nathan 29a

*W*e are the authors of what exists in the world today—we, Satan and his hosts. We, as we all well know, are full of compromises, contradictions, and depending on the way the wind is blowing, could do absolutely anything. We, as free moral agents, have the freedom, ability, and right to choose in whom we believe. **Sin is transferable — holiness is not.** For generations our ancestors have committed sins that have been passed down to us. Pride is the greatest sin of all. (Proverbs 14:3) Circumstances weigh heavily upon us. Our flesh is easily influenced by pressure. When one has not been born again, that one's spirit is cut off from life. Our five senses, being more developed than our spirits, influence us greatly and pull us from God into the things of the world and the flesh and the devil. The five senses are our ability to: see, hear, smell, taste and touch. To the spirit to whom we give our allegiance we become a door (not The Door) which enables that power to become a reality and force in the earth — either for good or evil. People are doors and when set apart for the use of the Lord they become altars. In the Old Testament to consecrate an altar was to "fill its hands", i.e. to put power in it. Atonement and purification took seven days. An altar could not be used until the eighth day. Consecration of a priest took seven days. He was consecrated or ordained by his hand being filled with power. David, as king of Israel, was anointed three times with: the Law, Grace and Perfection. Yet King David was not admitted to the outward profession of the Kingdom for a considerable time afterward.

1 Corinthians 15:21-22 For since by man (came) death, by man (came) also the resurrection of the dead. For as in Adam all die, so also in Christ shall all be made alive. ASV

Romans 5:14 Yet death held sway from Adam to Moses [the Lawgiver], even over those who did not themselves transgress [a positive command] as Adam did. Adam was a type (prefigure) of the one Who was to come [in reverse, the former destructive, the Latter saving]. AMP

Man is like a glove from which the Hand has been removed. Man is a half-alive creature with a moment of existence given to decide his eternity. All people will live forever, somewhere. Unredeemed man is full of fear and inferiority. He has no confidence to approach the Living God. Within himself he has no value or self-esteem. Guilt and condemnation plague him. Because he operates from knowledge gained through his five senses he knows within himself that he has no ability to handle what he is up against in this life. He is utterly powerless with no way of escape. He lives as a blind, deaf mute individual in a prison of his own making. He lives his life in oppression, under the hard control of another person or force. Over time he falls prey to various bondages. The natural man resorts to lying, stealing, envy/jealousy, manipulation and solitude to elevate himself above the people around him. When the covering protection of the previous generation is removed at their death, with great shock the innocence and purity of life is gone as the individual grapples not only with their own sins but the sins of those who have gone before them. William Osler 1849-1919, a Canadian-born physician, said, "The natural man has only two primal passions, to get and beget." Each individual will exist forever. The question is where? Will your existence be one of joy, bliss and contentment or one of eternal anguish? No one can decide for you. You alone have the authority and the right to choose your eternal existence.

Even more serious and worse than what is above described is the one who is enthralled with the world system. These individuals live lives of deception and delusion. Thinking they have joy and happiness their time is spent deviously conspiring to gain more and more, never satisfied. They seek position, power and wealth. There are others, filled with greed and lust, who crave and long for and worship things rather than loving people. They live for the thrill of physical stimulation and experience, yet have no peace. When still, they are consumed by unrest, torment and fear. There is only darkness and emptiness within. They are given over to wanderlust, ever seeking the unattainable. Ever learning they never come to the knowledge of the truth.

Worse still are those in various stages of possession by devils and satan, himself. Even those in the gall of bitterness in the world system recognize and are repulsed by the physical and mental sickness and evil of those so ensnared. First enticed to wickedness by greedy desire, they progress to actions of violence and evil. Then they are compelled and finally forced to harm themselves and others about them. Their end is eternal destruction in the depths of hell itself.

"The path of judgment is a clear one. Pride is the beginning. Pride giveth way to iniquity (self-will). Violence cometh next, carried about on the back of frustration. Wickedness is the result. All that is left is to make an end of it. The result is destruction and death. For when wickedness is come My soul departeth. (James 4)

"This is the pathway of abominations. It is the course of unregenerate man. For dying, he shall surely die. Every man is given the choice of life or death. Each one may go from life to life or from death to death. There is no middle ground. 'Man' is poised atop a razor blade of eternity. His free will determines which way he goes. Self must be removed if he goes the way of life. Light must be removed if he goes the way of death. This is an irrevocable law in My Kingdom. Many are called. Few are chosen. Death of self is a pre-requisite. Self-will is the most dangerous thing in the universe."

Yet man was not originally created by God to suffer this doom. In the Garden of Eden God had abundantly blessed His man, Adam. God gave Adam the abundance of all the earth and He gave him work to do. *Genesis 1:28-31 And God blessed them and said to them, Be fruitful, multiply, and fill the earth, and subdue it [using all its vast resources in the service of God and man]; and have dominion over the fish of the sea, the birds of the air, and over every living creature that moves upon the earth. And God said, See, I have given you every plant yielding seed that is on the face of all the land and every tree with seed in its fruit; you shall have them for food And to all the animals on the earth and to every bird of the air and to everything that creeps on the ground—to everything in which there is the breath of life—I have given every green plant for food. And it was so. And God saw everything that He had made, and behold, it was very good (suitable, pleasant) and He approved it completely. And there was evening and there was morning, a sixth day.* AMP

In the Artscroll Edition of the Stone Chumash commentary on Genesis 2:6, 7, 23 it is written, "God caused the deep to rise, forming low-flying clouds filled with water to moisten the dust, from which Adam was created. It is similar to a kneader who first pours in water and then kneads the dough. Here, too: First, *He watered the soil,* and then *He formed Man. And He blew into his nostrils the soul of life.* God thus made Man out of both lower (earthly) and upper (heavenly) matter: his body from the dust and his soul from the spirit. In the words of the Zohar, 'one who blows, blows from within himself,' indicating that Man's soul is part of God's essence, as it were. This soul made Man *a living being.* Which *Onkelos* defines as a *speaking spirit."* The blood of man contains the life of man. Human blood has the same percentage of salt as the ocean water has. Jesus told us to make sure our salt retained its savor. *And......"*Adam named her gender *Ishah* (Woman), because she was taken from *Ish* (Man); left unanswered, however, is why Man is called *Ish.* That name comes from *eish* or fire, because Man is unique among all living beings in the characteristics symbolized by fire: verve and enthusiasm, lust and initiative. These characteristics enable Man to achieve dominance, attain wisdom, and develop culture. But the same fire can cause the mass destruction that has marred humanity almost since the beginning of time. Controlled and directed, that fire can create spiritual kingdoms that surpass the angels."

In the Appendix to the Companion Bible, written
by E. W. Bullinger, four principal Hebrew words are
rendered "man". They represent him from four different points of view:

1. *Adam*, denotes his origin, as being made from the
   "dust of the *Adamah*" ground (Latin *homo*).
2. *Ish*, has regard to sex, a male (Latin *vir*).
3. *Enosh*, has regard to his infirmities, as physically
   mortal, and as to character, incurable.
4. *Geber*, has respect to his strength, a mighty man.

In addition to this, in Appendix 13 VI, E. W.
Bullinger writes, *Nephesh* is used of Man, and is
most often translated <u>soul.</u> Yet "the usage of the
word *nephesh* by the Holy Spirit in the Word of
God is the only guide to the true understanding
of it..............It will be seen that the word
'soul', in its theological sense, does not cover all
the ground, or properly represent the Hebrew word
'*nephesh*'. The English word 'soul' is from the Latin
solus = alone or sole, because the maintenance of
man as a living organism, and all that affects his
health and well-being, is the one sole or main thing
in common with every living thing which the Lord God
has made. The correct Latin word for the theological
term 'soul' (or *nephesh*) is *anima*; and this is from
the Greek *anemos* = air or breath, because it is this
which keeps the whole in life and in being."
In Appendix 9 V-VII, E. W. Bullinger writes, *Ruach*
is the invisible part of man (psychological) given
by God at man's formation at birth, and returning
to God at his death. It is also the invisible characteristics of man manifesting themselves in states
of mind and feeling and the whole person."
Thus we see that in his creation man is a composite being. The basic elements of fire, water, earth
and wind were used to create man's physical parts.
When God pronounced His righteous judgment upon man
at his fall, He said, "dying thou shalt surely die".

In his composite being, man's physical parts did not immediately die. Adam lived to be 930 years old. The spiritual parts of man died immediately with the physical parts to follow. The *Ruwach* or breath of the Almighty which had filled man with the spiritual light, power and energy of God vacated him at the time of his judgment. This is that that must fill man once more. This only occurs when one is born-again and filled with the Holy Spirit. The power and intensity of this experience has the potential to increase time and time again as one is filled with more and more of God. God is never limited and nothing is impossible to Him. We are able to have more and more of Him throughout eternity. Yet each container only has a certain capacity. For more and more of Him there must be less and less of me. Therefore, we must not limit Him with unbelief, darkness or ignorance. Each individual person must make a quality choice to repent and change. Each one must choose to be free of darkness, ignorance and unbelief. We must let go of it and receive new light and life from God so that we can walk upon His ways of peace and salvation.

To further compound the composite nature of humanity, the Woman was taken from one side of Man. Woman was not taken from the dust of the earth. Therefore Man was divided into two halves to bring multiplication of his essence. There is only one way for mankind to come into wholeness and that is in God. Man and woman are each the synergistic half of a whole and that "whole" is but a fourth? Of a greater whole because man and woman complete each other. This is not just about sex and the propagation of the species! VIRGINS: The reference is to the pollutions connected with the great religious system under antichrist. *These are they which were not defiled with women; for they are virgins. Revelation 14:4* In Scripture, "woman" spiritually represents a belief system.

The Tree of the Knowledge of Good and Evil is, in its essence, a division. It contains the lower, physical parts and the higher spiritual parts. It contains lies and truth. God desired Oneness in man and with man. But prior to his eating of the Tree of Life his integrity (oneness, wholeness) had to be proved. It was at this time that man fell. Man, of his own free will, chose two visions rather than one because his desire was to the flesh rather than to the spirit. Our desire is key to our relationship with our Heavenly Father. God speaks to this in Isaiah 58:3 when, speaking to His own people, He condemns the motives of their fasting. In the Garden of Eden Adam not only chose His wife's leadership over God's leadership but after he had made his choice, he hid what he did. He acted on his "knowledge of evil" (the fruit was fast acting) and lied. *Job 31:33-35 If like Adam or like [other] men I have concealed my transgressions, by hiding my iniquity in my bosom because I feared the great multitude and the contempt of families terrified me so that I kept silence and did not go out of the door—Oh, for a hearing! Oh, for an answer from the Almighty! Let my adversary write out His indictment [and put His vague accusations in tangible form] in a book! AMP* The Fall of Man in the Garden of Eden necessitated the righteous judgment of God to bring about the restoration of man and justice of God for all mankind. God promised to send His Seed into the earth to accomplish His end. Without God, man's existence is so fleeting, so temporary that he is incapable of comprehending the greatness of God and the huge scope of His plan for Man. God doesn't want anyone with Him who doesn't want to be with Him. Selfishness greedily longs for benefits and blessings without the attached responsibilities. Selfishness seeks isolated good and the control of that good while obedience lets go of all and surrenders to the leadership of another. Trust vs. control is another key to our relationship with our Heavenly Father. God never forces compliance. Once one surrenders all, He will bring the ultimate choice into being, even though ignorance and fear cloud the mind temporarily. Truth and understanding bring us up higher. Obedience moves us forward.

Many earthly religions have duplicated the soulish, emotional and intellectual benefits of what is morally right and good in God's character. Yet they have not Life! This duplication of moral goodness is, in itself, a deception that waylays an individual's progression to the Truth. Social programs of redemption that teach and train men to "be nice" and "do good" do not save their spirit, soul and body eternally. Only Jesus Christ has the needed Life within Himself. Jesus knew and understood Himself and the call of God upon Him when He was on the earth. He bought mankind back with His substitutionary death. Only the Holy Spirit has the needed Truth within Himself. There is only one true way to God. Rev. Dave Roberson teaches that Jesus Christ was the only man born spiritually alive since Adam. He is the only One able to give true spiritual life to you. Only God can fill you with His supernatural life, light and power. Only God can breathe His breath into your innermost being filling you with "joy unspeakable and full of glory". Man's religions merely curb the passions of the soul of man.

God is Good. His purpose in creating mankind was not selfish. He had and has not now any negative ulterior motives. His desire toward mankind is to love and to bless—to provide and to care for us. He desires relationship and companionship. God desires a Family. *Beloved is man, for he was created in the image of God; still greater was the love in that it was made known to him that he was created in the image of God. Mishnah Pirqei Avot 3:15*

When Jesus Christ was born, He was born of a virgin. A virgin is a person who has not been defiled spiritually with religion or physically with sex or in their soul with a lie. It is a scientific fact that a baby's blood comes from its father, bypassing the body of the mother in whom it is nurtured for nine months. Mary was highly developed in her faith. She was not in unbelief as Zacharias was. God favors those who believe Him. Therefore as Jesus Christ was conceived by the Holy Spirit, His blood came from

His Heavenly Father God. Why did God wait four thousand years for the fulfillment of His Promised Seed to crush the head of the serpent? Forty-two generations of mankind came and went before there was an Authorized Agent of such purified flesh as Mary, the descendant of King David, and Joseph, the descendant of King David, to provide suitable earthly parents for God's only begotten Son. Joseph kept his mouth shut. He was a person of integrity. Neither Joseph nor Mary discussed with anyone anything of what the angel had spoken to them. They obeyed instantly what God spoke through the angel because their faith was developed. They believed and obeyed God instantly. Forty-two generations had passed—each one fulfilling their Divine call from Almighty God. Thus the passage of four thousand years resulted in the purification of the flesh nature of the family line which brought forth the Messiah. Developed faith—trusting God easily, quickly and readily—takes generations to bring forth by God. Joseph was born of the visible, outward line of kings. Mary was born of the hidden, secreted line of prophets. Jesus was both the Son of Man and the Son of God. He is the true and rightful King of Israel. His composite parts found unity and oneness in God. He, and others about Him, heard the audible Voice of God three times in His earthly ministry. God called Him, *"My Beloved Son in Whom I AM well pleased"*.

God desires Oneness with Man as He has Oneness with the Trinity. Not all shall attain to these lofty heights of glory but some shall. God is looking for those who will sing Him "a new song". God's spiritual Seed shall not return unto Him void. It shall accomplish its purpose. God has made His Throne ready for "whosoever will" to come to it. God has made His banqueting hall ready for the Marriage Supper of the Lamb. He will have his hall filled with guests. He desires many fully restored sons of God to bring His will to pass on earth as it is in heaven. God's original intentions for man are His eternal intentions for man.

The precious Holy Spirit is the expression of God on earth today. He is the One Who brings the miraculous power of God to pass in this earth. The Holy Spirit is the Agent of Power to affect the will of God in humanity. God has delegated His authority to specific men, as Agents of Authority, conformed to the image of God in Christ Jesus for God's specific purposes and plan to be fulfilled. When the Agent of Power confirms the words of an Agent of Authority as they speak forth the rhema word of God, the will of God is performed bringing God's plan and purposes into reality in the natural realm.

In His original creation and commission of man in the Garden of Eden, God gave man a job to do. He was given a position or a job by God to 1) multiply himself and 2) guard and 3) care for the Garden in which he lived. Work is God's idea. God desires for us to work so that our needs will be met. God desires us to work that we have ability to give to others. The Bible teaches that if a man will not work he will not eat. Therefore to exist, man must work. When God commissioned man to guard the Garden of Eden He gave mankind the ability and the responsibility to protect what God has given him to enjoy. There are cultures on other continents that support the adage, "What's yours is mine." Yet God's initial commands to Adam and Eve don't support this. God desires man to care for what is given him. Maintenance is nine-tenths of ownership. It requires the most effort.

Man's multiplication began first when God created woman from him by taking his rib bone and creating her physically. God also took the parts of man needed to procreate and nurture and put them in woman. God put man's emotional identity in woman so that man was left with an intellectual identity. Man then, was best suited to leadership. As with the man, God blew His *Ruwach* into woman, giving her spiritual life. The woman is most affected by what she hears, while the man is most affected by what he sees.

God gave His Man power in the form of dominion, whereby Man was to guard and keep the Garden of Eden.

By the power of God Man knows who he, himself, is and Who God is. Many men are fascinated with God's power. When they think of God they think of His power. When men are young their power is exercised in the form of physical strength. As they grow older their strength is internalized more and more in the form of knowledge, and hopefully, as wisdom. Women tend to think of God's love when they think of God. Since the Church is lead primarily by men thoughts of dominion predominate. Herodotus (c.485-c.425 BC) in book 9 of his Histories wrote, "The most hateful torment for men is to have knowledge of everything but power over nothing."

God gave man the ability to exercise dominion when He gave Man the job or position of guarding and keeping the Garden of Eden. Who you have your position with determines what authority you are able to operate in. Who you are is your position in life. This is especially true for men. The job they perform often defines their concept of self. A man's position limits what sphere of influence he is able to operate in the natural realm. A man's position in life determines what his authority is capable of influencing. In a person's position in the natural realm in the world system their job frequently defines their persona.

With women this is true in regard to their relation to their womb. Historically, the womb is a woman's primary source of self-image. Whether or not a woman is successful in producing and rearing the man's offspring determines her ability to have positive self-worth. Currently, the world system has "liberated" women so that they are free to live as men. Just as Eve, the mother of all living, was deceived in the Garden of Eden because she desired to be wise, like God, so also do women today desire the benefits of being men and the benefits of being women, without any of the costs. A woman's five sexual functions have been reduced to the act of coitus. Abortion and marriage are being warred over in modern society. If a woman becomes pregnant she has the option of abortion. Thus her career can remain her main focus and identity. Women are no longer women, used of God to create and nurture life; they are merely human beings, spiritually deceived and bound by the world system and given work to do: i.e. slaves.

Humanism is the deification of self. Webster's Dictionary defines humanism as a doctrine, attitude, or way of life centered on human interests or values; especially a philosophy that asserts the dignity and worth of man and his capacity for self-realization through reason and that **often rejects supernaturalism.** When one is a Christian who is deceived by humanism, the ultimate end of that life will be lawlessness. W. E. Vine's Dictionary defines lawlessness as the rejection of the law, or will, of God and the substitution of the will of self. The thought is not simply that of doing what is unlawful, but of flagrant defiance of the known will of God. The display of lawlessness by the lawless one will be the effect of the attempt by the powers of darkness to overthrow the Divine government. In Christ, individuals do not determine their own path in life. Jesus Christ is Lord. That means He will tell each one what they are to do and how they are to do it. Joseph and Mary didn't try to figure it out. They believed God and they obeyed God. Submission and obedience are key to victory in life and eternity. God must receive all the glory!

The influence of authority created by one's worldly occupation is not valid for the true Christian, spiritually. Spiritually our ability to exercise power and strength is in direct relation to our position with God. This is determined by our relationship to Jesus Christ. This is why He is called The Door. When a human person receives the Seed of God in the Person of the Lord Jesus Christ by faith in His death, burial and resurrection they immediately become righteous before God. This is what the Church teaches us. It is the imputed righteousness of Jesus Christ that a person receives when they are born-again. God declares them "right". This is the gospel or Good News that the Apostle Paul proclaimed. God is holy and because of His holiness He demands righteousness. When we speak of God's righteousness, we speak of three things: His mandatory righteousness, His punitive righteousness, and His redemptive righteousness. God demands righteousness because His holiness is our standard for living. This righteousness was lost by Adam and Eve in the Fall. Yet the righteousness Christian mankind now has is far more important and valuable to us than the righteousness Adam and Eve had because it cost the life of Jesus Christ. How much of Christ's righteousness do you walk in, in reality? What God demands is justice, lovingkindness, and a humble walk with Him. God is intensely concerned with the *heart* of man. He is concerned with our attitude of life, that we grow in maturity in Jesus Christ so that we might become more like Him. He has given us the standard to be holy as He is holy. One day God will perfect us in holiness, but daily we are to grow in maturity and grow toward God's holiness to conform to His nature and character. One day God will judge the world in righteousness with true justice.

"In the course of time very often men and leaders become confused and err in that they impugn the righteousness of others unto themselves. For they do not stand in their own righteousness but in the righteousness of another. In this they do err. So it is with My Body. Very often men and leaders within My Body impugn the righteousness of others or of I, Myself, into their own lives when it is not a truth or a reality. For you see, My daughter, I impute My righteousness to those whom I choose—not those who choose themselves. I receive those who are of an humble, a

broken and a contrite spirit. It is these that I seek after. It is not merely those that seek Me that obtain My righteousness but those that I seek after. There is much confusion in My Body about this matter."

Proverbs 20:9 Who can say, "I have cleansed my heart, I am pure from my sin"?

Ezekiel 14:14 ...even though these three men, Noah, Daniel and Job were in its midst, by their own righteousness they could only deliver themselves, declares the Lord GOD.

Romans 3:19 Now we know that whatever the Law says, it speaks to those who are under the Law, so that every mouth may be closed and all the world may become accountable to God; NASU

"The Great Whore in the earth is the Church, the false bride of Christ Jesus. Many are called, few are chosen. It is the chosen of the earth who come into conflict with the whore. These are they who are uncompromisingly righteous. These are they who love not their lives unto death for they love light and life and truth more than they love self and position and power and wealth. These are they who are counted worthy to share My Throne, My honor and My glory. It is for such as these that I died. I have come to bring life to men not self. I have come to bring My glory not the precepts of men. All who live godly in Christ Jesus shall suffer

persecution. Righteousness is at odds with the trappings of the church world."

God freely gives His power to all His children. Yet it is the one who responds in love and obedience that gains His favor. That one is accepted by Him and gains entrance to more of Who He is by the transformation of their minds, with knowledge, and understanding with insight, of Christ Jesus. Yet even the heart motive of that person will be proved or tested by God.

It is important to note that Adam and Eve were never given dominion or authority over other human beings. They were given dominion and authority over the animal realm, the physical health of humans and animals and the physical environment. Mankind will never have authority over another human being. God did not conquer Man on the Cross of Jesus Christ. God sustains our right to our free-will choice. Man has not been given authority over other people. When Jesus Christ walked the earth in His three-and-a-half year ministry, He exercised dominion over satan, demons, all evil supernaturalism, provision, all sickness and disease, death, all natural elements such as water, etc. He was our spiritual pioneer. Jesus Christ has made the way for each son of God, conformed to His image, to live and walk in like manner in the earth today. The example of how He lived in His thirty-three years of life, His three-and-a-half year ministry; His death, burial and resurrection are our example today. The greatest authority a believer has is obedience.

When Man is initially born-again, as a composite being, their life is lived both in the natural realm of the world system and the spiritual realm of God's Kingdom. Thus their life is compartmentalized. However, it is God's plan and desire that we grow up in Him. God wants each person to be sold-out to Him. God has called "whosoever will" to be saved. He has called many to be sons. Many are called to positions of leadership in the Body of Christ. The question is, when you attain to the power and position of God what will you DO with it? The Apostle Paul prayed that we would be saved spirit, soul and body. He prayed that we would be saved with eternal glory. For this to occur we must submit to God's leadership. God has given us His Holy Spirit to accomplish this in our life. Submission means we lay aside our own ideas and ways and do it His way. In the mid-16th century it was said, "Every man for himself and God for us all." Yet we must not live for our self. Just because a person has heard God or another person say they are called of God to do great things for Him does not mean it shall come to pass if they refuse to obey God! We must learn to walk in love with other people. We must first of all, learn to hear the Voice of God and hearing Him, we must follow His leadership. We must listen to the Holy Spirit and follow His leading moment by moment. God must have first place in our life. Understand there is a price to pay for His plan.

If God did not conquer something then we have no authority over it. Jesus Christ's authority is over the things He conquered. Jesus has conquered and has authority over sin, disease, poverty, fear, failure, religion and all that satan is. Satan is a defeated foe. God desires believers to become disciples. God desires His children to grow to the maturity of sonship. He desires each one of us to be so filled with God, the Holy Spirit, that we have eyes that hear. What does that mean? It means that God wants us so alive in the realm of the spirit that when we merely look at a person or situation or circumstance, we hear His Voice giving us wisdom and instruction—at length—in paragraphs! It means we will walk with God through this life, as His friend, as His son, doing His will for His glory. These truths are not brought about in a person's life through mental assent to their veracity. Each individual has to personally choose to "do" what they know to be true. Each one must walk in the light they have and obey God. When we as born-again, spirit-filled believers in Christ

Jesus walk as children of light in obedience to the leading of the Holy Spirit to fulfill the purposes of the Father God time is stretched and expanded for us that God's will be supernaturally completed. Our walking in the light with Jesus connects time and light and furthers God's purposes in the earth. Rev. Mac Hammond has written, "So, as we walk in the light, we get closer to God until time begins to stretch and we accomplish more. Time is slowed for us. It goes further and lasts longer. We are on God's time. The truth about the supernatural is that it's simply God coming together with man. You and God have been joined by virtue of the blood of Jesus. The supernatural will carry anyone over any obstacle that the natural portion isn't sufficient to meet."

It is really important that you, as an individual, realize that you must seek after life, light and truth to live eternally with God. The answer to all God's commands are found when you walk in the light as He is in the light. Rev. Hammond wrote, "Since God is light and God and His Word are one, we can begin walking in the light by getting into the Word of God. Prayer will also bring us into the Presence of God. So walking in the light is not only reading and studying the Word, it's also praying and communing with God." Let your self life die so that you may obey God's will for you fully in the earth. Do the job He has called you to do. Don't follow after men, especially religious men. Don't be preoccupied with the darkness men tell you is in you. Focus on the light of life in Christ Jesus. God doesn't care whether or not you keep certain "rules". He does want you to be full of His joy. Keep your eyes glued on Jesus and run after Him. Enter into His Oneness with the Father and the Holy Spirit. Christ's Spirit must take over all parts of your body until your mind, emotions, and will blend with your spirit and are filled with the Holy Spirit and then you will have the Mind of Christ. People must be taught to follow the Holy Spirit not a ministry position. The epitome of spiritual success is not preaching from a pulpit. Ministry is not God. God is God. The Church has so glorified itself that many believers feel they must have a "ministry" to validate their existence. Otherwise they feel invisible and worthless. The ministry is only a tool that God sometimes uses to have relationship with individuals. A personal relationship with the Living God is greater than a ministry! God has other ways and means to have relationship. We are not to look at faults in ourselves or others about us. We are to keep our eyes on Jesus. Man will always lead astray. No man is filled with the Holy Spirit 100% of the time. Only God is God. Man will always sabotage your efforts. Man will always destroy the precious fruit of the vine. Trust Jesus. Please meditate on Ezekiel 14:1-11; Romans 10. We are to go to God with our need and our failure. God will use men in our lives. He will work **upon us** through men but we are not to seek God **through** men. God wants each individual to seek Him themselves, personally. Develop your relationship with God through prayer, God's Holy Word, the Bible, and through Church attendance and involvement. (There is a fine line here, but it is important in order to find God's best.)

It is also important to note that God, Himself, does not relate to man in time or from the vantage point of time. Rather He relates to mankind from His position in eternity. God is Eternal. There is no time in God. And although He operates legally, He is not legalistic. God sees the end from the beginning and the beginning at the end. He knows those who are His. God has said, "Whosoever will, let them come..." The Chosen, are chosen when they choose Him. He chooses all men. Individuals eliminate themselves from position with God through their choices. God gives each person the desire of their own heart. God will fulfill your motives. God's choice of an individual, ultimately, is predicated by their abandonment unto Him. An individual must ultimately choose God over their own existence. In other words, they must die to their own self and choose God. Thereby, God has removed Himself from The Chosen, in that they, as individuals, make the choice. God chooses whether or not to accept each one. God is only Good.

Cease from anger; forsake wrath. Know ye not that I am the Prince of Peace? Fret not thyself because of evildoers. Be not dismayed at the wranglings and strife of men. Rest in God. I, alone, am the fulfillment of all your desire. I, alone, am able to meet your need. Rest in God. Trust in God. Be at peace.

Psalm 67:3 Let the people praise thee, O God; let all the people praise thee. KJV

Ezra 4:4 Then the people of the land weakened the hands of the people of Judah, and troubled them in building. KJV

CHAPTER III

WHAT IS RELIGION?

*S*alvation has been shrouded in secrecy for the last two thousand years. Yet the Bible teaches us that God is Light. What He does He does in the Light. Why are even the most holy of God's ministers reluctant to discuss the nuts and bolts of the process of salvation? As Christians we must know what it is that causes and results in our salvation so that we are enabled to take that same salvation to multitudes of lost humanity. We must know what we have in Christ Jesus to be enabled to do it on a consistent basis. Is there anyone you want to go to hell? If there is, then you, my friend, are wicked. People who are wicked but have been born-again are in this condition, not because they have or do not have demons, but because they don't know their Heavenly Father. God is Love. If you don't have the Love of the Father within you, you become twisted and warped with unbelief. If you desire to use the truths in this book for selfish ends then you are wicked and violent in the eyes of God. Repent! Receive Life! Seek to know God for this is eternal life.

Evil is so far beneath God that it is not even a consideration in His thoughts. Have you ever observed the common house fly? Scripture says that God removes demons with the flick of His finger. It is a good example of the importance of evil in the eyes of God. God even gave this example a name—Beelzebul.

Then, you contend, where does evil come from because it definitely is present in creation. It comes from Satan and from us—from our own hearts and minds and wills. Satan is lord over the world system. Jesus Christ defeated him on the Cross of Calvary. Each generation must enforce that defeat until Jesus returns the second time and makes all things new. Religion is Satan's kingdom. Satan and demons are totally real and absolutely and totally evil. Satan is evil. Satan is a defeated foe. The demonic realm, where principalities and powers rule, exist to challenge God. This is the second heaven—the etheric plane. God through the Apostle John in the Book of Revelation tells us that Satan will ultimately be thrown into the Lake of Fire forever throughout all eternity. I choose to believe and act on that future event now just as Jesus acted upon the truth of the healing virtue of God before He had hung upon the Cross of Calvary to legally obtain God's healing virtue. 1 John 4:3-6 AMP.

When satan was created by God he was a son of God, a cherubim, perfect in all his ways until iniquity was found in him. Satan was created as a covering cherub, one of four, and given the name Lucifer. His job was to protect and guard God. Lucifer was in charge of all worship of God in heaven. At some point in eternity God gave him this earth, as a son, to lord and bring to God. Yet Satan desired the position at the right Hand of God, Himself. Rather than lead the worship of God, he desired to be worshipped. Iniquity is defined as self will. In other words satan exerted his will against the will of God for himself. He rebelled against God in heaven. He rebelled against God in the Garden of Eden when he deceived Eve and was the instrument of Adam's rebellion. *Ezekiel 28:16 By the abundance of thy traffic they filled the midst of thee with violence, and thou hast sinned: ASV* God calls using His power to fulfill personal, or others', desires or agendas "violence".

It was because of violence that Lucifer lost his place in heaven and became satan. This is how the Father deals with princes in His kingdom who rebel against Him. God's power belongs to Him and although He delegates His authority, His power must be used for the express purpose of fulfilling His will alone. Because of this satan was judged by God three times. His power and his authority were progressively limited and diminished when, first of all, he was cast out of heaven and fell like lightening to the earth; secondly, in the Garden of Eden God said he would crawl on his belly and eat the dust of the earth; and, thirdly, at The Cross of Calvary when Jesus Christ said, "It is finished!". His future judgment is to be thrown into the lake of fire for all eternity.

F - FALSE
E - EVIDENCE
A - APPEARING
R - REAL

Satan has no power over us unless we believe he does. And that is the key! **What do you believe?** When an evil report of unbelief comes to you how big you view the enemy and how big you view the problem is exactly what you will get and how the devil will see you. Start praying and ask God to make you positive. Whatever is not of faith is sin. Sin means separation from God. Fear is the medium of exchange in Satan's kingdom. Fear is the fuel that keeps Satan's kingdom running. Often individuals do not perceive themselves as fearful when, in reality, there are large, hidden lakes of fear within them. How much fear is within you? Ask God to show you what fears are within you and to remove them from you.

Faith is the medium of exchange in the realm of the spirit world. If you believe it, it is so. The only power satan currently has is your own faith. He wants you to use your faith in fear. He wants to use you and your own faith against you to defeat yourself. He has no power without the agreement of a born-again person. The only methods satan has left to him are his ability to lie to you in your thought realm, to work deception in your circumstances and life and create a bad atmosphere for your emotions. Satan's techniques, as at the beginning, are to question the Word of God, to present a lie wrapped in the truth and to quote the Word of God out of context. Satan is the father of all liars. John 8:44 His main tool is deception. Deception is satan's most powerful weapon. He desires to prevent Pentecost in each individual life so the Teacher won't teach humanity about the Father from the Word of God as we operate His revelation gift. We must choose, on purpose, to savour and desire the things of God rather than the things of man. Therefore, satan desires to use you against your own self to defeat you in life. In spiritual warfare, when dealing with sickness, disease, infirmity, pestilence and plague first deal with the fear of the thing, then deal with the spirit of the thing itself. Also know that unbelief in the head will never pass into the heart if it doesn't pass through the mouth. In juxtaposition to this: evil is not lost in the earth. Just as faith is not lost, so also, evil is not lost. When a human person believes for something and speaks it forth—somewhere, sometime it shall occur. We must keep our shields well-oiled and hold them high in faith being ever ready to speak the Word of the Father as the Holy Spirit gives unction. Never allow satan to have the last word. Do not face evil quietly. Protect yourself from random evil in the earth by the shed blood of Jesus Christ. "Plead the Blood" over yourself. Speak the Word of God in faith as the Holy Spirit unctions it.

Even when one is a Christian satan desires the destruction of your soul (mind, emotions, will) for eternity. One of the main ways he does this is through your own words out of your own mouth. The prophet Isaiah said in *Isaiah 14:16, 17, 20 "they that see thee shall narrowly look upon thee, and consider thee, saying, Is this the man that made*

*the earth to tremble, that did shake kingdoms; that
made the world as a wilderness, and destroyed the
cities thereof; that opened not the house of his
prisoners?...........because thou hast destroyed thy
land, and slain thy people: the seed of evildoers
shall never be renowned." KJV*

God gave this earth to satan to rule. Currently,
Satan is the god of the world system. Originally,
he had been invited as a son of God to save this
planet for God. I believe each inhabited planet must
be saved by a son of God, sent from God's throne to
bring love, life and light to the willing that all
of God's creation be delivered of darkness and filled
with the light of God. Yet satan failed to fulfill
his call. As an anointed cherub that covered the
Presence of God he was the chief worshipper of God
in heaven. Music is in him. Beauty is in him. Yet
pride was also found in him. *Ezekiel 28:17 Thine
heart was lifted up because of thy beauty, thou hast
corrupted thy wisdom by reason of thy brightness: I
will cast thee to the ground, I will lay thee before
kings, that they may behold thee. KJV* He desired the
position of Christ, at the right hand of the Father.
He was not content with his call. He walked up and
down in the midst of the stones of fire. Supernatural
power was his to command; yet not creative power.
He was in the Garden of Eden. Precious stones were
his covering. It is interesting to note that the
High Priest of Israel was also given these precious
stones as his covering. Each of these stones represented one of the twelve tribes, i.e. the twelve
sons of Jacob, collectively called Israel by God.
The order of the twelve tribes, according to their
birth, was engraved on the two stones on the High
Priest's shoulders (the place of strength, joy and
government). The order on the twelve stones of the
High Priest's breastplate (the place of love and
life) was according to the twelve tribes, as chosen
by Jehovah's love. These precious stones are also the
foundation stones of the city of God in heaven. At
that time they still represent the Tribes of Israel.

Only the arrangement of the stones (and the tribes) varies due to their obedience to the commands of God, the office to which they are given and the use for which they are used. Because of satan the cities of the world became a wilderness and the people under his authority became prisoners. He did not have the power to set his prisoners free. Satan caused the people given to him of God to be slain.

Satan, in imitation of God, has a highly organized hierarchy of evil. He is incapable of creation. He cannot create. He only imitates. His throne imitates the Throne of God. He cannot stop the fulfillment of God's will in seeking Oneness with His Man but he is endeavoring to keep the many from finding the path to the Throne of God. He will do everything in his power to blind mankind and keep them from receiving their inheritance in Christ Jesus. *2 Corinthians 4:4 For the god of this world has blinded the unbelievers' minds [that they should not discern the truth], preventing them from seeing the illuminating light of the Gospel of the glory of Christ (the Messiah), Who is the Image and Likeness of God. AMP John 8:31-32 Then said Jesus to those Jews which believed on him, If ye continue in my word, then are ye my disciples indeed; and ye shall know the truth, and the truth shall make you free. KJV* Satan's kingdom is one where the flesh of man is "fully alive". Personal wealth and power are considered to be the epitome of success. Jesus died to set mankind free. Satan desires to keep men bound. He lies and deceives with religion, false supernatural acts and false holiness. The leadership of his kingdom is an imitation of Who the Holy Spirit is and what He has done through the Church, the Body of Christ, in the earth today. His power imitates the gifts of the Holy Spirit. *Hebrews 2:14-17 Inasmuch then as the children have partaken of flesh and blood, He Himself likewise shared in the same, that through death He might destroy him who had the power of death, that is, the devil, and release those who through fear of death were all their lifetime subject to bondage. For indeed He does not give aid to angels, but He does give aid to the seed of Abraham. NKJV*

Satan has the power of death over the unredeemed flesh nature of mankind. His is the father of all lies. He is a destroyer. He is all bondage. Everything he does is opposite to, upside down to and in contradiction to the activity of God. His kingdom of the world system imitates the Kingdom of God. Satan's kingdom has a fourfold expression in the world system: Religion or Spirituality, Mammon or Economics, Dominions or Governments and Society. (Daniel 7) The greatest power in his kingdom is the cherubim because satan was originally the anointed cherub that covered the Presence of God. Yet there remains a segment of society, covering the whole of the Earth, which has remained in Satan's province. They have been his own peculiar treasure, as it were. There are those who are given to a finer sensibility than others. They are creative and artistic. Generally speaking, vocationally, they are involved in artistic pursuits such as drama, theater, writing, painting, singing, dancing and all manner of creativity. The expressions of creativity are myriad. They "march to the tune of a different drummer", so to speak. Sexually many are trapped in various perversions. Many are homosexual or lesbian, etc. As concerns them, they feel they see a brighter, whiter light. Yet that "light" is actually found in the deepest, blackest, darkness. It is now time to bring them into the true Light of the manifest Glory of God. This shall be accomplished when true worship is brought through the Body of Christ to the Father. As pure and holy worship is conducted through the Body of Christ by the Holy Spirit of God, Himself, and to Himself, these captives of Satan shall be set free.

Cherubim are creatures who cover God. The Lord of Hosts dwells between (enthroned above) the cherubim in the Old Testament. They are a celestial order of spirit beings. In the Greek language the word is *zoa* or *zoon, (a form of the Greek word zoe)* which means animal, living ones or living creatures. They are distinct from angels. One facet of their position was to hold in safe keeping what God committed to them. They walk up and down in the midst of the stones of fire that are beneath the Throne of God. The earth is Jehovah's footstool. Each cherubim's position round about, before and beneath (this causes me to think they move about) the Throne of God is beside a wheel within a wheel that is covered with eyes within and without. In Genesis 3:24 they were placed to keep or guard the way to the Tree of Life and preserve the hope of re-genesis for a ruined creation. Each cherubim has four faces {ox or calf, man, eagle, lion}, just as there are four gospels in the New Testament, each giving a different perspective of God. Cherubim are represented by the symbolic heads of the four great divisions of animate creation: the lion (king of wild beasts), the ox (lord of tame beasts), the eagle (divinity of heaven and of birds), man (of humanity). There are four cherubim and four is the number of Creation. Their song, when they speak, is of creation (Revelation 4:11) and is in connection with the earth. Redemption is a new song for them, relating to others. Cherubim have the ability to rearrange matter at a molecular level. A Biblical example of this is Pharaoh's magicians, Janes and Jambres. When Moses threw down his rod and it became a serpent, they threw down their rods to become serpents. They used the power of the evil cherubim to imitate the power of God through Moses.

Satan does not have the power or ability to create from nothing. Only God can do that. He also does not have the power or ability to raise the dead. Only God can do that. Satan has the ability to kill but not to give life. Therefore, satan and his kingdom are not to be taken lightly or are they to be ignored. The word devil means to penetrate. Satan desires to penetrate the life of man in order to control it. Satan and his minions, like large, carnivorous predators in the African savanna, seek their prey among those who live at the edge of the herd/Body of Christ. An old proverb from the early 16th century was, "Every

man for himself, and the Devil take the hindmost."
It was said of Jesus that satan had nothing "in
Him". Scripture does not record mankind maligning
or rebuking satan. It does, however, record people
who prayed that the Lord would rebuke satan and his
leadership. Jesus, Himself, also spoke directly to
satan with God's Word to defeat his purposes. *"...it
is written...Luke 4"* Scripture teaches us that when
we humble ourselves before God, submit to His will,
forgive all and speak His Word satan must obey it.

Above all, whatever demonic powers attempt against
God in this Age will finally serve to advance God's
plans and to bring about their own ruin. For in His
superior power and wisdom God directs their evil
action to a good end. Satan and his kingdom are not
to be feared. Fear gives him power over an individual because fear is part of his kingdom. Actually,
fear is the medium of satan's kingdom as faith is
the medium of God's Kingdom. We, as Christians, are
called to faith. We operate in the realm of faith.
We must learn to speak the Word of God in faith. A.
W. Tozer wrote, "Faith is an organ of knowledge, and
love an organ of experience. God came to us in the
incarnation; in atonement He reconciled us to Himself,
and by faith and love we enter and lay hold on Him."
Kenneth E. Hagin taught that we can never have faith
beyond our knowledge. We must take our position of
authority in Christ Jesus and exercise the dominion
of God over satan and his kingdom. Our faith in the
shed blood of Jesus Christ and in Christ's birth,
death and resurrection, has set us free from satan
and his kingdom. Scripture teaches us that satan is a
defeated foe. *1 John 4:4 Little children, you are of
God [you belong to Him] and have [already] defeated
and overcome them [the agents of the antichrist],
because He Who lives in you is greater (mightier)
than he who is in the world. AMP* Be set free of the
fear of satan by faith in Jesus' Name!

In Hebrews, Chapter Four, we are exhorted to labor
to enter into the rest of God. We must labor and
strive for godliness to attain the full salvation God

has already provided in Christ Jesus. What?! You say. Are you proclaiming salvation by works? No, most definitely, no. Salvation is an accomplished fact to be received by faith. It occurred two thousand years ago on the Cross of Calvary in Christ Jesus. The Bible declares that you get to heaven not by what you do but by Who you know. Yet to make one's positional truth in salvation experiential truth, spiritual growth must occur. The paradox of Christianity is that you are striving to become who you already are. When one receives Jesus Christ into one's heart they are saved. Yet God desires our soul to understand and to operate in the salvation He has provided in Christ Jesus. It is spiritual growth as we walk in the Way of Salvation we address in this work. The soul of man must be saved. Because of the fall of man in the Garden of Eden, mankind has the sentence of death within himself. Judgment does not come from without a person. It is within them. Our own fire comes from within us and consumes us. A person's own judgment was within them before their birth. To be saved from that judgment we must follow God's leading by His Word and His Holy Spirit (sanctification) through prayer until we attain to godliness. We cannot trust in our self. We must trust God, Who raises the dead. We are dead people in the process of being resurrected by a living God Who is the savior of all men who are believers in Christ Jesus. Salvation enables us to stand in the midst of the fire. There is fire in heaven and there is fire in hell. The difference is that, in heaven, people can withstand the fire because the Fire is within them. When Jesus Christ returns, everything that is, will be revealed with fire. **God is Love. God is a consuming Fire.** He has given us this lifetime to work out our own salvation with fear and trembling. We must be as saved as possible when we depart this planet. The Bride of Christ makes herself ready. She chooses to be a clean and spotless Bride with no spot or wrinkle whatsoever. If given free reign, Love will remove anything and everything that stands in its way. Choose Life people! Live! And be blessed!

Religion demands of us things other than what Jesus Christ accomplished on the Cross of Calvary. It adds to the work of Christ. Tradition takes our focus off of Jesus Christ and puts it on man and the ways of man. It subtracts from the work of Christ. Both religion and tradition are from hell and will lead a person to hell. *Revelation 22:18-19 For I testify unto every man that heareth the words of the prophecy of this book, If any man shall add unto these things, God shall add unto him the plagues that are written in this book: And if any man shall take away from the words of the book of this prophecy, God shall take away his part out of the book of life, and out of the holy city, and from the things which are written in this book. KJV*

God is not religious. God did not create a religion; He created a family. Only man and satan are religious. There is no religion in God at all. How is religion defined? Religion is satan's counterfeit of our relationship with the Living Christ in this earth. Religion is the most wicked thing in the sight of God! It is trying to get God to establish a covenant with the humanity (flesh nature) of man. Religion worships a god made either with the hands or with the imagination, but equally created. It consists of human merit and endeavor. Man must be saved from religion as he must be saved from self. Sin-consciousness is the parent of practically all human religions. Cults are established by those who seek to establish their own righteousness by ways not of God. T. L. Osborn said, "Religion uses sin and lives off of it. Jesus saves from sin." A Christian rock star, Bono, said "I learned that religion is often the enemy of God, actually…Religion is the artifice — you know, the building, after God has left it sometimes, like Elvis has left the building. You hold onto religion, you know, rules, regulations, traditions. I think what God is interested in is people's hearts, and that's hard enough." Religion is,

89

and ever has been, the greatest cause of blood-shedding. Holy wars are waged with cries of "Dominion, Dominion!" Whereas God's Word teaches we are to enter into His rest and live in peace and unity with one another. Anything other than God's vision results in murder. Religion forces compliance and obedience. God leads with love. Religion forces membership. It has rules and regulations because it is a Bondage. Please read what the Apostle Paul wrote about satan's use of Bondage in Galatians 4:16-31 in the Amplified Bible and the New American Standard Bible. Religion forces giving through emotion and fear of reprisal. The Pharisees doctrine was that the blessing of God you receive is in direct proportion to how much you give. Man cannot buy God's blessing and power. It is not for sale. It is a free gift. There is no money in heaven. God hates religion and the extortion of widows. The Pharisees used religion and doctrine to extort money from the sheep. There is no end to excess. The love of money is based on the love of self. Jesus said the love of money was the root of all evil.

Jesus was trying to save the Pharisees from hell. The love of Jesus was the original "tough love". You have to be blunt with religious people. You must say the truth sharply. Religious people are hard-hearted and it takes a sharp instrument to pierce hardness. Jesus did this so that they would believe. His motive was pure. Don't let the opposition of religious people stop you from doing what God wants you to do. The glory of God covers and protects you. Jesus was preaching about spiritual adultery—i.e. the love of money vs. the love of God. We are not in religion—we are in a family—the Family of God. Religion always limits the power and love of God. Religion lies when it says you must worship God from afar off. God desires to live in you and be one with you! God wants you to know Him up-close and personal.

Many who are attracted to the light, truth, and love that God is, begin in religion, but as they come to know Him personally, they rise up higher into true faith and belief in Christ; and thus religious control, form, and error, fall away. One of the four branches of satan's kingdom is religion. It is ruled by the Lying Strongman. Since Adam fell, man has desired relationship with God and the restoration of God's Kingdom on earth, but, failing to find the entrance or door to the Kingdom, man has substituted religion in its place. (Scripture teaches us that Jesus Christ is the only Door into the Kingdom of God.) In the Garden of Eden man fell from God's grace and lost His glory and therefore had to be covered with the skins of animals thereby necessitating the animal's shed blood and death. There is no life without the shedding of blood. This is true for nations as well as individuals. This was the beginning of religion. This is why God had Moses institute sacrifices by the Levitical priesthood of the Hebrew nation. It was a temporary stop-gap of that chosen nation's sin until the Seed of the Father came to redeem them. God provided for the nation of Israel while He was purifying the family line that brought forth The Seed. Jesus said that one could not "take a house unless he first bound the strongman". Religion is only an attribute of the Lying Strongman. Religion teaches and trains us to imitate God whereas true faith receives from God. True relationship to God encompasses participation in His Kingdom life. We must seek out the truth of Who God really is. This is more important than seeking for gold and diamonds.

The purpose of The Law was to point God's people, Israel, to God for salvation—to remind them of the covenant that Abraham, Isaac and Jacob had walked in. The Law did not change the Abrahamic Covenant. The Abrahamic Covenant has never ended as the Mosaic Covenant has. The promise of God to bless all the nations through Abraham is still continuing. The Law which came through Moses was given to drive men to The Life of God but instead men added unto it and made it religion. The Torah is the first five books of the Bible: Genesis, Exodus, Leviticus, Numbers and Deuteronomy. The Talmud is the amplification of the five books of the Torah. The Talmud has grown and grown and grown. This is religion. We are not to make religion out of God's Word. When you add to God's Word you actually subtract from it. The Book of Revelation has given severe admonition to those who add or subtract from God's Word. We are heirs of The Promise. Christ is the end of The (Mosaic) Law. We now live under The Royal Law of Love, which we keep by God's grace. The Law should be used to show man his sin and to confront him with his sin. We must show people how to receive God's grace. We use The Law lawfully to bring men to Christ.

The Jewish people failed to understand that Messiah was to come twice. They did not understand this truth. The Muslim people do not understand the truth of The Trinity. Jewish people did not see or understand that they, as a nation, had lapsed into religion. Dying, their relationship with God had surely died. They venerated the rules and laws of their religion rather than God Himself. God had created the rules and laws as tools that they might know Him. In fact, religion killed Jesus Christ. This was why He had to come to earth twice—once to do away with religion and twice to <u>fulfill</u> the Promise of the Father, the Holy Spirit's <u>fullness</u> in man. In this Age of Grace our experience of the Holy Spirit is but the down payment or earnest of our inheritance in God. In Moffatt's Translation of Holy Scripture in Matthew 12:18-21, as quoted from Isaiah 40-49 (specifically Isaiah 42:3), it is written, *"Here is my servant whom I have selected, my Beloved in whom my soul delights; I will invest him with my Spirit, and he shall proclaim religion to the Gentiles. He shall not wrangle or shout, no one hears his voice in the streets. He shall not break the bruised reed, he shall not put out the smouldering flax, till he carries religion to victory: and the Gentiles shall hope in his name."* It was and is God's determined purpose to see religion brought to victory! God has not and will not forsake Israel. The Hebrew people are God's Chosen People. God does not change. He is the same yesterday, today and forever. God will have relationship with His chosen people and with all people, whosoever will come. Therefore, their "religion", not in form, legality or practice; but rather in spirit, passed to the Gentiles. From thence it shall be done away with. This is the same "way" that God uses to do away with sickness and disease, etc. However, it is for "whosoever will". Understanding of this must come by faith. By that I mean, an individual must "see it" by faith and then they must "do it" by faith also.

Isaiah 42:1-4 Here is my servant whom I uphold, my chosen one, my heart's delight; I have endowed him with my spirit, to carry true religion to the nations. He shall not be loud and noisy, he shall not shout in public; he shall not crush a broken reed, nor quench a wick that dimly burns; loyally shall he set forth true religion, he shall not be broken nor grow dim, till he has settled true religion upon earth, till far lands long for his instruction. Moffatt Translation "I (the Father) have endowed him (the Son—Jesus Christ) with my spirit (the Holy Spirit)" is the Trinity (Father, Son, Holy Spirit). "He shall not be loud and noisy, He shall not shout in public..." is defined as ceremonial worship, which was a noisy song (a noisy iambus sung in honor of Bacchus) or wailing, clamoring. Satan was in charge of the music of worship in heaven. A "wick that dimly burns" is a type of the twisted world system that is painted over our lives like a cosmetic. God will not remove or harm it lest our perception of reality is damaged and we be deformed or harmed in His image. Matthew 13:1-30. He desires that we grow up in Him until we reach the fullness of God in Christ Jesus. A type of "religion carried to victory" in Scripture is Jehosaphat's victory through worship in 2 Chronicles 20:20-22.

Religion is hard work. Religious people attempt to overcome the world by removing themselves from it. They are rapacious and self-indulgent. Christians overcome the world by being other-worldly. They have

died to self (the flesh nature), just as Jesus Christ
died in His flesh on the Cross of Calvary. Religion
blinds people and causes them to look at the wrong
thing and follow the wrong leader. They are the
blind led about by the blind. We must not and can
not follow any man to find salvation, no matter what
position he holds in the Kingdom of God. We can
only follow our Lord and Savior, Jesus Christ. The
force of religion, if followed to its end, brings
deception and destruction — religion being that controlled form and order that is without the freedom
and life of the Spirit of God, and relationship with
the Living Christ. I believe a real Christian is one
of the happiest people on earth. A true Christian
is fully alive and full of joy. Religion has been
said to be man reaching up to God, without consideration of the ways in which God has reached down
to save man. Again, religion teaches and trains us
to be like God—to become "little gods" in the earth—
whereas faith receives from God. We cannot learn
what God expects from us as human beings through
our religious traditions. In his book, <u>The Image of
Righteousness</u>, Rev. Creflo Dollar has written, "I am
convinced that man-made doctrines of religious tradition are the greatest enemy of the church today.
This kind of religion creates a consciousness and
a system of beliefs that can cause us to completely
misunderstand our relationship with God. This form
of religion denies the life and power of the gospel
of Jesus." Our standard of righteousness must be the
Spirit of God, not religious traditions. Religion
always works from the outside in whereas Jesus said
we must be clean from the inside out. For example,
religious people frequently mock and deride the
Apostle Peter, who was the second son of God to be
born in God's Kingdom. He did not look "perfect"
from the outside. The glory of God is the expression
of His nature. Religion is rules because it is a
Bondage. Religion never helped anybody. Jesus Christ
was killed by the Pharisaical leadership of His day.
He was preaching and teaching life, light, love,

freedom and the Kingdom of God. The Pharisees wanted conformity to rules and regulations because **unredeemed humanity only understands, and is unafraid of, what it can control**. *Romans 8:15 For [the Spirit which] you have now received [is] not a spirit of slavery to put you once more in bondage to fear, but you have received the Spirit of adoption [the Spirit producing sonship] in [the bliss of] which we cry, Abba (Father)! Father! AMP*

Historically and in opposition to a fleshly desire for control, a whole denomination was created that focused on "anti-ordinance teaching". Their only law was to be led by the Holy Spirit. This was the Church of God: Holiness, in California which was founded in 1880. The Holiness Movement got into extremism by denying the Word, common sense and authority. They didn't like rules and regulations. Traditional Pentecostals, even today, are gun shy of denominations. All false religions are either overly separated, i.e. "doers" (Deists, Agnostics, Atheists) or overly belonging, i.e. "being" (Self-Deifying Religions, Mormonism, New Age Religions). The Roman Catholic Church has added great amounts of false doctrine to their theology that goes directly against the Word of God. False religions are a distortion of, an extreme of, an exaggeration of, and a perversion of the balanced truth that God is both Transcendent and Imminent, separate and belonging. To walk accurately in the spirit, speaking the truth in love, our faith must grasp the greatness of God. **Therefore balance and wisdom are key to your relationship with your Heavenly Father and to success in the spiritual life.** Jesus said, *Matthew 7:14 Because strait is the gate, and narrow is the way, which leadeth unto life, and few there be that find it. KJV*

Today the Church is in the same situation. Many preachers have little kingdoms that they want people to become members of and support with their time and work, their money and their prayers. In their hearts they believe certain people or families belong to them. Their members look to them personally for

salvation and are followers of men, not of God. Yet
God wants us to live in His glory, free of control
and manipulation; full of His life and His power,
walking in love with God and man. Each individual
Christian is able to see and hear God themselves and
obey the leading of the Holy Spirit from within. At
the same time we must ultimately submit to God, the
Holy Spirit, and to God's true Agents of Authority,
while walking with God personally. There is, therefore, no mediator between God and man but the Man,
Christ Jesus. The battle in America for the last two
hundred years has been for spiritual freedom. God
desires spiritual freedom for mankind. Pride, pleasure and self-will are ruling princes over America
and must be defeated by the Church. As a minister
our job is to know God, keep those given us of God
free of satanic oppression, feed them and minister
to their needs so they can grow up in Christ Jesus.
We must give them roots and wings. Religion desper-
ately seeks perfection in a person. One of the main
attributes of religion is, essentially, the deification of self. Religious people desire the power of
God but not His will for God's will shall destroy
their control of God's power. Even when they have
heard God's direction for their lives from the Holy
Spirit, illogically, they desire their kingdom on
earth to come using God's power rather than God's
will and His Kingdom to come. Their desire would have
to die and they would have to submit to God in this
life. Jesus said that if we lose our life, then we
will gain His life. He also asked us what it would
profit us to gain the entire world if we lost our
soul in the process. *Mark 8:35-37 For whoever wants
to save his [higher, spiritual, eternal] life, will
lose it [the lower, natural, temporal life which is
lived only on earth]; and whoever gives up his life
[which is lived only on earth] for My sake and the
Gospel's will save it [his higher, spiritual life
in the eternal kingdom of God]. For what does it
profit a man to gain the whole world, and forfeit his
life [in the eternal kingdom of God]? For what can*

a man give as an exchange (a compensation, a ransom, in return) for his [blessed] life [in the eternal kingdom of God]? AMP

The church of America is in very great danger of bringing judgment upon itself at this crucial hour. The following Scriptures sound all too true of the system of religion which has developed in our country: *Ezekiel 28:1-10 Thus saith the Lord GOD; Because thine heart is lifted up, and thou hast said, I am a God, I sit in the seat of God, in the midst of the seas; yet thou art a man, and not God, though thou set thine heart as the heart of God: Behold, thou art wiser than Daniel; there is no secret that they can hide from thee: With thy wisdom and with thine understanding thou hast gotten thee riches, and hast gotten gold and silver into thy treasures: By thy great wisdom and by thy traffick hast thou increased thy riches, and thine heart is lifted up because of thy riches: Therefore thus saith the Lord GOD; Because thou hast set thine heart as the heart of God; Behold, therefore I will bring strangers upon thee, the terrible of the nations: and they shall draw their swords against the beauty of thy wisdom, and they shall defile thy brightness. They shall bring thee down to the pit, and thou shalt die the deaths of them that are slain in the midst of the seas. Wilt thou yet say before him that slayeth thee, I am God? But thou shalt be a man, and no God, in the hand of him that slayeth thee. Thou shalt die the deaths of the uncircumcised by the hand of strangers: for I have spoken it, saith the Lord GOD. KJV*

There is nothing new under the sun. Corporately the church of America is rich, proud and wise beyond belief in its own eyes. The Church of America is currently getting along quite well with the world system. It has adopted many worldly ways. There are many truths of Scripture that have been compromised. Many churches are little kingdoms and are run like corporations. Many churches desire to be one with, and in control of, a political system. There is great error with regard to mammon and the love of it. Has it become a religious behemoth?

These Scriptures bring to mind Psalm 82:
God standeth in the congregation of the mighty; he judgeth among the gods. How long will ye judge unjustly, and accept the persons of the wicked? Selah Defend the poor and fatherless: do justice to the afflicted and needy. Deliver the poor and needy: rid them out of the hand of the wicked. They know not, neither will they understand; they walk on in darkness: all the foundations of the earth are out of course. I have said, Ye are gods; and all of you are children of the most High. But ye shall die like men, and fall like one of the princes. Arise, O God, judge the earth: for thou shalt inherit all nations. KJV

An interesting story that typifies many ministries was found in England. Located in the Cotswalds, Gloucestershire, the British Isles, the estate of Stamway has changed hands only once in 1,260 years, which takes us back to the early 8th Century. In 715, Stamway was given by two local Mercian magnates, Odo and Dodo, to the abbey of Tewekesbury. Four monks were established here, holding the land in what was known as "frankalmoign"—that is, in return for their prayers for the souls of the founders of the abbey and their descendants. This is much like the Prayer Ministries found in large churches and denominations today. In 1530, Sir William Tracy of nearby Toddington declared in his will that he relied for his salvation on faith, not on the prayers of the monks: in response his body was dug up and burned by the Church, an act which caused widespread and understandable revulsion. God doesn't have any grandchildren. We are each responsible to Him for our personal salvation. We cannot look to "spiritual leaders" or the church we attend, however good they are, for our personal salvation. No other person can "pray you in" to the grace of God unless you, yourself, have faith in the shed blood of Jesus Christ.

"Many, many times I come into a man and he receives Me. Then as time goes by his flesh is tickled. He is not humble and he does not wait upon Me. Therefore he receives a spirit of seduction and he is drawn aside unto the worship of some man rather than the worship of Me. Pray for My grace to be kept from seduction. It is a spiritual law that if you give in to seduction you will face the anti-christ spirit."

The church of the Lord Jesus Christ is in great danger due to the rigidity and legalism of its institution. It has quenched the freedom, light and love of the Holy Spirit of God and ministered fear and skepticism rather than life to many. Where is the validating power of God in our services? Continual preaching on dominion, dominion, dominion yet without the balance of love and kindness shown through the miraculous power of God to save, heal and deliver have ministered fear rather than faith. A focus on financial prosperity and self-realization, rather than on helping the poor and under-privileged, has resulted in "seeker-friendly" churches that cater to the affluent. A person does not have to be rich to be a Christian. There has been a strong drive to unify the Christian churches of America with its political leadership. The Church is called of God to preach Jesus Christ, crucified and resurrected. In America the Church has become a business and emulates many business systems of the world. Jesus said you cannot love God and mammon at the same time. He said that we cannot be His friend and the friend of the world at the same time. The Church has degenerated into schisms, denominations and a party spirit rather than allowing the life of Jesus Christ to bring us into true unity. Preaching about the things of God without preaching the principles of the kingdom and without preaching about Jesus Himself, the King of the Kingdom, produce error. Where is God's love in our churches?

The devil is stupid but he has experience—6,000 years of it. He has known that if he could get men to have a form of godliness but deny the power thereof he could bind humanity under the oppression of religion. Most people in America today are not ignorant of the Name of Jesus and the Word of God. However, they run from churches and the people of God because they do not see truth, love or power. They only see a form or tradition of religion. Religion judges from position rather than power and truth. Their souls hunger for truth. They hunger for the love of God. They hunger for the holy fire of God's supernatural power. But they cannot find it. They cannot approach it and lay hold of it because the power, love and truth of God in America is surrounded by such hypocrisy, such religious sham and form and such selfish gain that the common man must seek God for himself. He cannot compete with those moneyed and wealthy hypocrites that surround the throne of God's power in America today. The common man has nothing to compete with the religious stranglehold that separates truth, love, mercy and goodness from the godly authority and power of leadership. The devil has known that if he could merely separate the common man from true godly leadership he would be able to lock America in a vise of religious hypocrisy that would bind this country for an hundred years.

America is a very, very special nation to God. America is unique among the nations—all the nations. For in America there is freedom that exists in no other nation on earth. No other nation on this planet was formed by people of different races, colors and creeds. America contains people of every tribe and every tongue, every color and every creed. The one common denominator in America is the burning holy passion for freedom. A person of another language and another race can come from a different country and become an American by what they believe! People want freedom! People require love and they require freedom for life to prosper. It was the blood—innocent blood—of our founding fathers that provided the freedoms we have enjoyed these 235 years. Yet we are dangerously close to losing these freedoms. Why? Internationally we are no longer viewed to be the land of the free and the home of the brave but rather we are seen as an oppressive war mongers, power hungry over-lords and self-seeking. How did this happen and why? Currently, our government is changing from a democracy to a socialist system that operates well with the other governments of the world.

The devil knew that if he could separate the power of God from the truth of God he could pervert and imbalance the people of God and splinter the unity of the Body of Christ in America and the world. But God! God always has a plan! God always has a way. God hid the power of God underground for 100 years until the Azusa Street Revival at the turn of the century when he began to raise up a few common men and women in power and truth in pockets of this nation. These "seeds" as it were, lay dormant for years, all the while changing and being metamorphose into a strong and healthy vine of truth and power. Yet as this vine grew it was detected by the enemy of men's souls and wrapped around with worldly lust for prosperity, acceptance and recognition of self. Yet God still has a hidden church—the true church of America. It is now time for that church to arise and shake off the lies of the religious behemoth that has developed in the United States of America. It is time for those trapped in religion to rise up and come forth into a greater light of the glory of God! It is time for the power of God and the truth of God to be united with the people of God in the Love of God Almighty!

An area of confusion and contention among the leadership of the Body of Christ has to do with understanding the power of the Holy Spirit in the earth today. The spirit of religion only has the capacity for false holiness. Just because something is supernatural does not necessarily mean it is of the Holy Spirit or of God. The gifts of the Holy Spirit must not be used to manipulate the Church, one's children and family or any person. People who try to control are a terrible problem in the Church. Charismatic witchcraft is a greater problem than strongholds over cities.

Romans 1:17-22 For in the Gospel a righteousness which God ascribes is revealed, both springing from faith and leading to faith [disclosed through the way of faith that arouses to more faith]. As it is written, The man who through faith is just and upright shall live and shall live by faith. For God's [holy] wrath and indignation are revealed from heaven against all ungodliness and unrighteousness of men, who in their wickedness repress and hinder the truth and make it inoperative. For that which is known about God is evident to them and made plain in their inner consciousness, because God [Himself] has shown it to them. For ever since the creation of the world His invisible nature and attributes, that is, His eternal power and divinity, have been made intelligible and clearly discernible in and through the things that have been made (His handiworks). So [men] are without excuse [altogether without any defense or justification], because when they knew and recognized Him as God, they did not honor and glorify Him as God or give Him thanks. But instead they became futile and godless in their thinking [with vain imaginings, foolish reasoning, and stupid speculations] and their senseless minds were darkened. Claiming to be wise, they became fools [professing to be smart, they made simpletons of themselves].

Habbakuk 2:4-6 Look at the proud; his soul is not straight or right within him, but the [rigidly] just and the [uncompromisingly] righteous man shall live by his faith and in his faithfulness. Moreover, wine and wealth are treacherous; the proud man [the Chaldean invader] is restless and cannot stay at home. His appetite is large like that of Sheol and [his greed] is like death and cannot be satisfied; he gathers to himself all nations and collects all people as if he owned them. Shall not all these [victims of his greed] take up a taunt against him and in scoffing derision of him say, Woe to him who piles up that which is not his! [How long will he possess it?] And [woe to him] who loads himself with promissory notes for usury! AMP

It is impossible to add, subtract, divide or multiply the Word of God. Change does not come through the ministry of angels. Angels act on the spoken Word of God. Only the Holy Spirit can minister change to mankind. The Holy Spirit has been sent as the Promise of the Father to indwell each individual and minister life and light and love and truth to each one and through each one. When we receive Jesus Christ as our Savior and Lord, we become One with the Father. We are part of His family—the family of God. God does not entrust our eternal life and well being to any but a member of the family. The Holy Spirit is our Teacher according to Scripture. He is the Agent of Change for mankind. Only God, Himself, can change me! An angel or a spirit that is from without me cannot bring change and eternal life to me. Angels are created beings. The Holy Spirit is God. Jesus Christ, Himself, has spoken directly to this problem in several portions of Scriptures, including the following:

> *Matthew 7:14-23 A Tree and Its Fruit*
> *Beware of the false prophets, who come to you in sheep's clothing, but inwardly are ravenous wolves. You will know them by their fruits. Grapes are not gathered from thorn bushes nor figs from thistles, are they? So every good tree bears good fruit, but the bad tree bears bad fruit.*

103

A good tree cannot produce bad fruit, nor can a bad tree produce good fruit. Every tree that does not bear good fruit is cut down and thrown into the fire. So then, you will know them by their fruits. Not everyone who says to Me, "Lord, Lord," will enter the kingdom of heaven, but he who does the will of My Father who is in heaven will enter. Many will say to Me on that day, "Lord, Lord, did we not prophesy in Your name, and in Your name cast out demons, and in Your name perform many miracles?" And then I will declare to them, "I never knew you; DEPART FROM ME, YOU WHO PRACTICE LAWLESSNESS." NASU

Matthew 23:27-36
Woe to you, scribes and Pharisees, hypocrites! For you are like whitewashed tombs which on the outside appear beautiful, but inside they are full of dead men's bones and all uncleanness. So you, too, outwardly appear righteous to men, but inwardly you are full of hypocrisy and lawlessness. Woe to you, scribes and Pharisees, hypocrites! For you build the tombs of the prophets and adorn the monuments of the righteous, and say, "If we had been living in the days of our fathers, we would not have been partners with them in shedding the blood of the prophets." So you testify against yourselves, that you are sons of those who murdered the prophets. Fill up, then, the measure of the guilt of your fathers. You serpents, you brood of vipers, how will you escape the sentence of hell? Therefore, behold, I am sending you prophets and wise men and scribes; some of them you will kill and crucify, and some of them you will

scourge in your synagogues,and persecute from city to city, so that upon you may fall the guilt of all the righteous blood shed on earth, from the blood of righteous Abel to the blood of Zechariah, the son of Berechiah, whom you murdered between the temple and the altar. Truly I say to you, all these things will come upon this generation. NASU

God created this planet. He made it the way it is. Therefore, His ways of creation are the right ways. He does not need to change the order of creation to get the attention of mankind. His ways are already supernatural and they are good. Our change from being in the first Adam to being in the Last Adam will be accomplished through the power of the Holy Spirit Whom God, Himself, has sent to indwell us. We do not need to change God's order to accomplish His will. Angels or another person cannot bring eternal change.

There are personal spirits of religion, and there are corporate spirits of religion which are far more deadly. Persons, cities and nations can be controlled by spirits of religion, whether Christian (Catholic, Protestant, Charismatic, Pentecostal, Non-Denominational), Hindu, Buddhist or Animist etc. The ultimate tactic of a spirit of religion is that it would unite with a political spirit. This is satan's kingdom coming into a false unity which releases tremendous evil power. When corporate, this gives birth to **a Behemoth spirit**, described in the book of Job as the "first of the ways of God". In Scripture religion is frequently typified by the name of Babylon, which means confusion. It has to do with both political and religious spirits. Babylon is the fountain-head of all idolatry and systems of false worship. This is the "mystery of iniquity" seen in all the great "religions" of the world. As an example we currently see whole nations captive by the religious and political behemoth of the Muslim religion.

The "World Council of Churches" and the "League of Nations" are two of the most arresting signs of the times. This is the religious spirit's modus operendi. The strongman spirit that rules religious spirits is The Lying Spirit. When politics and religion are mixed the Church deteriorates. Jesus Christ is the only Head of the Church. Great persecution has come to true Christians in many different lands because of their faithfulness to Christ and their refusal to submit to political control. An example of this was seen in communist China during the twentieth century. In opposition to the Three Self Movement, many Chinese Christians were put in prison and endured torture because of their faith. Many died. Babylon was a place of safety for those who believed the Word of God through His prophets but a place of death for those who sought their own welfare. Religion is a place of safety for one who believes as long as they don't push the limits and desire more of God.

Christianity is supported by the doctrine of Monotheism. We believe in One God. His greatness is expressed in Three Persons: Father, Son and Holy Spirit. In His infinite wisdom He chose to separate the continents in the time of Peleg, secreting what we now call North and South America until mankind matured enough to seek out freedom. The United States of America was founded upon this desire for spiritual freedom of worship and faith in the Lord Jesus Christ. As a democratic republic it has grown to a position of dominance in the kingdoms of the world. I believe God has shown me it is His will for America that those He brought to the shores of this nation in two and threes and even in families be returned to the nations—they or their descendants—to bring His Life and His Truth. Yet in contradiction to God's will as the American culture has matured, its sin has also matured. Made up of many, many tribes, tongues and peoples, it has persecuted and oppressed tribes, tongues and peoples. It has matured to the point of the heresy of Henotheism or the worship of God from a tribal perspective. Tribalism affects the

Church in many ways. God is not with us and against our "enemies". The nation of Israel also fell into this sin. If God judged His chosen people do you not think He will likewise judge America? God loves America but God hates sin. God is not with America and against her perceived "enemies" because God is not political. Are we interested in preserving our civilization and our culture or in the salvation of the lost? As American Christians do we preach and minister the American culture or the Christianity of the Bible? We must love and reconcile the world to Jesus Christ. The Kingdom of God is open to all people. Satan is tempting the Church of America with enmity toward our political opponents by the heresy of Henotheism.

CHAPTER IV

RELIGION: THEN AND NOW

The History of Religion on Earth.

*W*hy do we study history? We must discover from God's revelation of truth the meaning of HIS STORY (events). We can never understand history until we understand the plan of God. Prophecy is the plan of God before it happens. History is the study of events and their meaning. Revelation gives meaning to events. The Bible gives meaning and revelation to history. We study Church history to learn God's direction today. Winston Churchill said, "Those who don't know history are destined to repeat it." Error flows in cycles and always contains a measure of truth. Therefore we study history to profit from the past experiences of others. Also we are inspired by accounts of faith, courage and the success of great people. We must learn to appreciate our heritage. Freedom comes with a price of the shedding of blood. We study Church history to observe the patterns and characteristics and conditions of Church outreach and growth.

Religion began when man fell in the Garden of Eden. *Genesis 3:7-8, 21 And the eyes of them both were opened, and they knew that they were naked; and they sewed fig leaves together, and made themselves aprons.*

And they heard the voice of the LORD God walking in the garden in the cool of the day: and Adam and his wife hid themselves from the presence of the LORD God amongst the trees of the garden........Unto Adam also and to his wife did the LORD God make coats of skins, and clothed them. KJV To cover the departure of His glory from man, God slew animals to make coats of skins for them, and hence the first shedding of blood occurred. *Hebrews 9:22 [In fact] under the Law almost everything is purified by means of blood, and without the shedding of blood there is neither release from sin and its guilt nor the remission of the due and merited punishment for sins.* AMP From this time forward man's discontent with God's Plan and Purpose evidenced itself in religious traditions and rituals. The di-vision (or two visions) begun in man's Fall were furthered in Adam and Eve's two sons, Cain and Abel. The solution is given in Genesis 4 in the persons of Cain and Abel. Here are presented and described the Two Ways of knowing God. The Way of God: *Acts 13:26 Men and brethren, children of the stock of Abraham, and whosoever among you feareth God, to you is the word of this salvation sent.* KJV and the Way of Cain: *Jude 11 Woe unto them! for they have gone in the way of Cain, and ran greedily after the error of Balaam for reward, and perished in the gainsaying of Core.* KJV These two "ways" are the only two religions which the world has ever seen. One: the true; the other: the false. True "religion" is one and unchangeable. Its language is "NOTHING in my hand I bring, simply to Thy Cross I cling." False religion is one and unchangeable. It has many varieties; its one language is "SOMETHING in my hand I bring." Men quarrel bitterly as to what that something is to be. They persecute, and burn, and destroy one another in the heat of their controversies about it. But however this "something" may vary, it is one, in that it is not "the way of God," not the way which God has appointed, but it is "the way of Cain," man's way. The one is "faith," the other is "works." The one is "grace," the other is human "merit." The one is the ancient and good way of "the path of life," the other ends in "the second death." God's revelation to man is two-fold, expressed in two Covenants. The Old Covenant and the New Covenant are God's sufficient testimony to man. And yet how different they are! The Law and Grace; Faith and Works! God's Word is One!!! It is not divided. There is no division in the Word of God. Yet there is growth and progression in mankind. Man must change to have relationship with an Holy God. God does not change. He is Immutable.

God found a man in Abraham who believed Him. Abraham believed the promise of God. His faith was accounted unto him as righteousness. His faith resulted in the birth of Isaac. Isaac fathered twelve sons through four women. Each son became the father of a tribe of people within the nation of Israel. Each one was also a type and a shadow for us today. It is interesting to note the names of Abraham's sons at their births, then the names of the heads of the tribes of the nation of Israel and finally the names of the tribes as listed in the Book of Revelation. Changes occur.

"Levi was given to self-will as was Simeon. Simeon was lost because he went the way of self, which resulted in death. Levi was chosen because he intermittently was given to obey My will. However, the self-will would creep in. For his own good I chained him to My law to help him and protect him. As a priest of the law he was constantly and continually responsible for the step-by-step procedures involved in My dealing with sin. Therefore, his self-will was bound, chained and caged, that his free-will might have opportunity to behold and gaze upon Me and, knowing light and love, that he might choose Life."

"So it is also today. Those who are called and anointed of Me but who are given to self-will must be chained to a 'system' to protect them from the destruction which lies within their own heart. Thus I incorporate them into the church system for their protection because they have not died to self and truly allowed Me to rule and reign and be Lord. Those who hear My Voice and walk by My Spirit and who are dead to self are few and far between. They are those who are chosen. I use them to do My works in the earth. For it is not how many generations of service there are in one's family line but how completely one has learned those lessons and obeyed these truths. Billy Graham is an example of one who has learned these truths and does not come from a line of preachers."

Genesis 29:33-34 And she conceived again, and bare a son; and said, Because the LORD hath heard that I was hated, he hath therefore given me this son also: and she called his name Simeon. And she conceived again, and bare a son; and said, Now this time will my husband be joined unto me, because I have born him three sons: therefore was his name called Levi.

Genesis 35:23 The sons of Leah; Reuben, Jacob's first-born, and Simeon, and Levi, and Judah, and Issachar, and Zebulun:

Genesis 49:5-7 Simeon and Levi are brethren; instruments of cruelty are in their habitations. O my soul, come not thou into their secret; unto their assembly, mine honour, be not thou united: for in their anger they slew a man, and in their selfwill they digged down a wall. Cursed be their anger, for it was fierce; and their wrath, for it was cruel: I will divide them in Jacob, and scatter them in Israel. KJV

Simeon = hatred. Levi = joined or chained—His motive for self-will was to bring about good. The evil [cruelty, murder] within them was used to bring good. They digged down a wall [that which separates God and man, i.e. sin.] It is better to go over a wall as Joseph did. Book of Leviticus = laws that grant access to an Holy God. Hebrews is the companion book in the New Testament. Its topic is seeking purifying of self to obtain divine favor, i.e. Life.

As was prophesied the nation went down into Egypt for four hundred years. They suffered bondage and severe oppression and cruel taskmasters. God raised up a deliverer in the person of Moses. God responded to man's need by rising up Moses and giving him The Law on Mount Sanai when the Hebrew people refused to come to Him on the Mount. The Law is not God. The Law cannot save man from sin. The Law was given to mankind to show them their sin. The Law acts like a mirror.

Exodus 32:25-29 And when Moses saw that the people were naked; (for Aaron had made them naked unto their shame among their enemies:) then Moses stood in the gate of the camp, and said, Who is on the LORD's side? Let him come unto me. And all the sons of Levi gathered themselves together unto him. And he said unto them, Thus saith the LORD God of Israel, Put every man his sword by his side, and go in and out from gate to gate throughout the camp, and slay every man his brother, and every man his companion, and every man his neighbour. And the children of Levi did according to the word of Moses: and there fell of the people that day about three thousand men. For Moses

*had said, Consecrate yourselves to day to the LORD,
even every man upon his son, and upon his brother;
that he may bestow upon you a blessing this day. KJV
Psalm 140—violence, evil imaginations*

We must refuse all gifts if we are to avoid corruption. The religious system provides for priests
continually with gifts—it helps break pride but compromises purity. There is a difference between a <u>priest</u>
and a <u>prophet/judge/deliverer/Christ spirit.</u> Before
God had the Levitical priests He had Melchizadek—a
priest after a different order. <u>Before</u> man desired
a king, God had instituted His judges—those who
judged sin in order to bring deliverance. The Feast
of Pentecost brought the law and likewise today the
Holy Spirit, when He comes into a person, convicts
them of sin and judgment, thus bringing about deliverance and leading to sonship relationship with the
Father. There is a relationship outside of the system
but pride, self-will and all sin must still be dealt
with. The Christ spirit must still be obtained. Pride
and self-will are ruling princes over America and
must be defeated by the Church.

Jesus Christ was never a part of the Levitical
priesthood. God said of Him that He was a priest
after the order of Melchizedek. The contrast between
the Melchizedek and Aaronic priesthoods is in <u>person,</u>
<u>order</u>, and <u>duration</u>. Melchizedek was a priest, prophet
and king as is Jesus. Melchizedek's ministry typi-
fies the eternal ministry of Jesus. Only Christ can
set one free from the bondage of sin. The Law of the
Spirit of Life in Christ Jesus has set us free from
the Law of Sin and Death.

The True Church has certain characteristics. In
the spiritual church Christ is the only Head. There
is only <u>one</u> mediator between God and man and that
is the Man, Christ Jesus. There is only one Name
under heaven whereby man must be saved. No other
person hung on the Cross of Calvary for my salvation but Jesus Christ. The Ten Commandments do not
save us but they are the standard of the moral life

of Christians. They are pillars at The Door, Who is Christ. *Matthew 19:17 And he said unto him, Why callest thou me good? There is none good but one, that is, God: but if thou wilt enter into life, keep the commandments. KJV* Rev. David Alsobrook has written, "Unlike all churches, the Kingdom of God is perfect. This is why no one in the early church preached the church. They all preached the Kingdom, in accordance with Jesus' command to them. *And as you go, preach, saying, The Kingdom of Heaven is at hand. Matthew 10:7* The Kingdom is the rule of God and is perfect. Church history is littered with the remains of mind-ruled men who were not 'Spirit governed' and never matured into full-grown sons (the literal meanings of 'led' and 'sons' in Romans 8:14). They are gone, but their leaven remains. Many who have been added to the church have been subtracted from the Kingdom (see Matthew 13:47-50). Many are called (*ekkaleo* and the church is the *ekklessia* or gathering of the called); few are chosen to rule and reign with Him in this life or in the Age to come (see Matthew 22:14; 2 Timothy 2:12). The Kingdom is hidden from the wise and prudent (those who are wise in their own conceits, which lean to their own understanding); instead it is revealed to babes, which is why prostitutes in the street can enter it before professionals in the pulpit (Matthew 11:25; 21:31). The One Who is bringing those who hunger and thirst for righteousness into His Kingdom is mighty to save. *We are receiving a Kingdom which cannot be shaken. Hebrews 12:28 For the Kingdom of God is not in word, but in power. 1 Corinthians 4:20 RV.*" How much of the power of God do you exercise?

Historically, the Church's revelation of the Kingdom of God has progressed in real time through the centuries from the building of physical containers for God, i.e. giant cathedrals, convents and monasteries and the political kingdom of papal authority in Rome (by definition a behemoth: a system of religion and politics); to a soulish evidence of the Kingdom of God in the making of denominations and ministry organizations with religious creeds and dogmas that are either intellectual, emotional or products of the will of man; to this new millennia which we now face. Will mankind progress from the physical expression of the Kingdom of God, past the soulish expression of the Kingdom of God into the spiritual expression of the Kingdom of God? God knows. I choose to believe that mankind shall enter into the realm of true spiritual worship of God because it is the desire of the Father God. After all, this is the Third Day of the Grace of God and the Christ Life in the earth. Not all shall enter in but there shall be some who will. Will you be one? God seeks for those who will worship Him in spirit and in truth. God is Love.

The Apostle John lived the longest of all the original apostles who had seen Jesus Christ and walked with Him. He is known as the Apostle of Love. His writings are the very last of Holy Canon. He walked into the Temple of Diana in Ephesus and cursed the idol. Untouched, supernaturally, it broke and fell to the ground. The Roman Emperor Diocletian declared himself to be 'GOD' but the Apostle John would not acknowledge or agree with his declaration so the Romans tried to kill John. They boiled the Apostle John in oil but he didn't die. He was given poison to drink but he didn't die. Next they exiled him to the Isle of Patmos. This is where he was when he received The Revelation of Jesus Christ— the last book of the Bible. The Book of Revelation is a continuation of the Book of Daniel, in the Old Testament. This last book of the Bible was the Head of the Church writing to the whole church for the whole Age, i.e. the message to the seven churches. The Apostle John would not compromise God's Word and the testimony of Jesus Christ. He was an overcomer.

In the Book of the Revelation of Jesus Christ the message from Jesus to the seven Churches can be interpreted different ways. Two ways of interpretation are: 1) to view the churches as progressive periods of time during the last two millennia and 2) to view the churches as expressions of the character of the Church at any given time. Christ's word to the seven churches of Asia is just as much to the Church today.

From 100 A.D. to 313 A.D. the Church was uncompromisingly righteous in its walk in the earth. *John 14:6 Jesus saith unto him, I am the way, the truth, and the life: no man cometh unto the Father, but by me. KJV* The world considered the Christians of this era atheists because of a lack of visible deity. The Roman Empire did not understand the spirit realm. It is much like the world system today. Thus this period of Church history is known as **The Persecuted Church, The Church of Smyrna.** They had no warning because they walked in the light they had and judged their own selves. The Church grew very fast during this period. Everyone spoke Greek and traveled on the Roman roads and trade routes. Egypt and North Africa quickly became Christian and developed great libraries. By the end of this period 17,000 people were fed to the lions in thirty days in the Coliseum of Rome. The Diocletian Pillar was erected in honor of the destruction of the early Christians in Rome.

In Revelation 2:4 **The Church of Ephesus** left their first agapeo love—that place of dependence upon God whereby we respond to Him personally and individually. This era is known as **The Loveless Church.** It is a good thing to depend on the Father God for everything—to have full, complete dependence upon Him. Whatever we do we must do it all in the Name of the Lord Jesus Christ. Jesus only did what He saw the Father do and spoke what He heard the Father say. We are to do the same. We are responsible to walk in the light we have. If we do and judge ourselves, keeping our conscience tender before the Lord, we will not be chastened, reproved, warned or corrected. We are to give heed, to listen and do what the Holy Spirit says to the Churches. God's tender mercies are over all His works. We must partake of the Tree of Life by faith when we believe in our heart and confess with our mouth the Word of God. For the Kingdom of God is within each one of us who are true Christians. It is that Kingdom which is the Paradise of God. *Proverbs 15:4 A wholesome tongue is a tree of life: but perverseness therein is a breach in the spirit. Genesis 3:22 And the LORD God said, Behold, the man is become as one of us, to know good and evil: and now, lest he put forth his hand, and take also of the tree of life, and eat, and live for ever: KJV* I eat of the Tree of Life in the Paradise of my spirit man and overcome evil by <u>faith and confession</u> of God's Word and obedience to the leading of the Holy Spirit as I walk in Love.

When the Emperor Constantine came to power in Rome the era of **The Imperial Church or The Corrupt Church of Thyatira** was born. Constantine had a vision of a Cross brighter than the sun with the words: **CONQUER BY THIS.** In the Edict of Milan/Edict of Toleration he proclaimed religious liberty throughout the empire. He filled government offices with Christians, made ministers' tax exempt and rebuilt and helped the churches prosper. The Roman aristocracy refused Christianity and the capitol was moved from Rome to Byzantine, which was renamed Constantinople and later Istanbul. In A.D. 325 The Nicene Council was convened and Jesus was proclaimed God. 318 Bishops were welcomed by Constantine. They officially proclaimed Jesus Christ as God.

However, as life became easier in the natural realm, the Church that had its roots in Judaism was cut off from its roots and <u>became a corrupt religion</u> instead of a relationship with the Living God. Because of Constantine, Christianity got a "king", the Pope, instead of every man relating to God personally and individually. Just as the nation of Israel desired a king, so the Church desired a king. It was in the fourth century of The Imperial Period that anti-Semitism got into the Church. Because the Church was cut off from its roots of Judaism it began to develop its own doctrines:

1. penance
2. trans-substantiation

3. political machine

However, the truth is that Jesus Christ is the cornerstone of the Church not the Pope (or Peter). The Church developed from this time as: a pastor, who was a Head; and spectators, who merely watched. The pastor supposedly fulfilled the demands of God for the people while they merely watched him and received the benefits of his action. The pastor acted as an intercessor for "his" people. **Yet, in reality, we are each personally responsible to God for our own salvation.** In ancient Israel this same event occurred when the heads of the tribes of Israel were invited to come to God on the mountain of God and they refused out of fear. They begged for Moses to be their mediator and this was granted them.

In Biblical prophecy fulfilled in history the Papacy became the heir of the superstitious and false philosophies of all ages from Babylon on down and so became the mystic Babylon of the book of Revelation. Because satan could not defeat the Church of the Living God through persecution, he changed his tactics and allowed the Church to become the world ruler of its day. The spirit of Rome entered into the Church and compromised it. The Church of the Middle Ages was both the religious and governmental center of power in the earth. It became a religious behemoth. Thus the era of **The Compromising Church, The Church of Pergamos,** began. Religion and politics united in the oppression of the common man. At that time the Church exalted its power over the power of the Word of God and the Spirit of God and commanded all men everywhere to submit to its leadership. Laymen were kept ignorant of the Word of God which was written in Latin. Salvation only came through the church and its religious traditions. "Indulgences" could be bought thereby lessening man's stay in Purgatory—something never mentioned in Scripture.

The church and state were united in A.D. 533 when Emperor Justinian issued his famous letter declaring the Bishop of Rome to be "the head of all the holy churches" and in another letter of the same year he was designated as "corrector of heretics." For the next 1,260 years (3 1/2 "days" in Daniel) religious leaders assumed presumptuous titles, authority and power over mankind. The Pope assumed the title of *Vicarius Filii Dei*, meaning Vicar of the Son of God. This spirit received a fatal wound to the head in 1798 when Napoleon's General Berthier entered Rome, took Pope Pius VI prisoner, and abolished the Papacy. The "deadly wound" was dealt to the Papacy in 1798 by the French armies. The healing began immediately when the Papacy was re-established, but with a dimming of its former glory, by the election of a new Pope, March 14, 1800.

The Inquisition was the result of the combining of the religious and political power of the Catholic Church. By definition it became a religious behemoth to God. Through the Inquisition Jews, Muslims and the unbelievers of the day were forced to comply with the understanding of a few men that resulted in rules and regulations. Only Satan himself could have been behind the horror that ensued. Were The Inquisition and The Crusades the actions of **The Church of Sardis, a church dying or dead?**

Jesus left on record these words, "My Kingdom is not of this world." Therefore it is clear that any power assuming earthly sovereignty as Christ's vicar or in the place of Christ may certainly be known to be hostile to Christ and His kingdom, which is entirely spiritual. The persecution of Jesus Christ by the religious Pharisees of that day was a defense of their authority and their law. If something is achieved by stealing, killing or destroying then what spirit is behind it? It is very important to note that since these truths are spiritual and not natural, people may be true Christians no matter what their religious affiliation is—whether Catholic, Charismatic, Baptist, or another. Whether an individual experiences salvation only in their spirit; their spirit and soul; or their spirit, soul and body is up to them individually and personally. The vital question is whether or not they have faith in the shed blood of Jesus Christ—in His virgin birth, His death on the Cross of Calvary, His burial for three days and three nights and His resurrection and eternal life. Do they look to Jesus for eternal life and have faith in His salvation? Yet the true facts of history help set us free from religious lies, error and heresy. **If you are going to be strong in God don't get involved in religious politics!**

Some believe Satan's greatest masterpiece of deception in the Church Age was the Crusades because it destroyed the Church from within. The enmity it created between Muslims, Jews and Christians has lasted one thousand years. The Crusades, too, were a religious behemoth before God. The Church, operating in Satan's ways and the spirit of Anti-Christ, violently oppressed the peoples of the Middle East, instilling a fear of the symbol of the Cross that has lasted for generations. The unified religious and political spirit that worked through the Church of its day brought such evil into the earth that we are still "paying for it" today. Muslims today view the armies of America as the expression of this spirit at work. Hitler also operated from the error of Henotheism as his soldiers wore the words "Deus vuit!" (God With Us) on their uniforms. Militant Muslims bent on terrorism and extremism cry "Allah Akbar!" in response. Is the Church of America going to join the war?

Why did God "allow" these events to occur? Have we become **The Lukewarm Church of Laodicea?** One doesn't get into this condition from being cold but, rather, from being hot and allowing coldness. The Laodicean Church was a trade and finance center, a crossroads of commerce. This Church has the appearance of salvation but they deny the power thereof. The Laodicean Church was founded in revival. They fell from grace into coldness perhaps two generations later. Many have preached that man has free will. They preach that man can "write his own ticket with God". Yet Scripture

teaches in several places that God is in control of
both good and evil. God is greater than all churches,
denominations, ministers and ministries. So why did
these events occur? God will not touch the free-will
of man. I believe one reason was that God desired the
salvation of Rome. God desires the salvation of all
men everywhere. God desires the lost to be saved. It
is God's #1 Priority. Persecution, torture and death
in this life are of little consequence when an eternity of blessings follows one's obedience. Yet the
salvation of one soul is so precious to our Heavenly
Father. Please read Romans 11. In like manner, many
have decried the fall of political conservatism in
America in recent elections. Fear is rampant due to
the stripping away of the military and political protection from this nation. America's doors are being
thrown open to her enemies and destruction seems
sure to follow. Church is largely viewed as a sham
that only the old and ignorant participate in. Why
has this occurred? I believe God desires the salvation of the Muslim nations. If a lukewarm Laodicean
Church would not obey Him when times were good then,
by their sins of omission, God will use that Church
to save the millions of Muslims who are destined for
hell without Him. Pride is sin. God's will shall be
accomplished. The Church that sought to be a unified
political power in the earth that would overcome its
"enemies" by strength and power has been defeated.
The political power of religion is not the way of God.
The Church can either obey God when it seems to be
hard or they will obey God through their own judgment and the seeds of their blood will bring forth
new life in their enemies. God has commanded that we
forgive. He desires us to be humble and to forgive
to be enabled to use us to save our enemies. When
the sinner, Mary, washed Jesus' feet with her hair,
He said she was forgiven because of her great love.
Just before His crucifixion Jesus wrapped a towel
around Him and washed the feet of the disciples as
our example. Peter taught that we were to be examples to the flock, not lords over them. Jesus wasn't

kidding when He told us not to fear men but to fear God, Who has the power of death and hell.

How Does Religion Prevail?

According to Rev. C. Peter Wagner, the spirit of religion is a high level demon that works collectively by enchanting, or casting a spell, or bewitching the leadership of a group. People under its influence do not recognize the subtlety of it at all. There are four strongman spirits that oppose the Spirit of Truth: antichrist, lying, seduction and error. For example, the Pharisees thought they were pleasing God by observing the traditions of the elders and executing Jesus of Nazareth. *2 Corinthians 2:11 To keep Satan from getting the advantage over us; for we are not ignorant of his wiles and intentions.AMP* The device of Satan is that we would not <u>presently</u> hear what the Spirit of the Lord is saying to the churches by [BELAW (Hebrew)-to wear out in a mental sense] wearing out our minds with past revelation through fear that position would be lost or that money, power or control would be lost. It fears harm to "self". The spirit of religion is the enemy of the mind of Christ in the earth. It is the enemy of the living Christ in the NOW. In the Middle Ages the Inquisition forced conformity of religious belief through torture and death. Religion frequently lapses into satan's ways of stealing, killing and destroying to enforce it's will on an individual. However, nothing and no one can control the human heart. Christians must not preach as doctrine what is merely of man and is inconsequential to eternal, spiritual matters. This is in regard especially to money, faith, food, clothes, appearance, etc. The power of God and miracles validate our preaching. Moral integrity and uprightness validate goodness and the motives of one's heart. How does the Body of Christ handle radical change?

Matthew 9:14-17 Then the disciples of John came to Jesus, inquiring, Why is it that we and the Pharisees fast often, [that is, abstain from food and drink as a religious exercise], but Your disciples do not fast? And Jesus replied to them, Can the wedding guests mourn while the bridegroom is still with them? The days will come when the bridegroom is taken away from them, and then they will fast. And no one puts a piece of cloth that has not been shrunk on an old garment, for such a patch tears away from the garment and a worse rent (tear) is made. Neither is new wine put in old wineskins; for if it is, the skins burst and are torn in pieces, and the wine is spilled and the skins are ruined. But new wine is put into fresh wineskins, and so both are preserved. AMP

God always has new wine but He wants to preserve the old wineskin. Change always meets with resistance but not from truly anointed leadership that is hungry for more of God. To be kept as new, a wineskin must be frequently rubbed with oil so that its skin is kept supple and flexible. Likewise, we humans must be continually anointed with the oil of the Holy Spirit to remain new and fresh with the *zoe* life of God.

Pastor Sharon Daugherty had a revelatory dream in which the Holy Spirit told her that the greatest enemy of the people of God in the last days was to be deception. Deception is satan's #1 tool. If the devil can not deceive you, he can not destroy you. When someone deceives you, he causes you to think on things that are not true. A liar is a giver of false impression. A liar tries to deceive you. Satan wants each Christian to walk away from their position with God so that they will automatically lose their benefits. Satan wants all men everywhere to think untruthful thoughts about God. He wants a person to think what God says is not the truth. If the devil can have you think untruthful thoughts about Who God is and what He does he can take you out of your position in Christ Jesus. Satan desires you to lose your eternal spiritual benefits in Christ Jesus. Sickness and disease are sometimes the result of someone thinking on things that are untrue. Fiery darts are thoughts, ideas and suggestions. Our thoughts have power. They initially appear as logical thoughts, not as lies. We must be more concerned about how we think than any other area of our life. We must control our thought life to have victory. Our personal shield of faith will maintain our thought life. Are we thinking thoughts of the Word of God?

The kingdom of darkness teaches you how to live in the flesh—by sight. The Kingdom of Light teaches you how to live in the spirit—by faith. Our minds must be enlightened by the Word of God so that we will grow in the grace and the knowledge of the Lord Jesus Christ. Blindness comes from deception. We must be free in our minds. We must be free from control by the world, the flesh and the devil. The blind in spirit are in prison. There are many, many "Christians" who are the blind led around by blind men. They continue to gaze upon sin and think upon lies.

The spirit of religion focuses on the mind. Jesus gave us The Mind of Christ. The spirit of religion persecutes us and attacks our thinking through mental suffering. Remember that the corporate spirit of religion desires to take all your time, to the end that it would wear out your mind. The greatest defense of those held captive by this spirit is denial. We must always show those held captive honor and respect. We must walk in love and entreat each one as the valuable spiritual sibling they are. Just as war is waged in our minds so also our victory comes through our mind. It has been said that true spiritual warfare occurs in our own mind. It is in our own mind that we overcome the strongholds, principalities, fortresses, reasonings and lofty thoughts of Satan and his kingdom.

2 Corinthians 10:3-6 For though we walk (live) in the flesh, we are not carrying on our warfare according to the flesh and using mere human weapons. For the weapons of our warfare are not physical [weapons of flesh and blood], but they are mighty before God for the overthrow and destruction of strongholds, [Inasmuch as we] refute arguments and theories and reasonings and every proud and lofty thing that sets itself up against the [true] knowledge of God; and we lead every thought and purpose away captive into the obedience of Christ (the Messiah, the Anointed one), Being in readiness to punish every [insubordinate for his] disobedience, when your own submission and obedience [as a church] are fully secured and complete. AMP

We must clothe ourselves with humility. We must accept correction and reproof. We must renew our minds with the Word of God as it is anointed by the Holy Spirit in the NOW, i.e. the rhema word of God. We convert the logos into rhema and we eat it. It becomes part of us. We must mix faith with the promises God gives us. We must hear the Voice of God. Renewing your mind by the Word of God and the Spirit of God as you walk in the Love of the Father is the Scriptural way to freedom in Christ Jesus. We must change our mentality from that of the Wilderness and enter our Promised Land. The children of light put off the old man by the renewing of their minds with the Word of God and the Spirit of God. Jesus Christ is our Standard of Righteousness. The new nature of Christ Jesus was put in you by God when you were born-again. What are we to possess then? What is our Promised Land? Jesus Christ is our Promised Land. The mind of man is the Promised Land that must be possessed. Therefore Jesus Christ and the spirit, mind and body of man must become one.

My job right now is to retrain my mind by the new nature possessed by the Holy Spirit within me. What is the mind? Is it just your brain? Does being made in the image of God mean that He is a giant Brain in the cosmos and you are a little brain made in His image? One definition of the mind is the human consciousness that originates in the human spirit of man, filled with the Holy Spirit of God, projected through the brain of man and manifesting in thoughts, perceptions, imaginations, feelings, will, and memory. Therefore the mind of man originates in his spirit and is focused through the physical organ of the brain. It, in itself, is intangible. The spirit of man has the ability to see, hear, taste, touch and smell. It is just like the physical body at its peak. The mind is ethereal.

Romans 12:1-3 I APPEAL to you therefore, brethren, and beg of you in view of [all] the   mercies   of God, to make a decisive dedication of your bodies [presenting all your members and faculties] as a living sacrifice, holy (devoted, consecrated) and well pleasing to God, which is your reasonable (rational, intelligent) service and spiritual worship. Do not be conformed to this world (this age), [fashioned after and adapted to its external, superficial customs], but be transformed (changed) by the [entire] renewal of your mind [by its new ideals and its new attitude], so that you may prove [for yourselves] what is the good and acceptable and perfect will of God, even the thing which is good and acceptable and perfect [in His sight for you]. For by the grace (unmerited favor of God) given to me I warn everyone among you not to estimate and think of himself more highly than he ought [not to have an exaggerated opinion of his own importance], but to rate his ability with sober judgment, each according to the degree of faith apportioned by God to him. AMP

We must be focused and move ahead. Our life in God is one of constant growth and movement. If we ever stop or become stagnant we are backslidden. Tommy Tenney has become well known in Christian circles for his writings about running after God. We are in a race, and we all run that we might receive the prize.

Offer your body as a living sacrifice to God which will result in spiritual growth into the perfect will of God. Our mind must be renewed. This is how to do that: *Romans 8:23-27 And not only they, but ourselves also, which have the firstfruits of the Spirit, even we ourselves groan within ourselves, waiting for the adoption, to wit, the redemption of our body. For we are saved by hope: but hope that is seen is not hope: for what a man seeth, why doth he yet hope for? But if we hope for that we see not, then do we with patience wait for it. Likewise the Spirit also helpeth our infirmities: for we know not what we should pray for as we ought: but the Spirit itself maketh intercession for us with groanings which cannot be uttered. And he that searcheth the hearts knoweth what is the mind of the Spirit, because he maketh intercession for the saints according to the will of God. KJV*

*Ephesians 4:22-24 Strip yourselves of your former nature [put off and discard your old unrenewed self] which characterized your previous manner of life and becomes corrupt through lusts and **desires that spring from delusion;** and **be constantly renewed in the spirit of your mind [having a fresh mental and spiritual attitude],** and put on the new nature (the regenerate self) created in God's image, [Godlike] in true righteousness and holiness. AMP*

As we pray we are conformed to the image of Christ Jesus. When you pray in tongues God's power pulls you out of the past and gives you miracles in the present thereby changing your future. Praying in tongues bypasses the human mind. Praying in other tongues changes who you are at your core. Therefore we are enabled by the Holy Spirit to interact with our Heavenly Father outside of the war zone of our own mind. When we pray in tongues at length we enter into the peace of God. God is enabled through your own prayer to pray out His will for your life.

Events and circumstances are changed ahead of you as He orders your days through prayer. When each of us obeys the leading of the Holy Spirit, moment by moment, we walk in continual victory. We are More Than Conquerors through Christ Jesus our Lord!

Feast of Pentecost = Law that enabled Old Testament persons to circumvent and deal with pride.

Pentecost = New Testament outpouring of the Holy Spirit with tongues which enables Christian persons to circumvent and deal with pride.

We must partake of the Divine Nature of God Almighty to become One with Him. We are transformed by the renewing of our mind. The Bible clearly states exactly how to do that.

1. the promises of God in the Bible given to each one, personally, by the Holy Spirit (God's Logos focused as Rhema)
2. praying in tongues, at length, as we read, study and meditate on the Word of God (revelation received this way)
3. the peace of God, given by Jesus Christ, which acts as our mediator
4. confession of who we are IN CHRIST JESUS by putting on God's Armor which God custom makes for each person individually and thereby conforming our "self" with the character of Christ
5. moment by moment obedience to the Voice of the Holy Spirit within our human spirit
6. training our "self" to think the Word of God in the personal, present tense as the Holy Spirit unctions the Word of God (moment-by-moment correction of our own thought life)
7. a humble heart of love and forgiveness in serving those about us, putting family before "ministry"
8. doing the "high call" of God the Father — staying where He assigns us on our own personal Cross

2 Peter 1:3-9 *For His divine power has bestowed upon us all things that [are requisite and suited] to life*

and godliness, through the [full, personal] **knowledge of Him** Who called us by and to His own glory
and excellence (virtue). By means of these He has
bestowed on us **His precious and exceedingly great
promises,** so that through them you may escape [by
flight] from the moral decay (rottenness and corruption) that is in the world because of covetousness
(lust and greed), and become **sharers (partakers) of
the divine nature.** For this very reason, adding your
diligence [to the divine promises], employ every effort
in exercising your faith to develop virtue (excellence, resolution, Christian energy), and in [exer-
cising] virtue [develop] knowledge (intelligence),
and in [exercising] knowledge [develop] self-control,
and in [exercising] self-control [develop] steadfastness (patience, endurance), and in [exercising]
steadfastness [develop] godliness (piety), and in
[exercising] godliness [develop] brotherly affection,
and in [exercising] brotherly affection [develop]
Christian love. For as these qualities are yours and
increasingly abound in you, they will keep [you] from
being idle or unfruitful unto the [full personal]
knowledge of our Lord Jesus Christ (the Messiah, the
Anointed one). For whoever lacks these qualities is
blind, [spiritually] shortsighted, seeing only what
is near to him, and has become oblivious [to the
fact] that he was cleansed from his old sins. AMP

God's method of change is to call those things
that be not as though they are, until they are, not
to call those things that are, as they are, to change
what they are. One definition of insanity is to continue to do the same things and practice the same
ways you have always done expecting to achieve a
new and different goal. The laws of the realm of the
spirit will override the laws of the natural realm.

We do not seek supernatural power. We do not worship supernatural power. Supernatural power is not
the goal of the church or the "end all" of our growth
in Christ Jesus, just as ministry itself is not our

goal. Yes, when we obey God, His supernatural power will flow through us in signs, wonders and miracles. However, that is not our goal. When we seek spiritual power without seeking the Heart of God, Himself, we perish by the way side. Our goal and that which we seek is JESUS CHRIST, HIMSELF!!! We seek Him because we desire to know Him and be One with Him. We do that because we love Jesus. We love God. Any other motive is wrong. Yes, we want to see hospitals emptied. Yes, we want to see ignorance and darkness banished. Yes, we desire wholeness and soundness in little children and in all people. Yet those goals are not enough. If we sought those goals only they would lead us into error and into defeat. The physical wholeness of humanity cannot and should not ever be our ultimate goal. God, Himself, is our goal!

Jesus said, " Mark 16:15-18 Go ye into all the world, and preach the gospel to every creature. He that believeth and is baptized shall be saved; but he that believeth not shall be damned. And these signs shall follow them that believe; In my name shall they cast out devils; they shall speak with new tongues; they shall take up serpents; and if they drink any deadly thing, it shall not hurt them; they shall lay hands on the sick, and they shall recover. Matthew 28:18-20 All power is given unto me in heaven and in earth. Go ye therefore, and teach all nations, baptizing them in the name of the Father, and of the Son, and of the Holy Ghost: Teaching them to observe all things whatsoever I have commanded you: and, lo, I am with you alway, even unto the end of the world. Luke 24:46-49 Thus it is written, and thus it behoved Christ to suffer, and to rise from the dead the third day: And that repentance and remission of sins should be preached in his name among all nations, beginning at Jerusalem. And ye are witnesses of these things. And, behold, I send the promise of my Father upon you: but tarry ye in the city of Jerusalem, until ye be endued with power from on high. John 20:21-23, 30, 31 Then said Jesus to them again, Peace be unto you: as my Father hath sent me, even so send I you. And when he had said this, he breathed on them, and saith unto them, Receive ye the Holy Ghost: Whose soever sins ye remit, they are remitted unto them; and whose soever sins ye retain, they are retained.........And many other signs truly did Jesus in the presence of his disciples, which are not written in this book: But these are written, that ye might believe that Jesus is the Christ, the Son of God; and that believing ye might have life through his name. KJV

Jesus Christ is our only worthy goal. He, Himself, is the only One Who is pure enough, holy enough, and righteous enough for us to seek. Jesus Christ is God! **GOD** is our goal! The good of humanity must not be the great goal. Even the actions and the attributes of God cannot and must never be the end we seek. We must seek the Person of the Heart of God, not only His Face/Mind and His Hand. This is crucial to our success as a race of beings. Without knowledge of the Heart of God we can never carry out the ways of God to their proper end. **The Heart of God Almighty must be that which we seek. We must have an intimate knowledge of God's Heart.** This is only achieved by time spent in His Presence in true worship and love. The Heart of God is found when we WAIT upon Him. How long are you willing to wait?

Jesus combs the earth seeking for those who love Him. Are you one of them? Let every motive and way within you be swallowed up in His love. (We must have) the power of God + the knowledge of God (which results in our) = edification. When we work for the Lord we must check our motive. Are we motivated by the heart? Are we motivated by love? Has God, Himself, instigated our action? Are we a "sent one"? Is our motivation to obey Him? Are we seeking His glory or our own glory? Does serving God give us fulfillment because it justifies our existence and validates us as an individual or do we obey Him because we love Him?

Every one that is perfect must be like his Master. Our standard of excellence is the Word of God and the Life of Jesus Christ. If we are willing and obedient we will eat the good of the land.

2 Chronicles 16:9
For the eyes of the Lord run to and fro throughout the whole earth to show Himself strong in behalf of those whose hearts are blameless toward Him. AMP
2 Chronicles 16:9
For the eyes of the LORD run to and fro throughout the whole earth, to shew himself strong in the behalf of them whose heart is perfect toward him. KJV
2 Chronicles 16:9
For the eyes of the LORD move to and fro throughout the earth that He may strongly support those whose heart is completely His. NASU

Are we, as the Body of Christ, moving past the Age of Grace or is God bringing the Body of Christ into a greater maturity? Is mankind, itself, growing past religion? Always remember that true Christians are full of joy. They are the happiest people on earth. This is a joy that is real—not a forced conformity to an ideology or the control of another person or by fear. It is a joy motivated by freedom and fueled by peace.

$$J \ = \ \text{Jesus Christ}$$
$$O \ = \ \text{others}$$
$$y \ = \ \text{you}$$

CHAPTER V

WHAT DID JESUS CHRIST ACCOMPLISH?

For the Son of Man has come to seek and to save that which was lost. Luke 19:10

For there is one God, and one mediator between God and men, the man Christ Jesus; Who gave himself a ransom for all 1 Timothy 2:5-6

*G*od gave us the whole answer to the whole problem at The Cross. He did it in the Person of Jesus Christ. God is so great and so big that He fixed an infinitely complicated problem in the simplest way and with a single event. Salvation is *what Christ did for us.* Salvation is given only by faith in Jesus Christ. Too easy! You say. Well you could take into consideration that it just might be possible that you don't realize how totally awesome and magnificent God really is. He is closer and more real than the breath you just breathed! In fact, He is the breath you just breathed. You live **in** Him and, if you are a Christian, He is in you. Every single person who has ever lived is eternal and an eternity. Every single person who has ever lived has a universe within them. Every single person who has ever lived on this earth is spiritually alive right now. Where are they? The question is, do they have Life? Can they stand in the midst of the Fire and live?

There is only one plan of salvation. What will **you** do with Jesus Christ? Jesus is the Way. Jesus is the Truth. Agapeo love is the essence of truth. If you do not have the Love of God in you the truth you seek is a deception. Jesus is the Life. Life is a Person—His name is Jesus. He is The Door. He is our Good Shepherd. Jesus is the Light of the world. He created everything that exists on the earth. Jesus Christ does not exist: Jesus is existence. Jesus has nothing: He is everything. He is the Word. He is King of kings and Lord of lords. He is the Beginning and the Ending of this earth. He is our Joy and the rejoicing of our hearts and much more. He is the Lord from Heaven: a quickening spirit. He has Life within Him. He gives Life to those who obey Him. He is all beauty. He is the Rose of Sharon and the Lily of the Valley.

It was good that Jesus Christ was nailed to the Cross of Calvary and that He was in the process of death because He became all sin, all evil, all perversion, all jealousy, all pride, all bondage, all poverty, all error, all seduction, all deception, all unbelief, all sickness, disease, infirmity, pestilence and plague <u>for you</u>. He was separated from God and He died spiritually <u>for you.</u> He was wounded for your transgressions. He was bruised for your iniquities. The chastening for your well-being and peace was upon Him. He did not have three trickles of blood and two bruises. He was so deformed you could not tell He was a human being. *Isaiah 52:14 [For many the Servant of God became an object of horror; many were astonished at Him.] His face and His whole appearance were marred more than any man's, and His form beyond that of the sons of men—but just as many were astonished at Him AMP* His blood was poured out. He was the sinless Son of God on the Cross of Calvary. Yet He was also the Son of man. Spiritually He was sick and evil and poor and proud and every wicked thing. He did it <u>for you</u>. Because He did this thing you are free. You can walk on by a free person. That is how much God loves you. If you think this is an exaggeration and error, then ask God to show you the truth—if you are brave enough. Even though He became sin yet He was the sinless Son of God and, as such, Jesus Christ spoke seven times from the Cross:

1. Luke 23:34 Then said Jesus, *Father, forgive them; for they know not what they do.* And they parted his raiment, and cast lots.
2. Matthew 27:46 And about the ninth hour Jesus cried with a loud voice, saying, *Eli, Eli, lama sabachthani?* that is to say, My God, my God, why hast thou forsaken me?
   Mark 15:34 And at the ninth hour Jesus cried with a loud voice, saying, *Eloi, Eloi, lama sabachthani?* which is, being interpreted, My God, my God, why hast thou forsaken me?
3. Luke 23:43 And Jesus said unto him, *Verily I say unto thee, To day shalt thou be with me in paradise.*
4. John 19:26-27 When Jesus therefore saw his mother, and the disciple standing by, whom he loved, he saith unto his mother, *Woman, behold thy son!* Then saith he to the disciple, *Behold thy mother!* And from that hour that disciple took her unto his own home.
5. John 19:28 After this, Jesus knowing that all things were now accomplished, that the scripture might be fulfilled, saith, *I thirst.*
6. Luke 23:46 And when Jesus had cried with a loud voice, he said, *Father, into thy hands I commend my spirit:* and having said thus, he gave up the ghost.
7. John 19:30 When Jesus therefore had received the vinegar, he said, *It is finished*: and he bowed his head, and gave up the ghost. KJV

2 Timothy 1:9-10 [For it is He] Who delivered and saved us and called us with a calling in itself holy and leading to holiness [to a life of consecration, a vocation of holiness*]; [He did it] not because of anything of merit that we have done, but because of and to further <u>His own purpose</u> and grace (unmerited favor) which was given us in Christ Jesus before the world began [eternal ages ago]. [It is that purpose and grace] which He now has made known and has fully disclosed and made real [to us] through the appearing of our Savior Christ Jesus, <u>Who annulled death</u> and made it of no effect and brought <u>life and immortality (immunity from eternal death) to light</u> through the Gospel. AMP*

How dare we ever say we have this sin or this problem or that error within us! What an affront to the death of Christ on Calvary! Positionally Jesus' death took it all away! God removed our sins in totality through the death of Jesus Christ! Now we possess the new nature of Christ within our selves. The Church has ministered such confusion, double-mindedness and darkness about this one truth. Just about every pulpit that exists preaches from either the intellect, the emotions or the will, of the soul of man. The congregation of such a church cannot rise above the revelation of its leadership. Where is there a church that ministers from the realm of the spirit? Where is there a church in which the leadership is so humble that it openly professes it is not God incarnate and that it seeks to grow and change into more of what Jesus Christ accomplished on the Cross of Calvary by His death and resurrection, thereby freeing its congregation to do the same?

What Jesus did at the Cross was no last minute contingency plan to fix a situation that had run amuck. God saw the problem and gave the solution before the beginning of the foundation of the earth. There was nothing sentimental about it. There was nothing religious about it. The Solution that He has given is extremely efficient and exactly what is needed. It is efficacious.

Five things accomplished in <u>the cross</u> of Christ Jesus:

1. *a complete work of grace was accomplished*
2. *a work of perfection was achieved—nothing need be added or subtracted*
3. *both judgment and mercy were fulfilled—God's holy nature was satisfied with fallen mankind*
4. *the compassion and love of God was fully expressed toward His fallen man*
5. *eternity was opened unto humanity and eternal life was made possible to man*

Thus the mending of relationship was accomplished not by man, who sinned, but by God, Who loved. The Cross reconciled heaven and earth in addition to reconciling God and man.

Yet our salvation has not come merely through the death of Jesus Christ on the Cross of Calvary. It has also come through His life and His three-and-a-half year ministry while on the earth. Everything about Jesus Christ and everything He was, is and will do is a gift to you, personally, from God Almighty. His life has been given for you to know God. Jesus Christ was the spiritual pioneer of our earthly walk as sons of God. Everything we know about how to live and what to do as sons of God on this earth we have learned from the life of Jesus Christ. *Romans 5:10 For if, when we were enemies, we were reconciled to God by the death of his Son, much more, being reconciled, we shall be saved by his life.* KJV Thus we see that His accomplishments are far more pervasive than initially thought. God did not just deal with mankind as a whole but has shown us in a personal and individual way how to live successfully and how to be overcomers in this life. There are answers to life's difficult questions. God has provided the means whereby we are enabled to escape the wrath of the world, the flesh and the devil. However, all this is predicated on the idea that we will be doers of His plan. We must not be hearers only. There is a cost—our self life. We must pay the price to obtain the blessing.

"The suffering and sorrow that you see and into which you have been baptized have been the same since the beginning and shall be unto the end. Each man who desires to walk in My ways and be like unto Me must be baptized in this even as I was. For it was into this baptism that I came in the flesh; for this is the fallen state of man. If you do not partake of this, you have no part in Me.

"The error of many peoples is that they do not receive the Lord in His fullness. They receive only the blessings of the Lord—His goodness, mercy, grace and prosperity. Because they only receive half of Me they have only half of Me—half of My wisdom, half of My truth, half of My guidance. They do not receive My pain, My sorrow, My suffering, My turmoil. Receive the fullness of the Lord and you shall have the fullness of the Lord."

One of the worst travesties of religious tradition is the original sin of separation created by rules and regulations demanding perfection in the soulish sense. The leadership of a church walking in this mind set has eaten from the tree of the knowledge of good and evil rather than eating from the tree of life. "Holiness toward God, righteousness toward man, and the control of the passions, rest on love, not merely to an abstract dogma, but to the person of Him who first loved us and bought us at the cost of His own blood." (from Fausset's Bible Dictionary, Electronic Database Copyright (c)1998 by Biblesoft) When an individual is unwilling or unable to conform to the societal standards of the church they visit, rejection is ministered to them — whether through body language, overt action or merely the omission of loving acceptance and kindness.

God must have first place in all things. We must accept all that God is. When we only receive or accept the good things of God and reject that which involves judgment, power, truth, etc. then we only possess half of God. How does this translate into "the real world"? The Biblical example began when the nation of Israel rejected the leadership of judges and asked God for a king. God gave them King Saul. When King Saul put the opinion of man first before the Word of the Lord through the prophet Samuel, God rose up David to be king in his place. God raised David up to a level of blessing and maturity and sent him into the wilderness where all those who were "in debt, discouraged and dissatisfied" were gathered unto him. David's throne was established on the bedrock of Israeli society. He had to deal with the dregs of humanity until God transformed them into mighty men of valor.

In America today this sequence of events is being painfully repeated. The visible church, having only received the good things of God and rejecting the poor, ugly, rebellious, stubborn, chronically diseased and disobedient who were sent to it, has become a select membership of the elect. Or, in other words, having put themselves in the place of God, knowing what is good and what is evil, rather than obeying God's simple commands and allowing God, Himself, to adjudicate, they have chosen only the good for themselves. What of the baser elements of society? The Muslim religion has gone into the slums and ministered acceptance and love to the prisoners, drug addicts and gang members, raising them up in knowledge and power to a force to be dealt with. Just as God led David into the wilderness to deal with the baser elements of Israeli society before he was made king, so the Muslims are dealing with those in the wilderness of American society. Who will be made king? What must we learn from this?

1. God must be put in first place and obeyed implicitly. "Seek ye first….."
2. We must accept all that God is, realizing this earth is His.
3. Acceptance and love must be ministered to all. All persons must be received and loved. Each will find their right place in God's Kingdom as **the Holy Spirit adjudicates** God's will.
4. All must receive life. No man is God. Only God is God. Ministers are servants not lords.
5. Restoration will be achieved from the realm from which it is ministered.

It is important to note that Jesus Christ is the only and very Son of God. At the same time He is the model for the sons of God that the Father desires to be conformed to His image. Confusion on this point has been a source of division and schism in the Body of Christ and ought not to be so. God desires many sons. For this reason He sowed the Seed of His Son in the earth—that He might reap a harvest of many sons, who are conformed to the image of His Only Begotten Son.

Genealogically Jesus ben Joseph was a direct descendant of King David ben Jesse through both His mother and His father. Mary descended through David's son Nathan—a prophet. Joseph descended through David's son Solomon—a king. King Solomon and Nathan, the Prophet, were half-brothers. Jesus was the true and rightful King of Israel. He was and is the true Prophet of God. King Herod was an Aramean imposter. When Pontius Pilate had the sign "The King of the Jews" nailed to the cross of Christ it was the truth. (He had asked, "What is truth?" God worked the truth through him. God is so-o Good!) The nation of Israel chose Cesear as their Emperor from fear of loss and said with their own mouths they would bear the judgment and blood of the death of Jesus Christ, their true king, upon themselves and their children. Once Jesus Christ was resurrected from the dead He never appeared in the world system or to the worldly people. His only appearances were to His own people who had of their own free will chosen Him. It is the same today.

All persons must receive Jesus Christ as their Savior. We Gentiles often believe we are a cut above the Jewish people because of Jesus Christ. Yet one of God's main purposes in sending Christ the Messiah was to deliver His chosen people, Israel's seed, from the grip of false religion and the bondage into which they had fallen. The Gentile Church is merely a parenthesis in the eternal purposes and plan of the Almighty God. The Jewish people are God's eternally chosen family. Yet all people belong to God. All people must be born-again by faith in the shed blood of Jesus Christ. One of the main purposes of Jesus Christ's first visitation to planet earth was to proclaim religion to the Gentiles and bring religion to victory. *2 Corinthians 12:9; 13:4 And he said unto me, My grace is sufficient for thee: for my strength is made perfect in weakness. Most gladly therefore will I rather glory in my infirmities, that the power of Christ may rest upon me........For though he was crucified through weakness, yet he liveth by the power of God. For we also are weak in him, but we shall live with him by the power of God toward you.KJV*

True salvation, like healing, progresses from the inside to the outside of man. It is not imposed from the outside in. Salvation is offered from God to man as a free will choice. When we receive the Seed of God, the Lord Jesus Christ, Who is Himself God, into the soil of our hearts, we are saved. God, the Father, has ordained our lives upon this earth to "walk out" this salvation, or rather that the Seed planted in our spirit man would come to fruition throughout our entire person: spirit, soul and body. The Apostle Paul prayed that we might be saved spirit, soul and body. He prayed that eternal glory would rest upon us. Thus, when we leave this earth we shall leave as one who is spiritually alive with Christ's life in us. We shall be a member of the new species of humanity created by God through the work of Jesus Christ. We will be spiritual fruit that remains unto eternity, brought forth unto the Father by the Lord Jesus Christ, Himself. We shall be able to stand in the midst of the Fire for the Fire, Himself, shall live in the midst of us. (Our God is a consuming Fire.)

The word salvation or Sozo, as it is in the Greek, includes in its meaning soundness, healing, security, deliverance and wholeness. The chief blessing of the New Covenant that Jesus Christ established between God and man is the salvation of the soul. It has been said by Rev. Rod Parsley that with only three nails and two pieces of wood Jesus Christ built a bridge between God and man that has lasted over two thousand years. It is the greatest spiritual blessing that Christ came to bring. Jesus Christ is the Saviour of the world. Theologically this "so great salvation" includes the benefits made possible by the New Covenant in Christ. We have pardon or the **forgiveness** of our sins, **justification** or a right-standing (**righteousness**) with God, **regeneration** or the miracle of the **new birth** (being **born-again**), **redemption** providing our ransom from eternal penalty for sin, **assurance** of our salvation, **sanctification** or holiness whereby we are set apart unto the Lord and His holy service or use, **adoption** whereby we are set into place in the Body of Christ as a son of God, **glorification** where we enter into oneness with God in His fullness, majesty and brightness with the powers of the Age to Come and **consecration** whereby we are made pure and holy and given a job to do. These expressions of God's grace are received by faith. (There exist various terms for these definitions of spiritual growth and some of them overlap.)

Jesus Christ **is** life on this planet. Everything that exists, exists because He initiated it. He holds all things together with His power. *John 1:1-5,*

14 IN THE beginning [before all time] was the Word (Christ), and the Word was with God, and the Word was God Himself. [Isa 9:6.] He was present originally with God. All things were made and came into existence through Him; and without Him was not even one thing made that has come into being. In Him was Life, and the Life was the Light of men. And the Light shines on in the darkness, for the darkness has never overpowered it [put it out or absorbed it or appropriated it, and is unreceptive to it]....... And the Word (Christ) became flesh (human, incarnate) and tabernacled (fixed His tent of flesh, lived awhile) among us; and we [actually] saw His glory (His honor, His majesty), such glory as an only begotten son receives from his father, full of grace (favor, loving-kindness) and truth.

Proverbs 8:22-31 The Lord formed and brought me [Wisdom] forth at the beginning of His way, before His acts of old. I [Wisdom] was inaugurated and ordained from everlasting, from the beginning, before ever the earth existed. [1 Cor 1:24] When there were no deeps, I was brought forth, when there were no fountains laden with water. Before the mountains were settled, before the hills, I was brought forth, [Job 15:7, 8.] While as yet He had not made the land or the fields or the first of the dust of the earth. When He prepared the heavens, I [Wisdom] was there; when He drew a circle upon the face of the deep and stretched out the firmament over it, when He made firm the skies above, when He established the fountains of the deep, when He gave to the sea its limit and His decree that the waters should not transgress [across the boundaries set by] His command, when He appointed the foundations of the earth— [Job 38:10,11; Ps 104:6-9; Jer 5:22.] Then I [Wisdom] was beside Him as a master and director of the work; and I was daily His delight, rejoicing before Him always, [Matt 3:17; John 1:2, 18.] Rejoicing in His inhabited earth and delighting in the sons of men. [Ps 16:3.] AMP Jesus Christ **IS** Wisdom.

1 Corinthians 1:30 But of him are ye in Christ Jesus, who of God is made unto us wisdom, and righteousness, and sanctification, and redemption: KJV 1 Corinthians 1: 30 But it is from Him that you have your life in Christ Jesus, Whom God made our Wisdom from God, [revealed to us a knowledge of the divine plan of salvation previously hidden, manifesting itself as] our Righteousness [thus making us upright and putting us in right standing with God], and our Consecration [making us pure and holy], and our Redemption [providing our ransom from eternal penalty for sin]. AMP

1 Corinthians 2:6-13 Yet when we are among the full-grown (spiritually mature Christians who are ripe in understanding), we do impart a [higher] wisdom (the knowledge of the divine plan previously hidden); but it is indeed not a wisdom of this present age or of this world nor of the leaders and rulers of this age, who are being brought to nothing and are doomed to pass away. But rather what we are setting forth is a wisdom of God once hidden [from the human understanding] and now revealed to us by God—[that wisdom] which God devised and decreed before the ages for our glorification [to lift us into the glory of His presence]. None of the rulers of this age or world perceived and recognized and understood this, for if they had, they would never have crucified the Lord of glory. But, on the contrary, as the Scripture says, What eye has not seen and ear has not heard and has not entered into the heart of man, [all that] God has prepared (made and keeps ready) for those who love Him [who hold Him in affectionate reverence, promptly obeying Him and gratefully recognizing the benefits He has bestowed]. [Isa 64:4; 65:17.] Yet to us God has unveiled and revealed them by and through His Spirit, for the [Holy] Spirit searches diligently, exploring and examining everything, even sounding the profound and bottomless things of God [the divine counsels and things hidden and beyond man's scrutiny]. For what person perceives (knows and understands) what passes through a man's thoughts except the man's own spirit within him? Just so no one discerns (comes to know and comprehend) the thoughts of God except the Spirit of God. Now we have not received the spirit [that belongs to] the world, but the [Holy] Spirit Who is from God, [given to us] that we might realize and comprehend and appreciate the gifts [of divine favor and blessing so freely and lavishly] bestowed on us by God. And we are setting these truths forth in words not taught by human wisdom but taught by the [Holy] Spirit, combining and interpreting spiritual truths with spiritual language [to those who possess the Holy Spirit]. AMP Jesus Christ really is our All in All! He is the **only** Door into heaven's eternity from this planet.

Jesus Christ came as both Savior and Servant. He is the King, Prophet and Priest of this planet. Yes, He did die for mankind's sin but He was resurrected that man might have eternal life. *Psalms 89:19 Then thou spakest in vision to thy holy one, and saidst, I have laid help upon one that is mighty; I have exalted one chosen out of the people. KJV* The second Person of the Holy Trinity partook of two natures—perfect God and perfect Man. Perfect Man indeed, but oh, how different! *Ecclesiastes 4:9-12 Two are better than one; because they have a good reward for their labour. For if they fall, the one will lift up his fellow: but woe to him that is alone when he falleth; for he hath not another to help him up. Again, if two lie together, then they have heat: but how can one be warm alone? And if one prevail against him, two shall withstand him; and a threefold cord is not quickly broken. KJV* God is Love. Love never fails. The three-fold cord of the Holy Trinity cannot be broken. Instead of enmity from his fellow, man receives help and agreement in Christ Jesus. Jesus is "the Faithful Witness". *Revelation 1:5-6 … from Jesus Christ, who is the faithful witness, and the first begotten of the dead, and the prince of the kings of the earth. Unto him that loved us, and washed us from our sins in his own blood, and hath made us*

kings and priests unto God and his Father; to him be glory and dominion for ever and ever. Amen. KJV
    Jesus Christ came to introduce mankind to the Father God. Before He came, men did not know that God was their Father. Yes they knew He was the Creator and they knew He was Jehovah with many names expressing the greatness of His being, but they did not know Him as Father. Jesus introduced us to Him. Jesus also introduced mankind to the love of God. Before He came men reverenced God, they feared and worshipped and served Him but they did not know of the Love of God. Grace and truth came through Jesus Christ. Everything God has given us in Christ Jesus has been given with the grace, not only to receive it, but the grace to walk it out. Jesus began to introduce the Person of God the Holy Spirit, Who is the Promise of the Father. Jesus and the Holy Spirit are BOTH our Intercessors and Advocates/Helpers. He taught us about the Kingdom of God and the will of God for all mankind. Jesus Christ came to show us Himself as the pattern of sonship to the Father God. He taught the disciples and us how to be sons of God. He taught us what Love is when He healed the sick and set the captives free. Jesus healed them all! For example many were healed when they touched the hem of His garment. The "hem of the garment" typifies a sanctified conscience. Jesus is our example of how to walk as God in the earth today. He has shown us how to be a supernatural son of God, building the Kingdom of God, for God's glory. When we become One with Jesus Christ and receive His glory what do we receive? We receive His standing with the Father as a true son of God. Currently we are to be Christ in the earth, working His works and performing the will of the Father—all for the glory of God. We are called to live out His life in our generation. Yes, Jesus Christ is truly our All in all. Rev. Gary Carpenter has said that the life of Jesus Christ is our Promised Land! Jesus is our Starry Night!
    Why did the solution have to be so messy, shameful and even embarrassing, you say? Why does it involve

146

blood? It is because the very essence of the answer, the Life, is in the blood. It is our faith in His shed blood, the blood of the Father, which saves us. (It is a scientific fact that the blood of a child passes, not from the mother who has been impregnated with the child, but from the blood of the Father.) God knows that each and every one born on this earth must personally come to a place of decision about His Blood. What do you believe about the blood of God?

The Roman government did not design crucifixion on a cross as an easy or quick death. It was designed to be slow and agonizing and to minister shame, disgrace and reproach. Those who died on the cross were naked and lifted up high for all to see them in their agony. It was the place for those who rejected instruction; who held to evil companions; who were proud, lazy, lustful, foolish, liars, stubborn, idolaters, hasty in speech, who mistreated their parents and who were juvenile delinquents. When we are "in Christ" we have no shame. God has delivered us from shame/guilt. Romans 8:2 Jesus endured the shame for the joy that was set before Him. That joy is YOU!

The good works of unsaved people, the Law which Moses was given by God, and which the nation of Israel traditionalized, and the Church which Jesus Christ initiated, can not and never will, save one person. Yes, God uses these institutions to teach us and train us to know and understand Him and His ways, but they will not, and can not, save us. Only your faith in the shed blood of Jesus Christ is able to save you. Do you have faith in the blood of Jesus Christ? That is the only question and there is only one answer. All we have to do is ask. (If you have yet to do this, please refer to the Prayer of Salvation at the end of the book.) There is only one answer. His name is Jesus. JESUS! He is our "I AM that I AM"!

What happened at the Cross? Death to Life. Despair to Hope. Problem to Solution. Black to White. The depths of hell to the heights of heaven. According to our faith it will be done to us—each one of us

147

on an individual basis. Whosoever shall call on the Name of the Lord shall be saved. Joel 2:32

Rev. James Stalker (1848-1927), a Scottish scholar and pastor, who was a professor of Church history in the United Free Church, Aberdeen, Scotland, wrote: "One of the great objects of the appearance of Christ was to break down the wall of separation between Jew and Gentile and make the blessings of salvation the property of all men, without distinction of race or language. But he was not himself permitted to carry this change into practical realization. It was one of the strange limitations of his earthly life that he was sent only to the lost sheep of the house of Israel." It was when Andrew brought the Greeks to meet Jesus that He knew the process of Calvary was to begin.

The Pauline Epistles give us a clear understanding of the revelation that the Apostle Paul received from Jesus Christ. The hidden purpose and sacred secret of the Omnipotent Father God, which is designed to secure submission to the Faith in the people of God and to lead us to obedience, even the Mystery of Godliness. Reverence for God's character and His commands are at the center of godliness. Our obedience and submission to the authority of His kingdom is pre-requisite to our godliness. It is Christ in us, the hope of glory. For, yes, when we receive Christ we become the temple of the Holy Spirit and God, Himself, lives in us. However, at the same time, we also enter into Him. We, corporately, as the Body of Christ, come to have our being in Him. It is this revelation of who we are in Him that Paul received from Jesus Christ. The Pauline Epistles teach the Church of the living God spiritual growth that each one might reach the goal of godliness. The institution of the Church is not the sacred secret that leads us to accomplish God's hidden purposes. The Church is merely the institution that God uses to train His children in His ways. It, in itself, shall pass away. Who we are in Christ Jesus shall never pass away! Our glorification and entering into oneness with Christ, as typified by the relationship of marriage or as typified by the human body, is God's hidden purpose. We shall be changed and transformed. Our physical bodies shall be made eternal. Sin and death no longer have power over us. Death shall be overcome by life in our physical bodies!

The Mystery of Godliness, Christ in us the hope of glory, is an abomination to the spirit of religion. It is an abomination to that spirit of antichrist and the spirit of the world and satan himself. This hidden purpose of God is such foolishness to the ungodly that they are unable to see its value. It can only be perceived and understood by men of pure conscience. It creates such uproar and fight among all but the people of God that there are few that receive it and believe it. There are fewer still that walk in it. Yet this is that that Jesus Christ accomplished on the Cross! The Mystery of Godliness. Christ in us the hope of glory. The essence of the Mystery of Godliness is Christ enthroned in the hearts of His people, so as to impart His nature and holiness to them. It is our restoration — the restoration of man-kind — to whosoever will come. "See" Jesus. He is the Word of God. Let images of Him and the Word be your thought, not the images of the world. Let Him become your hope. Visions of the Living Christ must be your imagination. Only what the Word says must be on the inside of you. God changed what Abraham "saw" on the inside—i.e. the imagination of his heart. Our imagi-nations must be directed by the Holy Spirit. We must get a new hope. We must conquer our understanding. Our mind must be renewed with the Word of God. Our hope must be alive. It must be more real than the circumstances we deal with daily. Jesus Christ is our "starry night"!

Isaiah 53:10-12 Yet it was the will of the Lord to bruise Him; He has put Him to grief and made Him sick. When You and He make His life an offering for sin [and He has risen from the dead, in time to come], He shall see His [spiritual] offspring, He shall prolong His days, and the will and pleasure of the

Lord shall prosper in His hand. He shall see [the fruit] of the travail of His soul and be satisfied; **by His knowledge of Himself [which He possesses and imparts to others] shall My [uncompromisingly] righteous one, My Servant, justify many and make many righteous (upright and in right standing with God),** for He shall bear their iniquities and their guilt [with the consequences, says the Lord]. Therefore will I divide Him a portion with the great [kings and rulers], and He shall divide the spoil with the mighty, because He poured out His life unto death, and [He let Himself] be regarded as a criminal and be numbered with the transgressors; yet **He bore [and took away] the sin of many and made intercession for the transgressors (the rebellious).** *AMP*

Jesus Christ sowed thirty years of life on this planet, three-and-a-half years of ministry, and three days and three nights in the grave to accomplish the Divine will of the Father God; that God might have a Family made up of many sons. He has reaped or received in return three "days" and three "nights" of God's grace, i.e. three thousand years known as the Church Age and the Millennium (The Age of Grace) to obtain His Bride, the Bride of Christ and see His life and the rule and reign of His Kingship brought forth. The Lord first lived and then died; whereas we first receive His death by faith and then live His earthly life by faith.

Colossians 1:18-23a He is the Head of the body made up of His people—that is, His church—which He began; and He is the Leader of all those who arise from the dead, so that He is first in everything; for God wanted all of Himself to be in His Son. It was through what His Son did that God cleared a path for everything to come to Him—all things in heaven and on earth—for Christ's death on the cross has made peace with God for all <u>*by His blood*</u>. *This includes you who were once so far away from God. You were His enemies and hated Him and were separated from Him by your evil thoughts and actions, yet now He has brought you back as His friends. He has done this through the death on the cross of His own human body, and now as a result Christ has brought you into the very presence of God, and you are standing there before Him with nothing left against you—nothing left that He could even chide you for; the only condition is that you fully believe the Truth, standing in it steadfast and firm, strong in the Lord, convinced of the Good News that Jesus died for you, and never shifting from trusting Him to save you. This is the wonderful news that came to each of you and is now spreading all over the world.* Living Bible

Isaiah 42:6-7 I the Lord have called You [the Messiah] for a righteous purpose and in righteousness; I will take You by the hand and will keep You; I will give You for a covenant to the people [Israel], for a light to the nations [Gentiles],to open the eyes of the blind, to bring out prisoners from the dungeon, and those who sit in darkness from the prison. AMP

Jesus Christ came to initiate a new species of humanity on earth. As the only man born spiritually alive since Adam he gathered all disparate races of mankind and accomplished the one act that allowed God to breathe the breath of life into the new man thus created by faith in God's grace. God had given mankind the Law through the nation of Israel that mankind might know and understand what sin is. The Law showed us our sin. Once knowing our sin we were unable to refrain from it. As sinners, we sinned. *Ephesians 2:4-5 But God—so rich is He in His mercy! Because of and in order to satisfy the great and wonderful and intense love with which He loved us, even when we were dead (slain) by [our own] shortcomings and trespasses, He made us alive together in fellowship and in union with Christ; [He gave us the very life of Christ Himself, the same new life with which He quickened Him, for] it is by grace (His favor and mercy which you did not deserve) that you are saved (delivered from judgment and made partakers of Christ's salvation). AMP* Jesus Christ dissolved the enmity in His own flesh. God has quickened His new

151

creation by the same power that raised Christ from
the dead. The Law of Sin and Death has been legally
overcome by the Law of the Spirit of Life in Christ
Jesus. The result of all this is peace. We, as individuals, have peace within. As the race of mankind
in community we have peace. All divisions and sep-
arations are done away with. There are no longer
races, genders, colors, religions, creeds or nations
in Christ Jesus. There is one vision, one man, one
goal. The question is, "Are you in Christ?"

Jesus Christ came to earth a pure and holy vessel,
born of the blood of the Father God. He carried in
His own person the sin, transgression, iniquity,
grief, sorrow, sickness, disease, infirmity, pestilence, plague, poverty, lack, debt, want, affliction,
rejection, insecurity, judgment, death and every
evil thing. He did this for every human being on the
face of the planet throughout time. Jesus identified
with each of us. He owned who we are by His identification. He bought humanity as gold tried in the
fire. Because He had knowledge of, and understood Who
He is and what He was doing, and He accomplished
the act as a pure vessel, without sin, born of pure
Blood, spiritually alive; He bought humanity back
from Satan. He was crucified in the place of Adam
and thereby bought **all** of humanity back from satan.
He was not crucified in the place of Abraham. It was
my sin that killed Jesus. Genealogically, Jesus ben
Joseph, son of David, was the true King of Israel. He
was the innocent victim of your sin and mine. Jesus
Christ's substitutionary suffering and death on the
Cross of Calvary enables every human being that will,
to walk free of sin, sickness and all evil. When
Jesus Christ was accused of our sins by Herod and by
the High Priest of Israel He did not defend Himself
because He was guilty, in a substitutionary way, of
our sins. This enables me to open my mouth and defend
myself to satan. I do this when I speak the Word of
God unctioned by the Holy Spirit. Confession must
be made of the Word of God. If you confess the Word
of God your confession will be primarily about God.

If you don't confess the Word of God your confession will be about man. Jesus is LIFE. Jesus is TRUTH. However, each individual must receive Christ Jesus into their life personally. The salvation God provided must be received and acted upon personally by each individual. Unless this occurs the individual is doomed to eternal hell. The Life of God, i.e. His Seed, must enter into each person to be saved.

Jesus Christ was responsible to God for all of mankind. He fulfilled His responsibility. While hanging on the Cross, beaten beyond recognition, He forgave those who crucified Him. Jesus is the Truth that supersedes all fact. He is positive Truth. Nothing was impossible to Him and nothing is impossible to those who believe Him now. He makes the way where there seems to be no way. He opens the door that no man can shut and He shuts the doors that no man can open. He drank to the dregs the cup of God's judgment upon mankind because of our sin and now God judges no more. He partook of the baptism of death for all mankind whereby man no longer tastes of death in Christ. He was content with God's will for His life. Having all power, wisdom and knowledge He obeyed God by living a small, seemingly unimportant, unsuccessful life of obedience to His Heavenly Father and died young. He actively did the will of the Father, always. He always obeyed the Father. Jesus is all mercy. He was and is always kind. He healed them all.

Eternity was opened unto humanity and eternal life was made possible to man. To literally and in reality pass through the birth canal of one's own soul in this world system into true spiritual eternal life while yet walking and breathing on this planet **there is only one way.** (It's like being turned upside down, inside out.) After one receives Jesus Christ as Lord and Savior and is filled with His precious Holy Spirit, then one must **trust** the Most High Father God and **obey** the Voice of the Holy Spirit in one's own heart. This is not a trite platitude. It is of the utmost importance as there is no other way to success. Realize that God does not need your intellect

153

and your understanding to save you. He does need you to obey Him. Obedience without understanding is one way of defining faith. Remember that to know God is eternal life. Your eternity begins the moment you trust Jesus Christ as your Savior and obey Him without question. Each individual has as much of God—as much of His salvation—as they want to have or as much as they have been allowed to have. There are weak individuals who are in such bondage that only another strong and powerful Christian can help them out of that bondage. God knew this and that is one reason He created the Church and ordained that we have pastors. It is the mercy of God for the majority of the Body of Christ to be in the Church system. There are also many individuals who are part of dead churches and have only been taught error and false doctrine that they are the modern-day blind, led by blind men. They live in ditches, which is only a grave with both ends opened.

In John 17, Jesus prayed that we would know God, be one in unity, have the Father's love within us and that we would believe God's words. He prayed we would have eternal life, i.e. that we would know God. He prayed God would keep us in His Name. He prayed God would keep us from the evil one. He prayed we would be one with God as the book, Song of Songs, teaches us. In Romans 5:5 the Apostle Paul states that the "love of God is shed abroad in our hearts by the power of the Holy Spirit". When we believe God's words we are enabled to "see" God. Our minds are renewed by the Word of God. This is sanctification. We are removed forever from the world. In contrast to the empty boasting and covetousness of satan in Isaiah 14:12-14, Jesus Christ accomplished the will of the Father in the lives of those given to Him by God. He said, "I have given them the words which Thou gavest Me I have given to them; and they received them, and truly understood that I came forth from Thee, and they believed that Thou didst send Me........I guarded them........I have given them Thy Word...." Jesus also said, "And the glory which

Thou hast given Me I have given to them; that they may be one, just as we are one....." "I have made Thy name known to them, and will make it known; that the love wherewith Thou didst love Me may be in them, and I in them." Jesus Christ fulfilled His mission from God. He is the Real Winner!

Jesus Christ was born in poverty in an animal's stable and placed in a feeding trough at birth. He grew up with his needs met as the son of a carpenter but without kingly wealth. His example is another way God has shown me that true salvation and true life has little, if anything, to do with money. This teaches me that the world systems of work and finance have little, if anything, to do with my eternal life. This life will soon pass but eternity is F-O-R-E-V-E-R! Jesus knew the Father and understood great revelatory truths about Him when he was twelve years of age and had had no formal education. This teaches me that spiritual truth does not have to be learned from other men. God, Himself, will teach and train me. Jesus put priority upon hearing and doing the will of His Heavenly Father before doing the will of his earthly father. This teaches me that though family was and is created by God that it must not have pre-eminence before God. Jesus was led from within, only speaking and doing what He heard and saw His Heavenly Father speak and do. This is my pattern for right living. Jesus healed the sick, raised the dead and cast out devils. This was a major way He expressed the Love of God to people. He exercised the authority of the Father God. Jesus confronted religion and error at every turn. Jesus was not moved by the opinions and motivations of people. He knew what was in the heart of man. Therefore, I must not be moved or led by men but only by God, Himself, Who indwells me. At the same time I must walk in love with those about me, serving them and meeting their needs as God leads me. Jesus Christ was provided for and His every need was met in His life and mine will be too. Jesus Christ was protected His entire life, both naturally and supernaturally, until the

appointed time for the plan of the Father God to
be fulfilled. This teaches me that I, too, shall be
protected in this life as I obey the Holy Spirit's
leading. I must not fear men but I must fear God, in
a positive, reverential way. Jesus Christ grew in
faith and in His obedience to God and so must I in
this life.

Jesus Christ sweat great drops of blood while in
prayer in the Garden of Gethsemane. He bore the crown
of thorns upon His head. His beard was plucked from
His face. His physical body was bruised thus producing internal bleeding. He bore the thirty-nine
stripes upon His back. He was slapped, mocked and
spit upon. In each of His hands He was nailed to the
Cross with an iron spike. His feet were nailed to
the Cross with an iron spike. His side was pierced
with a spear. In each of the aforementioned places
upon His Person Jesus shed His blood. Each drop of
His blood is holy unto God the Father. Each drop of
His blood accomplished a work for the human race.

He sweat great drops of blood while in prayer in
the Garden of Gethsemane that our wills would be
sanctified unto God, that our souls — our minds, wills
and emotions — would be submitted to the will of the
Father. He bore the crown of thorns that we might
have the mind of Christ and our memory be blessed.
Jesus wore the Crown of Thorns that we might wear
the heavenly crowns of glory in eternity. His beard
was plucked from Him that we might have the wisdom of
the ages, prudence, discernment, insight with understanding, the counsel of the indwelling Holy Spirit,
and blessing. His body suffered bruising and internal
bleeding that our emotions would be made whole. Upon
His back He bore the thirty-nine lashes for our
healing, health and divine life. All sickness, disease, infirmity, pestilence and plague emanates from
thirty nine source diseases. His shoulders and arms
were wounded that the government might be upon His
shoulders (the place of strength). His shoulders,
hips and lower legs were beaten, wounded and bruised
that our desire would no longer be for one another

but for God. His thighs were beaten that we might have a true, Godly, fear and reverence of God.

His hands were nailed to the cross that we might have the power of God at work through us, both in judgment and blessing, and do His will in the earth and cause His Kingdom to come on earth. His feet were nailed to the cross for our peace and humility that we might walk according to His will, experiencing spiritual growth and doing works of service. The nail through His feet provided for anointed preaching that men might be saved. His side was pierced through, blood and water gushing forth, that the Church, the Bride of Christ, might be brought forth into the earth. Just as Adam's rib was fashioned by God to form Eve, the mother of all living, so the Bride of Jesus Christ was brought forth through the second Adam. The Church of Jesus Christ is one of God's mysteries. The Age of Grace is hidden in the eternal timetable of God for the perfecting of the Bride of Christ which is to come out of the Church. God desires a family. He desires multiplication of His Love. All that we have and all that we are in the realm of the spirit came through Christ. Jesus Christ is the ONLY savior of this planet.

These sacrificial actions of the Lord Jesus contain much more revelation for the Body of Christ and must be received through prayer, fasting, study of the Scriptures and waiting upon God. There is still much more to be known, learned and experienced. When present with His disciples, Jesus said He had much more to teach them but they could not bear it then. God rose up Saul of Tarsus, i.e. the Apostle Paul, and from the revelation he received we have spiritual growth expounded in the epistles. Randy Alcorn has written that "after Columbus discovered the new world, Spain minted coins with the Latin slogan *Plus Ultra*. It meant 'More Beyond'. This was a horizon-expanding message to people who had always believed that the world they knew was all there was. *Plus Ultra* — there will always be more to discover about our God. In his new universe, there will always be more beyond."

Proverbs 4:18 NASB *"The path of the righteous is like the light of dawn, that shines brighter and brighter until the full day."*

So, get on the path, pilgrim, and RUN!

CHAPTER VI

WHO ARE WE WHEN WE ARE **IN CHRIST?**

*W*e, as Christians, are never told by God to get ourselves into Christ. We are not told to get ourselves there, because we are already there. However, we are told to remain where God has placed us. Every true spiritual experience means that we have discovered a certain fact in Christ, and have entered into His experience. Just as God once opened our eyes to see our sins laid upon Christ, so once again He must open our eyes to see our own selves in Christ. This is something He delights to do. Every Christian growth is achieved due to a greater revelation of **Who Christ Is.** We must know who we are in Christ, Who Christ is to us, and Who will Christ be through us.

The Way of Salvation is not in God making us good, but in His saving us out of Adam and putting us into Christ. This is our reality today. For when we are in Adam — in the flesh — we practice sin; and when we are in Christ — in the spirit — we practice righteousness. In the minds and hearts of many believers lies an error: the expectation that God will change us. It is very important to understand the truth. God does not and will not ever do anything in us; instead, He will put us in Christ. We are in Christ <u>positionally</u>

by faith in what Jesus did at Calvary. Christ is in us <u>experientially</u> when **we choose** to believe, think, speak and act out His Word and follow the leading of His Holy Spirit in obedience. In this way the life of Christ is lived through us. We must work out our own salvation with fear and trembling. When God put us in Christ, the Seed of Christ was put within us. The Seed of Christ will grow up, mature, flourish and bring forth fruit that remains unto eternity if allowed to do so. Mere intellectual knowledge is not enough to recommend men and make them acceptable to God. The righteous and holy life of Christ must be the object of the trust we have in God, held in our hearts, and it must be the pattern of our walk and practice in the natural realm before men.

In order to be translated from glory to glory or to grow in God you must have revelation because one part of man alone cannot grow. All parts together are required to change and grow and be translated from glory to glory. In other words, the spirit cannot grow without the soul growing and the body increasing in grace. All the parts of the spirit, all the parts of the soul and all the senses of the body are required to grow together for translation from glory to glory to occur. Your body is not "you"; it is the house you live in. Yet God does not hate your body and He doesn't want you to hate it either. Contrary to popular "Christian opinion" of most super-saints God did not create us spirits with irritating sin-laden bodies that we are burdened to deal with in this life. God created mankind to live in bodies and He likes them. God loves all of us! Friedrich Schiller (1759-1805), was raised a Pietist. "As an adult, he translated his heartfelt religion into a plea that education, indeed society itself, should recognize that the feelings are as necessary as the senses and the intellect to the attainment of full humanity." The error of Gnosticism was believing that matter was evil and emancipation comes through knowledge. Spiritual growth does come through knowledge but matter is not evil. This first century error

is a fine example of a lie embedded in a truth—one
of the ways of satan. Therefore, we conclude that
what God is interested in, is our full humanity—our
wholeness. Part of the definition of salvation is
wholeness and soundness. We must have the truth but
that truth must be a balanced truth that is ministered in love, not in hate.

Many people have been conformed to the image
of the church rather than being conformed to the
image of Christ. We are not to be conformed to the
apostle, the prophet, the evangelist, the pastor or
the teacher. We are to be conformed to Christ Jesus.
It is He, Himself, Who hung on the Cross for us not
a man or men. Yes, we are commanded in Scripture to
follow our godly leadership but, as is plainly stated
in Scripture, only AS they follow Christ. It is His
power that saves us and changes us from glory to
glory. We must remove ourselves from beholding with
our physical eyes that which we might perceive in
the sense realm and look unto the unseen Christ! He
alone is our Savior and our God! We are to be filled
up with God, with Jesus Christ and with the Holy
Spirit. We are not to be a reflection of a person or
an institution or even a product thereof. Doctrine
is a tool. It is not God. It can be likened to a
flashlight. Doctrine describes God. It must not be
worshipped. The Person of Almighty God is the object
of our worship. When we relegate the things of God
to methodology we have taken a step back from the
Person of Christ. We cannot live to fulfill prophecy.
God fulfills His Words. We can only live to seek and
worship God and to hear His Voice and obey His commands. Yes, these are very fine lines of distinction
but we must "hit the mark" with our faith. So many
have missed the mark by holding onto these slight
errors of faith. We must push past the fallen and
go on to victory!

Oneness with the Trinity of God, through <u>faith in
Christ,</u> comes through **glory** that is matured by the
<u>love of God,</u> through **trust** developed by God's faith-
fulness, and our **obedience** to the <u>leading of the Holy</u>

Spirit, over **time**. In this sense glory is defined as all the outward manifestations and appearance and the opportunities they bring. *John 17:18-23 As thou hast sent me into the world, even so have I also sent them into the world. And for their sakes I sanctify myself, that they also might be sanctified through the truth. Neither pray I for these alone, but for them also which shall believe on me through their word; that they all may be one; as thou, Father, art in me, and I in thee, that they also may be one in us: that the world may believe that thou hast sent me. And the glory which thou gavest me I have given them; that they may be one, even as we are one: I in them, and thou in me, that they may be made perfect in one; and that the world may know that thou hast sent me, and hast loved them, as thou hast loved me. KJV* When we are One with God time ceases. There is no time in God. We enter into eternity. When we live the Kingdom life of the Most High time ceases. We live in the NOW. We are dead to self and alive to God. We have nothing yet all things are ours. We are dead but Christ is alive in us and through us. We lay down our lives that others may live.

Spiros Zodhiates, Th.D. has written, "Dreams of perfection in the flesh would be little entertained if we kept clearly in view the distinction between what we are in Christ and what we are in ourselves. To be **in Him** is to be saved once and forever from the condemnation of sin, but not immediately from the presence and inworking of sin, as the lives of the saints testify. We are saved from the guilt and power of sin, but not from its presence while in this body and world. That is a state of being that will yet come when our bodies are redeemed when our resurrection takes place (Romans 8:23). Christ had sin upon Him, though there was no sin in Him. Therefore, he that is in Christ has no sin upon him (in the sense of condemnation), though he still has sin in him in the form of the sin-nature in the mortal body. The believer is unconditionally saved from sin and conditionally saved from the power of sin. Victory is

conditioned in proportion to the believer's unequiv-
ocal obedience to Christ and His command."

We are justified when sin is driven out by the
destruction of all evil desires deriving from the
body. The very fact of desire is of major importance in the spiritual arena. Anything you give up
for God you will receive it back 100 times in this
life with persecutions. If you keep something God
has given you freely He will take back what you
desired. In the Garden of Eden it was Adam's desire
for his wife that led him to knowingly sin. Eve fell
through deception but Adam knew what he was doing.
Eve was present in his life in the flesh. Adam loved
and desired Eve. Yes, God created marriage. Yes,
God created family. Yet to be one with God we must
put Him in first place before anyone else and anything else. Jesus said we must seek first the Kingdom
of God and His righteousness and all things would
be added unto us. Adam had oneness with God yet he
desired Eve; just as Samson was given the supernatural power of God yet he desired Delilah. As a result,
Samson chose Delilah so God took back His supernatural power. Adam chose to follow Eve's leadership
so oneness with God died. What do we desire? Who do
we desire? Why do we desire it? The true truths must
be grappled with in our innermost heart. We must
acknowledge the divine judgment to be righteous. God
does help the sinner to the position and status of
one who is righteous in His eyes. Love will remove
all things but a fervent desire for Him.

**"Holiness is a separation from the world
but it is also an open doorway into My
Heart. Being holy is in regard to what
you desire. Are your desires toward Me or
toward the world?" Where there is holiness there is beauty: where there are
beauty and holiness, there is omnipotence.**

Who are we in Him? What do we possess? What do
we do? We become Christ (the Anointed One) in the
earth. As Rev. Creflo Dollar defines it, we become
the anointed one and we carry his anointing — that

burden removing, yoke destroying power of God that is well able to set the captives free, loose the bonds, heal the brokenhearted and the sick, restore sight to the blind and hearing to the deaf, cause the lame to leap and raise the dead. Yes, we do His works, think His thoughts and live His life! He receives all the glory, honor, praise and majesty! God the Father has called us to BELIEVE. Jesus Christ the Son has given us the authority to FORGIVE. The Holy Spirit our Paraclete gives us the MINISTRY OF RECONCILIATION. The world views these three actions as wimpy and powerless yet the very opposite is the truth. If we are in Christ, all that is Christ's is ours. The victorious life that I seek in Christ is actually something I already possess positionally but must work out experientially by faith.

Romans 12:4-11 For as in one physical body we have many parts (organs, members) and all of these parts do not have the same function or use, so we, numerous as we are, are one body in Christ (the Messiah) and individually we are parts one of another [mutually dependent on one another]. Having gifts (faculties, talents, qualities) that differ according to the grace given us, let us use them: [He whose gift is] prophecy, [let him prophesy] according to the proportion of his faith; [He whose gift is] practical service, let him give himself to serving; he who teaches, to his teaching; he who exhorts (encourages), to his exhortation; he who contributes, let him do it in simplicity and liberality; he who gives aid and superintends, with zeal and singleness of mind; he who does acts of mercy, with genuine cheerfulness and joyful eagerness. [Let your] love be sincere (a real thing); hate what is evil [loathe all ungodliness, turn in horror from wickedness], but hold fast to that which is good. Love one another with brotherly affection [as members of one family], giving precedence and showing honor to one another. Never lag in zeal and in earnest endeavor; be aglow and burning with the Spirit, serving the Lord. AMP

1 Peter 4:10-11 As each of you has received a gift (a particular spiritual talent, a gracious divine endowment), employ it for one another as [befits] good trustees of God's many-sided grace [faithful stewards of the extremely Diverse powers and gifts granted to Christians by unmerited favor]. Whoever speaks, [let him do it as one who utters] oracles of God; whoever renders service, [let him do it] as with the strength which God furnishes abundantly, so that in all things God may be glorified through Jesus Christ (the Messiah). To Him be the glory and dominion forever and ever (through endless ages). Amen (so be it).

We are no longer Jew, "Christian" or Gentile, male or female, slave or free, black, white, red or yellow but as we grow in the grace and knowledge of Jesus Christ and enter into the Presence of the Trinity of God we are His child—nothing more and nothing less.

Just as Jesus did, when we are in Christ we are called to glorify the Father. We glorify the Father by accomplishing the work He gives us to do. We are to manifest God's Name to those given to us of God in order that they would keep God's Word. God keeps Christians in His Name that we may be one even as the Trinity is One. God keeps us from the power of the evil one. He sanctifies us in His Word of Truth. God's grace leads us to His glory. God gives us His glory for the purpose of bringing us into oneness. One purpose of the glory of God is to replace the veil of our flesh nature with His Presence that we are able to bear the transition from darkness to light.

The revelation that Jesus Christ brought to His people was the revelation of the Father. Prior to His coming the Jewish people did not know God as Father. They knew Him as Yahweh, the Lord of Sabbaoth, the Lord of Hosts. They knew Him as Jehovah in all His redemptive names and purposes. Yet it was Jesus Christ that introduced Him as our Heavenly Father, our Abba, or Daddy God. Jesus said that He and the Father are One. He prayed that the love of the Father might be in us, even as it was in Him.

165

Therefore, when we are "in Christ" we are One with the Father. We are "in Him". Scripture is full of God's Promises and truths about who we are "in Him". In 1 John the Apostle teaches us that when we have the Son we have the Father also. God is Love. When we are in Him we are permeated with His Love. *Romans 5:5 ...because the love of God is shed abroad in our hearts by the Holy Ghost which is given unto us. KJV* Scripture mentions those who do not have the love of the Father in them. We are commanded not to love the world because if we do, the love of the Father cannot be in us. *1 John 2:16 For all that is in the world, the lust of the flesh, and the lust of the eyes, and the pride of life, is not of the Father, but is of the world. KJV* We have all known Christians who are baptized with the Holy Spirit and speak in tongues yet they have no love within them. They can be mean as snakes! It is because they have not known the Father God, Who is Love. These three things, the love of the world, the lust of the eyes and the pride of life, constituted the original sin of mankind in the Garden of Eden. They oppose and are opposite to the love of the Father. In Luke 4 Scripture recounts Jesus' temptation by Satan in each of these three things. He overcame in each area. We appropriate His victory by faith in His shed blood. When faced with temptation in any of these areas Jesus Christ's over-coming of satan paves the way for us to overcome him in like manner by faith in His redemptive acts. Each one called of God and chosen by Him will face these same three temptations. What were they? 1) food when fasting 2) proof of our call and knowledge of what God has called us to do and 3) ability to enter into our call without death of self.

Rather than loving the world, we are to be joint heirs with Jesus Christ and enter into His Oneness with the Father. We are to walk in the Holy Spirit as sons of God in this life. Those who are led by the Holy Spirit are sons of God. Just as Jesus Christ is the Son of God so are we to be sons of the Father. He was the only sinless Son of God. Yet we are to walk as sons of God and do His works thereby allowing Him to live His life through us. All glory must be given to God. *Romans 8:29 For whom he did foreknow, he also did predestinate to be conformed to the image of his Son, that he might be the first-born among many brethren.* The daily life of the Christian can be summed up in one word: receive. The distinctive feature of true Christianity is that it compels people to receive. Our purpose is to fulfill the righteousness of the law. We are to walk in life and peace, spiritually minded, at rest with God and man. *Colossians 2:9-10 For in him dwelleth all the fulness of the Godhead bodily. And ye are complete in him, which is the head of all principality and power KJV* We are complete in Christ.

Jesus did not do anything unless He first "saw" the Father do it. He did not "say" anything unless He first heard the Father say it. He was led from within. He waited upon God. He spent long nights in prayer seeing, listening and waiting upon God. He prayed and waited upon God and studied the Scriptures. I believe that as He read the Word of God, He read it in the first person. In other words He read it as though it were written to Him and not about Him. This is the way we are to read the Word of God. God is speaking to me in the first person — not about Jesus Christ Who died two thousand years ago. He only did those things that the Father instructed Him to do in God's timing. Because He was absolutely obedient to the Father's leading, the power of God through Him was unlimited. I must also add here that Jesus is God. He is Very God. Jesus had the Holy Spirit without measure because He was the first man since Adam to be born spiritually alive. The plans, purposes and pursuits of God emanated from His spirit. (In the Old Testament the plans, purposes and pursuits of God emanated from the soul of man only, as there was no man in the entire world who was spiritually alive.) Jesus was born under the Law and, therefore, was obligated to fulfill the Law. Rev. Dave Roberson teaches that since Adam, Jesus Christ was the only one spiritually alive in all creation through all time. Jesus Christ set both Jews and Gentiles free of slavery to sin and the Law. He progressed beyond the Law into the Age of Grace. Through the work of Jesus Christ on the Cross of Calvary a new species of mankind exists on the earth today. Mankind spiritually alive, covered with the blood of Jesus Christ, obedient to the Father God as led by the Holy Spirit from within their own human spirit exist today. It is this species of being that have Christ within them, the hope of glory.

Living as a son of God can not be done on a part-time basis. The life of God can not be compartmentalized. Many people have been taught, traditionally, that to be a success in life and to really live a balanced life, they must fulfill the demands of God by serving Him in tithes and offerings and Sunday Church attendance; they must fulfill their familial and marital demands by being a good spouse and parent and child; and they must fulfill the demands of the world in their work ethic. Each area of their life is covered by laws and requirements. Rather, Jesus said that there was one law to fulfill. We must love the Lord our God with all our heart, our soul, our mind, and our strength and love our neighbor as our self. This is what is most important. God is Love. God has called us to integrity in wholeness and soundness. Satan divides. God does not. Satan gives multiple visions. God is One. We are called to be conformed to His image. Jesus told us to seek first the Kingdom of God and His righteousness and all things would be added unto us.

Therefore, how are we conformed to His image? How do we become one with God? How do we begin? There are practices, called virtues, mentioned in Scripture that have been practiced for centuries among Christians. These help us to grow in Christ. They enable our spirit man to gain preeminence over our flesh nature and to prevail. There are many virtues: prayer, fasting, confession of the promises of the Word of God, solitude, silence, meditation, assimilation of the Word of God (study), dancing, singing, praise, worship etc. These may be practiced individually and/in community.

When we are "in Christ" we live supernatural lives, just as Jesus did. Miracles, healings, resurrections are the marks of a son of God. We must do His works, just as He did. We allow the Holy Spirit of God to move through us in His "Gifts". Jesus even said that we would do the greater works because He was going to the Father. The ability to quicken and give spiritual life to a spiritually dead person is the greatest work of all. We bring the Kingdom of God into reality in this earth realm. We cause the will of God the Father to be performed on earth as it is in heaven. Jesus made the way for us to pray for people to be born-again and filled with the Holy Spirit. The miracles that Jesus did exhibited His power over the natural, physical realm, sickness and disease, provision and multiplication, the forces of nature, demons, Satan and the entire supernatural evil kingdom, death and resurrection life. The miracles of Christ exhibited and manifested His Omnipotence and Sovereign Authority. What He did, He did simply and easily. Yet Scripture suggests that even Christ's faith grew.

His growing faith was manifested over water. In Scripture water is a type of baptism. It is also a spiritual type and shadow of the peoples or nations. In His very first work of power **He changed the water into wine.** (This is a tremendous New Testament type and shadow of the salvation of mankind, filled with the Holy Spirit.) Some time later, when He and His disciples were crossing the Sea of Galilee in a ship a storm arose and He was fast asleep on a cushion. As the storm grew in intensity his disciples became terrified *"And they came to him, and awoke him, saying, Master, master, we perish. Then he arose, and **rebuked the wind and the raging of the water: and they ceased, and there was a calm.** And he said unto them, Where is your faith? And they being afraid wondered, saying one to another, What manner of man is this! For he* *commandeth even the winds and water, and they obey him." Luke 8:24, 25* A third incident demonstrated His mastery over water. *Mark 6:46-47 And when he had sent them away, he departed into a mountain to pray. And when even was come, the ship was in the midst of the sea, and he alone on the land. And he saw them toiling in rowing; for the wind was contrary unto them: and about the fourth watch of the night he cometh unto them, **walking upon the sea,** and would have passed by them. But when they saw him walking upon the sea, they supposed it had been a spirit, and cried out: For they all saw him, and were troubled. And immediately he talked with them, and saith unto them, Be of good cheer: it is I; be not afraid. And he went up unto them into the ship; and the wind ceased: and they were sore amazed in themselves beyond measure, and wondered. For they considered not the miracle of the loaves: for their heart was hardened. KJV*

Jesus' growing faith was manifested over death. To raise the dead takes the Gift of Faith, Gifts of Healings and the Workings of Miracles—all three power gifts. When Jesus raised the dead He first raised **Jairus's daughter**, who had only been dead a short time. He next resurrected **the son of the widow of Nain,** who had been dead a few hours or a day or so. Then He resurrected **Lazarus** who had been dead four days. This was also significant because in Jewish tradition a dead person's spirit left the vicinity of the body after three days thereby making impossible its resurrection. (At every turn Jesus blasted religious tradition and legalism.) He exerted **His faith in His own resurrection,** rose from the dead and showed Himself to over 500 over many days and by many proofs. Finally, He has spoken through the Apostle Paul His faith in the resurrection of **all who are in Him.** *1 Thessalonians 4:14, 16, 17 We believe that Jesus died and rose again and so we believe that God will bring with Jesus those who have fallen asleep in him…For the Lord himself will come down from heaven, with a loud command, with the voice of* *the archangel and with the trumpet call of God, and the dead in Christ will rise first. After that, we who are still alive and are left will be caught up together with them in the clouds to meet the Lord in the air. And so we will be with the Lord forever.* The faith of Jesus Christ is still at work. He is still at work. He is the Living Christ. He is coming for many brethren. Are you one of them?

What makes all this possible? It is eternal life or the Zoë of God. Whoever possesses eternal life possesses the power of His Life. Christ in us the hope of glory. The eternal life of Jesus Christ is our answer. It is what Jesus came to give all mankind. Zoë or eternal life is the tangible substance that made Jesus different than any man on earth. In John 10:10 Jesus said: *"I have come that they (all Believers) might have life (Zoë), and that they (all Believers) might have it (the Zoë life of God) more abundantly.* When we receive Christ and are born-again we are made the righteousness of God in Christ Jesus. We immediately have eternal life (the Zoë life of God) and we are made sons of God. This eternal life makes us one with Christ. This eternal life of God makes us God-men. We are more than conquerors and always are victorious. Eternal life delivers us from Satan's dominion. *Romans 8:2 For the law of the Spirit of life in Christ Jesus hath made me free from the law of sin and death.* We have the capability to walk in divine life and health. We do this by faith in Christ's shed blood, His death and resurrection. Jesus came to restore mankind to God as He originally intended for us to be in creation. Therefore, as born-again sons of God we are a new species in creation — in the same class of beings as God, angels and Satan. Though in the same classification as spiritual beings yet we are not God. There is only one God and there is only one sinless Son of God. Nothing is impossible to God and nothing is impossible to those who believe God. We are changed from glory to glory as we grow in the grace and the knowledge of the Lord Jesus Christ.

F. F. Bosworth said that we can have so much of eternal life on the inside of us that it starts to live its own life within us. It will take us over spirit, soul and body.

How do we receive the Zoë life of God? The Son of God has Life in Himself. When we hear His Word and believe on Him that sent Christ we have everlasting life. We cross the boundary between death and life. Jesus will raise us up at the last day. The Lord Jesus was lifted up on the Cross of Calvary for the sake of giving spiritual life to men; likewise, if we desire to cause people to have spiritual life, we, too, must be lifted up on the Cross so that the Holy Spirit may flow out of us as well. Whoever does not know the death of the Cross does not have the life of the Cross for other people. We must know the life of the Cross as well as its death. Having the death of the Cross, we die to sin and our old nature; but having the life of the Cross, we daily live in the spirit of the Cross. It is only as the Cross is allowed to burn into our own hearts through the fire of sufferings and adversities that we will be able to see it reproduced in the hearts of other people. We are only able to give to others what we, ourselves, have experienced. Intellectual knowledge alone cannot produce life on purpose. Ephesians 3:21 teaches that love is greater than knowledge. True agapeo love tried in the fires of adversity will produce life. Just as a forest, in the natural, is a seedbed of life, so also is spiritual life produced in the hidden, dark and secret places of our existence. The places where life is produced are holy to the Lord. Life is brought forth from union and communion. Life is fire and it is light. Life results when God's Word provokes the darkness within us and yet we choose God and His ways. *Luke 8:11 Now the parable is this: The seed is the word of God......... John 12:24-25 Verily, verily, I say unto you, Except a corn of wheat fall into the ground and die, it abideth alone: but if it die, it bringeth forth much fruit. He that loveth his life shall lose it; and*

he that hateth his life in this world shall keep it
unto life eternal. KJV

When both my father and brother died of cancer and
fifteen other family members had died, I was faced
with the Scriptures that Jesus Christ healed them
all. Even though I had stood on these Scriptures
personally, in faith believing, they had all died.
It was at this place of deep darkness in my life
that I chose God through His Word. I decided that
I believed God's Word with regard to healing even
though it had not been my experience—even though all
I dearly loved was destroyed and demolished—yet I
chose God. I decided if it cost me my life I would
believe God. I decided if no one was ever healed
when I prayed for them I still believed God simply
because the Bible said so. I chose to believe the
Bible was and is the Truth. I chose the Word of God
as my standard of reality. I did not choose myself,
another person or an organization as my standard of
reality. Nothing changed when I made this decision.
All remained dark and hopeless for years. Yet in my
heart of hearts I had decided and nothing would ever
change that decision. I chose Jesus. It was from that
decision that life sprang forth. The whole direction of my life changed. I received a new and higher
light of revelation of Christ Jesus. When it came to
be my turn to be tried in the furnace of affliction
with the plagues that had afflicted other members of
my family, I walked on in life. I was healed by God
of cancer. Today I and my family walk in Divine Life.
We have and are continuing to learn what this means.

When we eat the spiritual flesh of Christ Who is
the Bread of Life and drink His spiritual Blood we
have eternal life and live by Him. This is Communion.
Jesus said, "If you don't eat My flesh and drink
My blood you have no part in Me." (John 6:44-58)
As long as satan is present we can't eat or drink
Jesus. Only victorious, sanctified man can eat and
drink of Christ. We must have union with God that
is beyond Communion. Scripture enjoins us to sow to
the spirit for from it we shall reap eternal life.

173

Rev. Paul Yongghi Cho teaches we are to live in the fourth dimension. The third dimension is the merging of time, space and material — which is the realm of the natural, physical world. It is only the fourth dimension, or the realm of the spirit, that over-comes this natural world.

The law of sin and death is a law in this earth. Just as gravity is a law, it cannot be overcome unless it is overcome lawfully. Gravity is over-come when thrust exceeds lift. Sin that leads to death is overcome by the Law of the Spirit of Life in Christ Jesus. The way to enter into this life is through faith in Christ Jesus. He is the Door. The human mind is pivotal to the operation of the Law of the Spirit of Life in Christ Jesus. *Romans 8:6 to be spiritually minded is life and peace.* We must keep our thoughts on things above not on things of the earth. First our minds must be renewed with the Word of God and then we must train them to be spir-itually minded. It is the renewing of the mind, not the regeneration of the spirit, which causes you to walk in newness of life. There is a Holy of Holies in every man where only God can dwell. The mind must be renewed for this to come to pass. Our minds and our hearts must abide in Christ.

Knowing what eternal life is and how to use it is pivotal to the supernatural. The earth should reflect heaven. One of the greatest keys in the whole Bible is knowing what you possess. When you know that you have it, then you can use it. Knowledge is a power. The Presence of God hides the power of God. It is a quality of life to be lived on earth and used for God's glory. Eternal life is a merging of our self with heaven. How well do you work with God to do something?

Jesus Christ is real to every believer. His Presence belongs to every Christian. Christian, by definition, means anointed one. The power of God is legally mine not because of my works, talents, gifts, spirituality, intelligence, etc. but simply because I'm a Christian. God's anointing belongs to all in

Christ Jesus. God's anointing is mine. (Please say that out loud.) GOD'S ANOINTING IS MINE! Everything we have as a Christian comes as a result of the anointing. Every time God answers your prayers it comes from the anointing. We must focus on what God focuses on. God wants to use you to save the lost. God's anointing is abundant. The anointing is mine in fulness. God's power = God's anointing. The Presence of God hides His power. Look for God's Presence and His power will be hidden in it. Within His Presence is His Power if you know how to release it. The Word of God is the vehicle that releases the anointing. People need the meat of the Word. Dig deep. Search. The wise man dug deep in the rock. The key is the Word of God.

GOD'S PRESENCE	GOD'S ANOINTING
Attributes	
Face/Heart	Hand/Feet
Ways	Acts
Presence	Power
Grace/Glory	Anointing
Shadow	

God's anointing is not God's Presence. God's Presence = God's glory. Moses cried out for God's Presence. When Moses was in God's Presence he lost sight of himself. He didn't know his face shone. In contrast, when Adam fell in the Garden of Eden, he gained sight of himself. God's Presence lifted off of him. God's Presence cancels self. When you see God, self is gone. To see the Face of God is to be certain of His Presence and grace. (The face is the most important part of the human body. It is controlled by the significant number seven.) It's a "good idea" to spend at least one hour a day gazing at His Presence—not intercession, praise, church work, Bible reading, etc. We must make Him the center of

175

our seeking—not our needs, or even His work. Then we begin to know Him. However, seeing God involves the greatest peril, for man necessarily perishes before God's holiness.

Rather than trying to kill the flesh of people it is more effective for ministers to teach them to so love God that they lose sight of themselves by entering His Presence. God's Presence brings heavens realities into your life. God's Presence will take over your life. Telling people repeatedly, "Die to self! Die to self! Die to self!" without telling them how to do it, other than practicing Christian virtues and praying in tongues brings great harm to the Body of Christ. To love God and to seek Him because you love Him more than you love life is a natural, good and healthy path of progression in life: To focus on death to self is a negative. Focus on the negative does not bring forth the positive.

God's Presence is quite different than God's anointing. God's Presence will still you. God's power will excite you but God's Presence will quiet you. This is the entrance into the gifts of the Holy Spirit. Because God's power and anointing is a gift, once given, it is not rescinded. Our power in the Holy Spirit is in direct proportion to the degree we honor Him. If we have sudden heaviness we must realize we have grieved the Holy Spirit and we must repent. Our thoughts must be holy—God's thoughts— as well as all else. It is extremely important to your well-being that you never minister God's power without His Presence. To do so would be to grieve the Holy Spirit of God. If the Presence of God is not there God will honor His Word but dishonor you. Conviction and fruit and healing will not remain. Therefore we must learn to walk with God on a daily basis as, before he fell, Adam walked with God in the cool of the evening. The Presence of God waters the ground of the human heart and keeps it moist. The dew falls, and then the manna falls. God's Presence and quietness is the result of abundance. That Presence becomes prayer. When stillness is so deep prayer is at its best. Words become inadequate in God's Presence. His Presence will permeate your being and will cause you to walk into heaven in the spirit. No flesh will glory in His Presence. It must be all of God. His Presence is brightness. The glory shines there. The Presence of God shines for us in the Face of Christ. The highest spiritual attainments are the easiest to reach. This is not a matter of the intellect but rather it is a matter of the heart. Let go! Let God! Be willing to let go and give up anything but His Presence. Jacob wrestling with God was all about his self. Only those that lean are changed. John leaned upon Jesus' breast at the last supper. There is no such thing as independence in the Christian life. *2 Corinthians 4:4-6 For the god of this world has blinded the unbelievers' minds [that they should not discern the truth], preventing them from seeing the illuminating light of the Gospel of the glory of Christ (the Messiah), Who is the Image and Likeness of God. For what we preach is not ourselves but Jesus Christ as Lord, and ourselves [merely] as your servants (slaves) for Jesus' sake. For God Who said, Let light shine out of darkness, has shone in our hearts so as [to beam forth] the Light for the illumination of the knowledge of the majesty and glory of God [as it is manifest in the Person and is revealed] in the face of Jesus Christ (the Messiah). Genesis 1:3, 4 And God said, Let there be light; and there was light. And God saw that the light was good (suitable, pleasant) and He approved it; and God separated the light from the darkness. AMP*

God's Presence is not felt—it is <u>known</u>. His Presence is more than feeling. In the spirit realm there are realities greater than the soul realm—greater than your intellect and your emotions. When His reality overwhelms you—your reality is lost. He is so great.

The throne of the Universe is the Cross of Jesus Christ. There actually is a galaxy in the cosmos which exhibits the shape of a Cross. The Cross of Calvary is the seat of all authority, power and victory. Dr. Roy Hicks said, "If you will fully understand the work of the cross you will never have another weak, sick day nor shall you die prematurely." When you come to Jesus you begin to die to self. Repent is the first word of the Gospel. The Cross is the only place of safety from the world, your own flesh/self, satan and his demons. Get on the Cross. Stay on your Cross. Pray against your SELF on your Cross. Satan will offer you a cross-less life. All power was Jesus' when He was on the Cross. *Jesus said, "Carry your own cross and follow Me..."* Grain must die to bear fruit. We must die to follow Him. Be very pliable. The good way, the ancient pathway, where death is swallowed up by His life comes when one lives in the Presence of God. God's Presence causes your life to be so inconsequential that you do not notice its absence. He that is dead is freed from sin. It's impossible to tempt a corpse with anything. Self-effort is swallowed up in the Presence of the Lord. When we live to worship Him and love Him we ride the winds like an eagle. Joy is overwhelming. Beauty of spirit is at every hand. He will never leave us or forsake us. He is with us forever. Only the expression of His glory changes but its continuation does not fail. Learn to ride the winds of the Holy Spirit in Christ Jesus for the glory of Almighty God.

People are doors and when set apart for the use of the Lord they become altars. In the Old Testament to consecrate an altar was to "fill its hands", i.e. to put power in it. Atonement and purification took seven days. An altar could not be used until the eighth day. Consecration of a priest took seven days. He was consecrated or ordained by his hand being filled with power. Believers in Christ Jesus must rise up into overcoming perfection. David, as king of Israel, was anointed three times with: the Law, Grace and Perfection or Maturity. Yet King David was not admitted to the outward profession of the Kingdom for a considerable time afterward. In the Old Testament the High Priest wore the Breastplate of Judgment that contained the Beauties, Lights and Perfections of God. It contained the Urim and Thummim. In Christ Jesus the Church of the Living God is growing to maturity and fullness. The mighty spirit of Cyrus (Cyrus was the son of Queen Esther) is appointed to lay the foundation of this third temple. We must receive God's glory. We must be absolutely humble. Surrender all in His Presence. We must receive the seven spirits and seven eyes of God and enter into the Order of the Priesthood of Melchizedek. We must receive and be sealed with the mark of Divine authority, absolute unction and anointing whereby God will be ALL in ALL. This Manchild Company must be birthed forth from the Church Age wilderness and come to fruition in the earth. Only the Father God knows the times and the seasons and only He can rise up these hidden stones that are tried by the fiery breath of God. This manifestation of the true Bride of Christ is to come at the very end of the Church Age.

THE MINISTRY OF JESUS CHRIST

OLD TESTAMENT TITLE PRE-INCARNATE CHRIST	NEW TESTAMENT OFFICE	HUMANITY SENT TO
WONDERFUL	Apostle	poor
COUNSELOR	Prophet	brokenhearted
MIGHTY GOD	Evangelist	captives
EVERLASTING FATHER	Pastor	blind
PRINCE OF PEACE	Teacher	bruised

Rev. James Stalker, quoted earlier, has presented Paul's Pneuma Concept in his book, Life of Paul. I have included my understanding of what each Christian has according to the New Testament, in Christ, spiritually:

Mark 11:23 we speak spiritual words and have spiritual authority

John 5:21-29,39,40	Jesus came to give us spiritual life when we hear and believe His words and come to Him
John 6:27-63	Communion—eat Jesus' spiritual flesh and drink His spiritual blood; Jesus speaks spiritual words
Romans 1:9	worship and serve God in the spirit
Romans 1:11	established by receiving spiritual gifts
Romans 2:28, 29	the new birth is a circumcision in your heart
Romans 5:5	spiritual love shed abroad in your heart by the Holy Spirit
Romans 8:2	Law of Spirit of Life in Christ Jesus set me free from Law of Sin and Death
Romans 8:4	walk in the spirit
Romans 8:5, 6	have a spiritual mind, which is life and peace
Romans 8:9-11	Spirit of Christ dwells in you and you belong to God;spirit is alive by righteousness; spirit quickens your mortal body; by spirit you put to death the deeds of the body; those led by Spirit of God are sons of God
Romans 10:8-10	pneuma (spirit) faith = spiritual new birth
1 Cor. 2:9-16	natural man receives not the things of the spirit-they are spiritually discerned: spirit of the world-spirit of man-Spirit of God: understanding & growth comes by comparison of spiritual words, thoughts and principles -spiritual person lives outside of judgment of man, yet judges all things
1 Cor. 3:1	unity in the Body of Christ
1 Cor. 6:17	we are joined to the Master by our spirit
1 Cor. 10:4	we drink from the spiritual Rock which is Christ
1 Cor. 12:1-11,13	have spirituals—gifts and manifestations
1 Cor. 14:2,14-16	pray in the spirit, worship and sing in the spirit, singing and making melody in your heart

1 Cor. 15:44-46	we begin in the natural and grow in the spiritual and are raised a spiritual body
Galatians 5:16	walk in the spirit
Galatians 5:18	led and directed by the spirit
Galatians 5:22	have the fruit of the Spirit
Galatians 5:25	live and walk in the spirit
Galatians 6:1	in the spirit of meekness spiritual persons bring restoration to those in sin
Galatians 6:8	sow and reap in the spirit
Ephesians 1:3	blessed with every spiritual blessing in Christ
Ephesians 1:17	spiritual wisdom and revelation
Ephesians 2:4-6	spiritual life and spiritual dominion
Ephesians 6:17	spiritual sword which is the Word of God
Colossians 1:9	we grow in the knowledge of His will and spiritual understanding
1 Timothy 4:8	spiritual exercise
2 Timothy 1:7	spiritual power, love and a sound mind
Hebrews 12:9	God is Father Spirit and the Father of all spirits
1 Peter 2:5	as living stones we are built into a spiritual house to offer up to God spiritual sacrifices

CHAPTER VII

WHAT HAPPENS AS SALVATION OCCURS?

"It is not thy hold on Christ that saves thee; <u>it is Christ</u>. It is not thy joy in Christ that saves thee; <u>it is Christ</u>. It is not even thy faith in Christ, though that be the instrument; <u>it is Christ's blood and merit</u>."
Charles Haddon Spurgeon

When we are first born—again and the light of God shines within our person, we receive a revelation of Jesus Christ. If we hold fast to that which we have received at the beginning God, Himself, will conform us to that image we received of Christ. We will become Christ in the earth, the hope of glory for all about us to know God. Jesus Christ, Himself, will live His life through our person. Rev. T. L. Osborn once said, "If they can get to me, they have gotten to God." If that seems arrogant to you, you must realize there are stages to spiritual growth, like there are stages for the lift off of a rocket. Rev. Tim Stemple teaches that in the first stage it is all about the individual believer and their blessing. In the second stage it is all about Jesus Christ and the death of self. In the third stage it is all about Jesus Christ working through the believer to bring the will and purposes of the Father to pass in truth and love. Jesus has told us that if we try to save our life on this earth we will lose it. If we lose our life for Him, it will be saved for all eternity. We are merely the glove which His Hand occupies to do its work and live its life in this earth. All His desires for mankind of health, provision, healing, deliverance, protection, wholeness and soundness will be brought to pass. God desires to restore His vineyard. Nothing is impossible to God and nothing is impossible to the one who believes God. We do the greater works of the Father. The life of God takes place in the continuous present. It is progressive and yet unchanging *in Him*.

Hebrews 3:14 For we have become fellows with Christ (the Messiah) and share in all He has for us, if only we hold our first newborn confidence and original assured expectation [in virtue of which we are believers] firm and unshaken to the end. AMP

Hebrews 3:14 We have come to share in Christ if we hold firmly till the end the confidence we had at first. NIV

This first image of Christ is received in our heart not in our intellect. In Biblical terms the heart (kardia) is the source of the real person and is sometimes called the bowels (splanchna) or the source of affections. In psychological terms this is the Id, the source of a person's unconscious instinctive impulses and desires. *Proverbs 4:23 Keep thy heart with all diligence; for out of it are the issues of life. KJV* If we do not surrender to unbelief in its many and varied forms and give ourselves over to hardness of heart we shall be conformed to the image of Christ we have beheld. We will enter into the rest of God. We become one with Him in the revelation of Him we have received. When this revelation is first received the intellect is totally unfruitful. Our soul realm is unfruitful. We must follow the leading of the Holy Spirit over time and through circumstances, i.e. "the Valley of the Shadow of Death:", to bring about the death of the self life, that the resurrection life of Jesus Christ will surface within our person, thus bringing the revelation of the image of Christ we first received to fruition. Rev. Dave Roberson teaches that the fulfillment of the "born-again trail" is our return to our original inheritance. Some ministers have taken this truth and preached that we must remain in the same church that we first attended or under the same leadership that first led us to Christ. However, I do not believe this is a proper revelation of this truth. It is the revelation of Christ that we behold that must remain the same not our obedience to an individual person.

1 John 2 expounds upon these truths. Pay special attention to verses 24 through 29:

I John 2:24-29 As for you, keep in your hearts what you have heard from the beginning. If what you heard from the first dwells and remains in you, then you will dwell in the Son and in the Father [always]. And this is what He Himself has promised us—the life, the eternal [life]. I write this to you with reference to those who would deceive you [seduce and lead you astray]. But as for you, the anointing (the sacred appointment, the unction) which you received from Him abides [permanently] in you; [so] then you have no need that anyone should instruct you. But just as His anointing teaches you concerning everything and is true and is no falsehood, so you must abide in (live in, never depart from) Him [being rooted in Him, knit to Him], just as [His anointing] has taught you [to do]. And now, little children, abide (live, remain permanently) in Him, so that when He is made visible, we may have and enjoy perfect confidence (boldness, assurance) and not be ashamed and shrink from Him at His coming. If you know (perceive and are sure) that He [Christ] is [absolutely] righteous [conforming to the Father's will in purpose, thought, and action], you may also know (be sure) that everyone who does righteously [and is therefore in like manner conformed to the divine will] is born (begotten) of Him [God]. AMP

It is as we are conformed to Christ Jesus in thought, word, deed and action that the supernatural life of God occurs. For this to happen, our soulish, fleshly, self life must first be done away with. Then that which is of God can rise to the surface of our being. This is no small endeavor! This process can be compared to an enormous ball of fine twine that has been repeatedly knotted and reknotted, again and again. The "knotting" of the twine would have begun many generations before the birth of the person and would continue in even greater intensity during their lifetime. The salvation process would consist of unknotting each and every knot until the twine is laid out straight, entirely free of knots. It truly is a narrow path that very few find and even fewer still enter upon. For success to occur one must truly love God with all their heart, mind, soul and strength and love others as they love themselves. The joy of the Lord is essential to have the strength of God for this endeavor. We must trust and obey God. There is no other way to be happy in Jesus, than to trust and obey! Though infinitely complex, Jesus said His burden was easy and His load was light. It is as we walk in the light of life with Christ, quickly obeying His every known command, that we are enabled to easily follow Him into the fullness of God. Nothing is impossible to God.

I must insert here that in the example of the plan of the tabernacle it is not those who are without the tabernacle that affect those in the Holy of Holies. It is not even those who are in the Outer Court who will affect those in the Holy of Holies. It is those who are in the Inner Court who will affect those in the Holy of Holies. There is much confusion, false doctrine, error, heresy, deception and plain lying that occur in spiritual matters. We must keep the wonderful love of God we first received when born-again. We must keep the spiritual freedom Christ has died to give us. Live in the wonderful glory of your Heavenly Father!

Genesis 49:18 I have waited for thy salvation, O LORD. KJV E. W. Bullinger wrote about this verse in his Companion Bible: "These words are repeated three times (and in three different ways) by every pious Jew, morning and evening… Salvation is put for Him Who brings it." In the Jerusalem Targum it is written: "Not to the salvation wrought by Gideon, the son of Joash, does my soul look, for it is temporal. Not to the salvation wrought by Samson, the son of Manoah, is my longing directed, for it is transient; but to the salvation, the completion of which Thou hast promised, by Thy everlasting Word, to bring to Thy people the descendants of Israel. To Thy salvation, O Jehovah, to the salvation of Messiah the son of David, Who will one day redeem Israel and bring her back from the dispersion, to that salvation my soul looks forward; for Thy salvation is an everlasting salvation."

We as intercessors for the lost must understand the work of God in the heart of man that results in the salvation of the soul. God has given us life on this earth to find Him and receive His salvation. We are born in sin with the nature of the first Adam. Let us understand the greatness of the salvation that our Father has provided. There is only one gospel—one plan of salvation. It's our job to understand and communicate it properly. The act of salvation is a continuing present. Our present redemption is founded upon the solid hope of an eternal manifestation of our adoption. Salvation is not so much about what we believe or an action we take, although that is true, but it is about putting ourselves in the proper position and place, through our obedience, to have the salvation God has provided worked **upon** us. Jesus Christ is the Open Door that God has provided to enter the spiritual realm. Yet for most of us, there is a window of time that this Door will remain open. To do the perfect will of the Father and fulfill His High Call we must move quickly and obediently. We must follow the leading of the Holy Spirit within our own heart not men who are without us. We must overcome the world around us, our own flesh nature and the work of the devil.

Acts 4:12 says, *"There is no other name under heaven given among men by which we must be saved"* (NKJV). Salvation is not a man-made system or organization, but it is a gift of God. It was bought and paid for by the eternal Lamb of God, Jesus Christ, Who was the infinite sacrifice. He shed His blood on the Cross of Calvary for an infinite amount of sins so that we could come by faith and receive His free gift of salvation. That's why we call it "good news". It is the true power of God Himself available to each and every one of us.

In its simplest form as an outward act, conversion or salvation is a four-step process of change:

1) an offer of salvation by God through Christ in the convicting energy of the Holy Spirit
2) our personal heartfelt decision to receive and follow Christ
3) when God sees that our repentance of our sin is genuine, He accepts us
4) God makes us part of His Body

When salvation occurs the spirit is instantly and completely made perfect in the image of God. The Seed of the Lord Jesus Christ is planted within the spirit of the saved person. At the time of the Rapture of the Church or at the second coming of Christ the body will be transformed into a supernatural spiritual body that will live throughout eternity with Christ. *1 Corinthians 15:44 "It is sown a natural body; it is raised a spiritual body. There is a natural body, and there is a spiritual body."KJV* However, during our life on earth we have been given time to work out the salvation of our souls. God created mankind in His image — we are spirits, we have souls and we live in an earth suit, a physical body. The human soul is comprised of our mind, our emotions and our will. The salvation of the soul is a growth in grace and the knowledge of the Lord Jesus Christ that results in the removal of the spiritual veils upon our hearts and minds (the flesh or self nature), upon our ability to understand, hear and see God.

Isaiah 53:10-12
Yet it pleased the Lord to bruise him; he hath put him to grief: when thou shalt make his soul an offering for sin, he shall see his seed, he shall prolong his days, and the pleasure of the Lord shall prosper in his hand. He shall see of the travail of his soul, and shall be satisfied: by his knowledge shall my righteous servant justify many; for he shall bear their iniquities. Therefore will I divide him a portion with the great, and he shall divide the spoil with the strong; because he hath poured out his soul unto death: and he was numbered with the transgressors; and he bare the sin of many, and made intercession for the transgressors.

Jesus Christ's soul was made an offering for sin, yet Scripture does not guarantee the salvation of all our soul. In heaven God will make all things new. There will be no more sorrow, pain or grief or anything that defiles. In 1 Thessalonians 5:23 the Apostle Paul wrote, *"And the very God of peace sanctify you wholly; and I pray God your whole spirit and soul and body be preserved blameless unto the coming of our Lord Jesus Christ."KJV* This indicates that we have the authority and ability to make choices that will result in our spirit, soul or body not being entirely saved. Both we and the literal earth or land we live upon can be sinned against by sinning against God. Sins against God comprise sins of idolatry and witchcraft. Sins against the soul comprise broken relationships, sins of temperament and offense, slander, gossip, lying, etc. Sins of the body comprise sexual sins, addictions, intemperance, gluttony, etc. It is these things that Christ has redeemed us from. However, as the spirit is made perfect in the image of God the soul must take up its cross and work out its salvation with fear and trembling. We each have the choice as to whether or not we will follow the leading of the Holy Spirit and the instruction of the Word of God moment by moment as we abide in Him. Abiding in Christ is pivotal to our salvation. It is possible to attain to a place in God where we "waste our lives" upon Jesus. After all, it is only what is done for Christ—at His bidding—and in Christ, which will last. Eternity is forever!

The Way of Salvation.

The following portion of Scripture is pivotal to understanding God's plan of discipleship. There are fourteen different actions that occur in the life of one chosen out of the people to be fully restored and to enter into the image of Christ Jesus. What the prophet Ezekiel calls restoration to the land we would more fully understand to be death to the self life and identification and/or participation in the life of Jesus Christ through conformity to His image or likeness. Major portions of Scripture are type and shadow of these truths: i.e. the salvation of the nation of Israel over hundreds of years. God foretold of Israel's bondage in a foreign land and His deliverance of them into their own Promised Land. We may clearly see God's ways exemplified through an entire nation of people over a period of several millennia.

Ezekiel 20:33-44
As I live, declares the Lord GOD, surely with a mighty hand and with an outstretched arm and with wrath poured out, I shall be king over you. I will bring you out from the peoples and gather you from the lands where you are scattered, with a mighty hand and with an outstretched arm and with wrath poured out; and I will bring you into the wilderness of the peoples, and there I will enter into judgment with

you face to face. As I entered into judgment with your fathers in the wilderness of the land of Egypt, so I will enter into judgment with you, declares the Lord GOD. I will make you pass under the rod, and I will bring you into the bond of the covenant; and I will purge from you the rebels and those who transgress against Me; I will bring them out of the land where they sojourn, but they will not enter the land of Israel. Thus you will know that I am the LORD. As for you, O house of Israel, thus says the Lord GOD, Go, serve everyone his idols; but later you will surely listen to Me, and My holy name you will profane no longer with your gifts and with your idols. For on My holy mountain, on the high mountain of Israel, declares the Lord GOD, there the whole house of Israel, all of them, will serve Me in the land; there I will accept them and there I will seek your contributions and the choicest of your gifts, with all your holy things. As a soothing aroma I will accept you when I bring you out from the peoples and gather you from the lands where you are scattered; and I will prove Myself holy among you in the sight of the nations. And you will know that I am the LORD, when I bring you into the land of Israel, into the land which I swore to give to your forefathers. There you will remember your ways and all your deeds with which you have defiled yourselves; and you will loathe yourselves in your own sight for all the evil things that you have done. Then you will know that I am the LORD when I have dealt with you for My name's sake, not according to your evil ways or according to your corrupt deeds, O house of Israel, declares the Lord GOD. NASU

The Way of Salvation
Restoration to the (land) image of Jesus Christ

1. out from the peoples and their lands (images)
   with wrath doubly poured out
2. into the wilderness of the peoples

3. face to face judgment of God
4. pass "under the rod"
5. bring into the "bond of the covenant"
6. purge the rebels and the transgressors
7. false religious ways condemned
8. serve God on His "mountain"
9. God will accept you
10. gifts, contributions and holy things given to God
11. God will prove Himself holy
12. bring you into your land—Christ in you, the hope of glory
13. bring you into self-judgment by remembrance of your own ways and deeds
14. God deals with each one for His Name's sake (not according to their ways and deeds)

There are three phrases couched in prophetic terminology that bear closer study in these passages. The first is to "pass under the rod". What does this mean to us today? According to Strong's Concordance a rod is a symbol of authority in the hands of a ruler. In 2 Thessalonians 2:7-12 Scripture teaches that Jesus will destroy the Wicked One with the breath or spirit of His Mouth. The Greek word translated breath or spirit is the same Hebrew root word for rod. Therefore rod, in this sense, denotes severe judgments upon satan and/or those who practice wickedness. In another portion of Scripture, Jeremiah 51:19-23, the nation of Israel is described as the "tribe of God's inheritance". This same Hebrew word *sheber* which is defined as rod is also defined as a tribe, clan or family. The above portion of Scripture describes a family, clan or tribe that shatters. A rod of iron is power over nations. There are three other portions of Scripture that are important in understanding this term rod. They are Isaiah 11:4, which states the action taken by the Messiah against the wicked; Psalm 2:9 and 23:4, which is one of the Bible's most beloved Scriptures. King David's famous words: *Psalm 23:4 Yes, though I walk through the* *[deep, sunless] valley of the shadow of death, I will fear or dread no evil, for You are with me; **Your rod [to protect]** and Your staff [to guide], **they comfort me.*** AMP The rod of iron is symbolic of power over sin and an unbreakable rule. It is about measuring and judgment. Jesus Christ is our Shepherd and our measuring rod. The Holy Spirit is our Comforter. Together they bring us to the Father.

The second prophetic term is "the bonds of covenant". This refers to a journey into oneness with God. An entire book of Holy Canon has been written with reference to the subject of oneness: i.e. The Song of Songs. There are many terminologies in Scripture that refer to the process of coming into this oneness. Each individual must die to self and be conformed to the image of God in Christ Jesus, for example. God is Love and oneness with Love is a process that not all attain to. The Hebrew word, covenant, has to do with a devisory will or a contract, agreement or compact. The English word, covenant, means a "coming together", which signifies a mutual undertaking between two parties or more, each binding himself to fulfil obligations. These obligations are not necessarily equal in their demands. It also refers to a promise or undertaking, human or divine. Therefore we may understand "the bonds of the covenant" to mean the requirements that God demands of each of us, individually and personally, to bring us into oneness with Himself.

The third prophetic term or phrase is to "serve God on His mountain". Intercessors have power to remove veils and break the coverings over nations. In Scripture this is referred to as breaking the covering over mountains. Therefore we see that mountains often refer to nations or world kingdoms in Scripture. Breaking a covering or veil off a person, family, city, or nation is the work that the Lord Jesus Christ and the Holy Spirit are doing in the now. This phrase, therefore, denotes being active in the work of the family business of the salvation of mankind; i.e. working in God's Kingdom. The holy mountain of God in Scripture is Mount Zion. Zion means a parched place, fortress and sunny. Mt. Zion is a type of the ruling power of the Son of David's tabernacle; it is also a type of worship and praise, the New Covenant and the spiritual priesthood. Every mountain mentioned in Scripture is a type or shadow of spiritual truth and bears study. Mount Ebal is a symbol of the Mount of Cursing. Mount Gerizim is a symbol of the Mount of Blessing. Mount Moriah is a type of sacrifice, substitution, the Temple site and foundation. Mount Sinai is a type of fear, bondage, legalism, the Commandments and the Covenant of Law. These are only a few of the most prominent mounts in Scripture. Where has God called you?

What is Repentance?

God created man in His image, male and female He created them. God created man from the dust of the earth. The Lord described the hearts of men like different types of soil and the Father as the owner of a fruit orchard. In the Parable of the Sower Jesus describes four different types of hearts. The <u>first</u> is like seed that falls upon the path or the "way side". It is the heart that has no understanding. In it the birds devour the seed sown. In other words, the truths of the gospel that are taught are robbed from the mind of the hearer by the devil because the one who is hearing does not understand the truth shown him. He is spiritually blind and dull. <u>Secondly</u>, the seed falls in stony places or where there is rocky, thin or scanty soil. Therefore, the seed sown grows up quickly and does not develop a strong root system to sustain it and becomes scorched and withers away. In other words, the hearer of gospel truths receives truth with great joy and endures for a short time but can not hold out long and when suffering or persecution comes it causes offence and they give up and turn away. Offence, or as it is originally called in the Greek, the Spirit of Skandalon, is the cause of the fall of many. A lack of character is evidenced in this believer. A depth of soil that will sustain deep roots is needed. The <u>third</u> type of soil is thorns. This heart hears the gospel but has the life choked out of it by the cares, anxieties and worries of life. The focus of this life is upon the world system rather than upon the Saviour. The glamour and delight of wealth and the deception caused by it stops the growth of the heart and no return of His investment is given to the Lord. The pride of life or rather, the Spirit of Defiance, evidenced by humanistic motivations prevents the needed repentance in this believer's life. The <u>fourth</u> category of heart is good ground. The seed sown falls on rich ground in which abundant fruit is brought forth. This is the believer that hears and understands the Word of God taught to him and retains that Word in a good and faithful heart. This believer is obedient. This believer perseveres in the walk of the Spirit, overcoming obstacles by changing his ways and dying to his self life, until he brings forth fruit that remains. In some good hearts there is a thirty fold return, in some good hearts a sixty fold return and in some good hearts an hundred fold return. This is the heart that hears the Word of God and understands it and yields a good return of His investment to the Lord, either one third, two thirds or all His investment. Only 8% of people bring a 100% return unto God; that is eight people out of an hundred who have good hearts. Only 25% of Christians have good hearts, so 8% of 25%, or two people out of one hundred, enter into all God has provided. When Israel left Egypt only two men over forty years of age, out of six million +, entered The Promised Land. Not even Moses entered into the land. God's standards are set. It is we who must attain to them. As Christians today, Jesus Christ is our Promised Land. He is our Starry Night. We enter into the rest of God in Christ Jesus.

Jesus taught in Luke 13:6-9 that repentance is the fertilizer of the spirit, thus enabling God to enrich the soil of our heart. When fruitfulness is lacking the soil must be irrigated and fertilized. In the parable of the sower and the soils Jesus explains the different types of hearts with which He works. In Ezekiel 15 God tells of His attitude toward the unfruitful. Praise God that He is merciful and His mercy triumphs over judgment! Thus He shows us and has made a way for us to escape the wickedness and evil of our sinful hearts. **Repentance!** The original word means literally an afterthought, or a change of mind, a change of view. Now to think after, or take a second thought, is often to think differently, and to think more justly and truly; hence, to repent of the first thought. The idea pre-supposes that the mind has received some new and better light with regard to life and its duties, and its relations to God and man; which new light within, makes a change inevitable, a change of thought and purpose and intention. The Wycliffe Bible Commentary says that repentance on the part of man involves a turning about in a new attitude toward God. Repentance on the part of God is a change of approach toward man on the basis of man's changed attitude toward God. As with salvation, healing, blessing or any other action of the spirit realm, for true change through repentance to occur it is best achieved when the individual heart is full of faith and humbles itself before the power of a constituted authority. It is the friction between the faith and the power that spark the life of God, thus bringing about change in the individual. Many churches and ministries have taught that the individual Christian's life may be lived alone before God. For example: In the Middle Ages when one desired to follow God fully, they would enter into a cloister and take vows of silence. However, Jesus Himself told His followers to "go into all the world and preach…" Yet I have watched people die who held to this error. However, power is released in the interaction of the body of Christ operating that "which every joint supplies". This is how we grow into the fullness of the love of God.

Ephesians 4:14-27 That we henceforth be no more children, tossed to and fro, and carried about with every wind of doctrine, by the sleight of men, and cunning craftiness, whereby they lie in wait to deceive; but speaking the truth in love, may grow up into him in all things, which is the head, even Christ: From whom the whole body fitly joined together and compacted by that which every joint supplieth, according to the effectual working in the measure of every part, maketh increase of the body unto the edifying of itself in love. This I say therefore, and testify in the Lord, that ye henceforth walk not as other Gentiles walk, in the vanity of their mind, having the understanding darkened, being alienated from the life of God through the ignorance that is in them, because of the blindness of their heart: Who being past feeling have given themselves over unto lasciviousness, to work all uncleanness with greediness. But ye have not so learned Christ; if so be that ye have heard him, and have been taught by him, as the truth is in Jesus: That ye put off concerning the former conversation the old man, which is corrupt according to the deceitful lusts; and be renewed in the spirit of your mind; and that ye put on the new man, which after God is created in righteousness and true holiness. Wherefore putting away lying, speak every man truth with his neighbour: for we are members one of another. Be ye angry, and sin not: let not the sun go down upon your wrath: Neither give place to the devil. KJV

Does repentance need to take place for the initial act of salvation to occur? NO! A resounding NO! must be and is the only answer. The pathway into all God's fullness is clearly marked in Scripture, however, and whether it be before, during or after salvation and/or during the course of growth in the Christian life, repentance and, I might add, baptism and communion, are real and vital aspects in Christian life and growth. Therefore, it bears close examination and real understanding. God has made provision in His Word for both the sinner to repent and for the

Christian to repent, be baptized and participate in communion. Change is the name of the game. If we desire spiritual success in the realm of eternity we must not allow the devil to penetrate us. Rather than a serpent shedding its skin, we must shed our veils of flesh nature and allow the life of God to shine out from within us.

1 John 1:5-10 This then is the message which we have heard of him, and declare unto you, that God is light, and in him is no darkness at all. If we say that we have fellowship with him, and walk in darkness, we lie, and do not the truth: But if we walk in the light, as he is in the light, we have fellowship one with another, and the blood of Jesus Christ his Son cleanseth us from all sin. If we say that we have no sin, we deceive ourselves, and the truth is not in us. If we confess our sins, he is faithful and just to forgive us our sins, and to cleanse us from all unrighteousness. If we say that we have not sinned, we make him a liar, and his word is not in us. KJV

Daniel Defoe, 1747, author of <u>Robinson Caruso</u>, has written....."how incongruous and irrational the common temper of mankind is, especially of youth, to that reason which ought to guide them in such cases, viz. that they are not ashamed to sin, and yet are ashamed to repent; not ashamed of the action for which they ought justly to be esteemed fools, but are ashamed of the returning, which only can make them be esteemed wise men." Let us not be as those who call themselves believers in the Lord Jesus Christ yet live lives of defiance to God and His ways of truth. *Isaiah 9:9-14 And all the people shall know, even Ephraim and the inhabitant of Samaria, that say in the **pride and stoutness of heart**, the bricks are fallen down, but we will build with hewn stones: the sycomores are cut down, but we will change them into cedars. Therefore the Lord shall set up the adversaries of Rezin against him, and join his enemies together; the Syrians before, and the Philistines behind; and they shall devour Israel with open mouth.*

197

For all this his anger is not turned away, but his hand is stretched out still. For the people turneth not unto him that smiteth them, neither do they seek the Lord of hosts. Therefore the Lord will cut off from Israel head and tail, branch and rush, in one day. KJV Let common sense guide us in life! Take the path provided by God in His inestimable mercy and walk in the way of repentance!

There are three primary elements of repentance. First, a change of mind and intention caused by new and better light or knowledge that enables the soul to see itself and God and the world in higher and truer aspects. Secondly, there needs to be a change of conduct corresponding to this change of mind. As our thoughts precede our actions and our actions inevitably follow correct thoughts so it naturally follows these two events will be in harmony with one another. Thirdly, this change of thought and conduct will be accompanied by sorrow for the past and strong prayer to God for help to change. Genuine humility before God, and broken-heartedness and contrition of soul constitute the true repentance that is received by God. We must have Godly sorrow for our sin. Repentance is more than an act of the human will. Repentance is an operation of the mercy and grace of God upon the human soul, changing the heart that once despised God into one which loves Him. We must dig deep and sink our foundation upon the rock of Christ that we be not shaken in the judgment which is to come. In the lake of fire there will be no mercy, no grace, hence, no repentance will be offered to man. The shed blood of Jesus Christ is the atonement God has provided to wash away the guilt of our sin. Therefore, let's go receive it! Proper repentance brings us a peace of conscience; not deadness, but a sense of rest and approval.

As says a noted preacher: "When a man undertakes to repent towards his fellow-men, it is like repenting straight up a precipice; when he repents toward law, it is like repenting into a crocodile's jaws; when he repents toward public sentiment, it is throwing himself into a thicket of brambles and thorns; but when he repents toward God, he repents toward all love, gentleness and kindness. God receives the soul as pure waters a swimmer, and returns it again cleaner, whiter and happier than he took it."

Therefore our repentance must be to God and not to man. Yet God has ordained that His authority is delegated to ministry offices that true growth will occur. God has deigned that His Body on this earth is interdependent one of another. As we all know from bitter experience, those who are religious only judge after the flesh and make our bondage more severe. Therefore, we must obey God's ways, sanctifying Him in our hearts as Lord and God, and not look to man for our redemption. Yet our repentance is best achieved when made to God via His constituted Agent of Authority. Even when that authority is corrupt and unbelieving God will honor the office and according to our faith it will be done unto us. God has a plan! We must conform ourselves to that plan.

Ephesians 4:11-13 And he gave some, apostles; and some, prophets; and some, evangelists; and some, pastors and teachers; for the perfecting of the saints, for the work of the ministry, for the edifying of the body of Christ: Till we all come in the unity of the faith, and of the knowledge of the Son of God, unto a perfect man, unto the measure of the stature of the fulness of Christ: KJV

2 Samuel 24:14 David said to Gad, "I am in deep distress. Let us fall into the hands of the LORD, for his mercy is great; but do not let me fall into the hands of men." NIV

1 Samuel 1:9-19 So Hannah rose up after they had eaten in Shiloh, and after they had drunk. Now Eli the priest sat upon a seat by a post of the temple of the LORD. And she was in bitterness of soul, and prayed unto the LORD, and wept sore. And she vowed a vow, and said, O LORD of hosts, if thou wilt indeed look on the affliction of thine handmaid, and remember me, and not forget thine handmaid, but wilt give unto thine handmaid a man child, then I will give him unto the LORD all the days of his life, and there shall no rasor come upon his head. And it came to pass, as she continued praying before the LORD, that Eli marked her mouth. Now Hannah, she spake in her heart; only her lips moved, but her voice was not heard: therefore Eli thought she had been drunken. And Eli said unto her, How long wilt thou be drunken? put away thy wine from thee. And Hannah answered and said, No, my lord, I am a woman of a sorrowful spirit: I have drunk neither wine nor strong drink, but have poured out my soul before the LORD. Count not thine handmaid for a daughter of Belial: for out of the abundance of my complaint and grief have I spoken hitherto Then Eli answered and said, Go in peace: and the God of Israel grant thee thy petition that thou hast asked of him. And she said, Let thine handmaid find grace in thy sight. So the woman went her way, and did eat, and her countenance was no more sad. And they rose up in the morning early, and worshipped before the LORD, and returned, and came to their house to Ramah: and Elkanah knew Hannah his wife; and the LORD remembered her. *KJV*

As faith without works is dead, being alone, so saving faith is invariably preceded by repentance, accompanied with confession, and followed by obedient action. If Christ frees us, He is to have control of us from that time forward and forever. We are no longer our own, but His; spirit, soul and body and all else. Many have a deep fear of any control other than their own yet, spiritually, fail to realize they are blind, deaf, mute and halt and it is only the mercy of the God Who is Love that would lift them from their destitute condition to one of life and life more abundant, thus setting them into the true freedom for which their soul really longs. Jesus Christ received the judgment of God (in His own Person) upon the sins of mankind even though He is the sinless Son of God and, in truth, God Incarnate. How can we not receive God's righteous judgment upon the truth of our sinful lives? We must do this and we do this by our agreement with His just judgment of our sins through our repentance.

Robert G. Voight, Ph.D. wrote, "I believe there are two concepts that we need to keep constantly before us: 1) repentance (*metanoeo*) which means to 'change your mind,' and 2) confession (*homologeo*) which means to 'speak the same thing.' You repent; God forgives. You change your mind; God changes your heart. You confess; God regenerates. For a time, I refused God's claims upon my life. Then I repented, I changed my mind, and I confessed what God said about me. God had said that I was a sinner, and if I believed on the Lord Jesus Christ as my savior, I would be saved. I changed my mind about myself: I confessed I was a sinner, and I confessed that Jesus was my Lord and Savior, and I was saved." The Hebrew word *Yadah* means to throw, to cast, to speak out, to confess, to praise, to sing, to give thanks, to thank. Essentially, it is the acknowledgment of sin, man's character, or the nature and work of God. According to the Apostle John, God wants us to be cleansed through confession (1 John 1:9). This constant acknowledgment maintains a proper relationship with God. In ancient Israel this included personal repentance and confession, corporate repentance and confession and national repentance and confession. This is crucial in the experience of salvation. Confession must be made of the Word of God. Rev. Kenneth E. Hagin taught we must speak God's Word precisely. If you confess the Word of God your confession will be primarily about God, and you shall be conformed to His image. There is a trend in the Church today that greatly disturbs me. Leadership takes the Scriptures of the Word of God and has "dumbed them down" (like Outcome Based Education in America's public school system) by personalizing and paraphrasing the general intent of a principal of God's Word. If you don't confess the Word of God your confession will be about man which leads to humanism.

This new attitude is defined by God as wisdom. The desire to walk in wisdom is the desire to walk upon the royal road of God, on the ancient paths. Lester Sumrall emphatically wrote that he was determined to keep to the old paths of the gospel. To reign eternally with God we must hold wisdom in honor. *The very first step towards wisdom is the desire for discipline, and how should a man care for discipline without loving it, or love it without heeding its laws, or heed its laws without winning immortality, or win immortality without drawing near to God?* Wisdom 6:21, 22 Knox Translation

A new attitude.

A changed attitude is a changed way of thinking, a changed mind or disposition. It is a changed perspective or way of looking at life. We are to have *the same attitude that was in Christ Jesus, Who, being in the form of God, thought it not robbery to be equal with God: but made Himself of no reputation, and took upon Him the form of a servant, and was made in the likeness of men; and being found in fashion as a man, He humbled Himself, and became obedient unto death, even death on a Cross!* Philippians 2:6-8 J. B. Phillips translation reads, *"Let Christ Jesus be your example as to what your attitude should be."* The Amplified version says, *"Let this same attitude and purpose and humble mind be in you which was in Christ Jesus — let Him be your example in humility."* In the Message Bible it is written thusly: *"Think of yourselves the way Christ Jesus thought of Himself..."* and a few verses before, *"If you have gotten anything at all out of following Christ, if His love has made any difference in your life, if being a community of the Spirit means anything to you, if you have a heart, if you care — then do me a favor: Agree with each other, love each other, be deep-spirited friends. Don't push your way to the front; don't sweet-talk your way to the top. Put yourself aside, and help others get ahead. Don't be obsessed with getting your own advantage. Forget yourselves long enough to lend a helping hand."* Joyce Meyer has said that attitude is a posture you take in life, your thought life turned inside out, the prophet of your future, your best friend or your worst enemy. Attitude draws people to you or repels people from you. She says patience is waiting with a good attitude. Attitude determines whether or not you will live in the Promised Land as a Christian or whether or not you wander around in the wilderness of your own soul. We must be responsible to be set free.

In Isaiah 14:12-14 God speaks through the prophet revealing Satan's attitude of heart:

"How you are fallen from heaven,
O Lucifer, son of the morning!
How you are cut down to the ground,
You who weakened the nations!
For you have said in your heart:
*'**I will** ascend into heaven,*
***I will** exalt my throne above the stars of God;*
***I will** also sit on the mount of the congregation*
On the farthest sides of the north;
***I will** ascend above the heights of the clouds,*
***I will** be like the Most High.' NKJV*

These five "I will's" show satan's deification of self and his great ambition. In contrast, Jesus Christ, in His high priestly prayer in the gospel of John, chapter 17, in the King James Version, says in verse 4, "**I have** glorified Thee on earth: **I have** finished the work which Thou gavest me to do." And in verse 6 "**I have** manifested Thy Name unto the men which Thou gavest Me out of the world…" and in verse 8 "**I have** given them the words which Thou gavest Me." And in verse 12 "**I have** guarded them" and in the previous phrase "I kept them safe in Thy Name". What a contrast! This contrast of our Saviour and satan clearly exposes the diametrically opposing focuses of good and evil. Jesus' attitude and focus was of a humble servant giving life to others whereas satan's desire is to glorify himself. Jesus accomplished

God's will perfectly and completely. Satan is a miserable failure and a defeated foe. Yet while Christ was alive on the earth the opposite appeared to be true because history records only what occurs in the sense realm and does not take into account the supernatural realities of a vast spiritual realm.

John 17:4-13

*I **have** glorified You down here on the earth by completing the work that You gave Me to do. And now, Father, glorify Me along with Yourself and restore Me to such majesty and honor in Your presence as I had with You before the world existed. **I have** manifested Your Name [**I have** revealed Your very Self, Your real Self] to the people whom You have given Me out of the world. They were Yours, and You gave them to Me, and they have obeyed and kept Your word. Now [at last] they know and understand that all You have given Me belongs to You [is really and truly Yours]. For the [uttered] words that You gave Me **I have** given them; and they have received and accepted [them] and have come to know positively and in reality [to believe with absolute assurance] that I came forth from Your presence, and they have believed and are convinced that You did send Me. I am praying for them. I am not praying (requesting) for the world, but for those You have given Me, for they belong to You. All [things that are] Mine are Yours, and all [things that are] Yours belong to Me; and I am glorified in (through) them. [They have done Me honor; in them My glory is achieved.] And [now] I am no more in the world, but these are [still] in the world, and I am coming to You. Holy Father, keep in Your Name [in the knowledge of Yourself] those whom You have given Me, that they may be one as We [are one]. While I was with them, I kept and preserved them in Your Name [in the knowledge and worship of You]. Those You have given Me I guarded and protected, and not one of them has perished or is lost except the son of perdition [Judas Iscariot—the one who is now doomed to destruction,*

*destined to be lost], that the Scripture might be
fulfilled. [Ps 41:9; John 6:70.] AMP*

The motivation of an individual's attitude is
foundational to all his life. This is a crucial truth.
Satan's five "I will's" versus Jesus Christ's five "I
have's" demonstrate the black and white difference of
hell's desired ambition versus God's accomplished
love for mankind. As we meditate these Scriptures we
come closer to the exact center of what salvation is.

It is interesting to note that the emphasis of
the early church seemed to be on giving, denying
and surrendering self — pouring out one's life for
Christ even to the point of martyrdom. The blood of
the martyrs has been said to be the seed bed of the
Church. The emphasis of the last day church seems
to be the building up of self — what I can gain,
what I can know and have and do in Christ. It's been
taught that we can write our own ticket with God.
Which is right? What did Jesus do? How few today
are truly concerned for others. Jesus did not count
equality with God a thing to be grasped. I am very
concerned about the present day Church of the Lord
Jesus Christ. Many in the Church are very close to
entering into the error of satan as it is written
in Ezekiel 28:1-10. We must never forget that we are
men and not God. Is it right to walk in what Jesus
accomplished by faith and yet use His attainments for
selfish purposes, i.e. to deify self? Having attained
God's Power and Anointing have we also attained to
the right to kill and make alive according to our
own will and purposes? We do not have record of
Jesus Christ "offing" those who got in His way. We
do have record of Him raising the dead. God, Alone,
is the Judge of all the earth. If one pursues God
long enough and hard enough they will find that all
Scripture and all obedience to the Holy Spirit lead
to the Servant's Heart.

Matthew 20:28

Even as the Son of man came not to be ministered unto, but to minister, and to give his life a ransom for many. KJV

Satan did desire to be "like the Most High". Jesus was a servant and satan wants to be served. Yet the Bible also teaches we are joint heirs with Christ, we have dominion over the earth, and we are to possess the land. What is God's will? Where are the balance and the truth? Could it be that Jesus has given us power and dominion and has put all things under our feet (His feet) in order that we might be truly like Him — a love slave? Could it be that our goal is not to attain wealth and power for "the Kingdom of God" on earth in the building of huge cathedrals or in the creation of denominations and ministry organizations with creeds and religious systems of belief with rules and dogmas but for the Kingdom of God that exists in the hearts of men? Could it be that our goal is to attain wealth and power in order that we might continually pour it all out for others? That we might serve others, wash their feet, meet their needs and be true stewards of God? Is this truly what Zoë and Agape are? Loving God is doing His Word and the fruit of the Spirit in action but isn't the culmination of the Word of God love? God so loved that He gave… Love is giving and receiving without asking or expecting. The proof is in the pudding, so to speak; what is it that we **do**? Are we overcoming evil with good? Are we forgiving those who have despitefully used us and persecuted us? Do we give our enemies what they desire of us? How valuable are people to you?

Galatians 5:13-14

For, brethren, ye have been called unto liberty; only use not liberty for an occasion to the flesh, but by love serve one another. For all the law is fulfilled in one word, even in this; Thou shalt love thy neighbour as thyself. KJV

The heart of the matter.

There remains yet undescribed the deepest and the controlling part of man's nature; that part which governs his action, determines the moral character of his thoughts, directs his will; in a word, the ruling power in man. This is the love of his heart or the heart's desire. Every man pursues that end and object of life which not only commends itself to his mind, but which he really and in his heart loves; and whenever there is antagonism between the decisions of reason and the love of the soul, as all know by experience, the love in the end triumphs and carries the man captive. The center of God's Being is that He is Love and as we are created in His image it follows that we, ourselves, are led and governed by love. The fleshly heart of man desires to control, own and dominate all that is around it. It is only unafraid of and can only understand what it has power over. This is diametrically opposed to the ways of God. He is all gentleness and love and kindness and His desire is to give us life and set us free from the black hole of self. Indeed our selfish love so subjugates the intellect that very speedily a man comes to believe just that which he loves is the right; while the will of man is only the executive power that carries out the heart's desires. Now, being "born again," or born from above, is to have this ruling, sinful love of the heart turned away from self and the world, to God and truth. The born-again spirit of man must be the leader of the soul and the body; subjugating self to the will of God. Our love must be focused upon meeting the eternal needs of others, not upon building earthly kingdoms for our soul.

Salvation is, after all, a progression of the grace of God in the soul of man. Our entire life on this earth must be devoted to the goal of the salvation provided by God. God's goodness that leads us to repentance, and then our seeking after and obtaining

His grace are the beginning steps toward God's glory. In other words, if God's grace is followed fully, it will result in God's glory. God's glory is more than just the favor of God upon an individual. God's glory is becoming one with Him. The Name brings the glory on the scene. The Blood brings the glory on the scene. The Presence of God is the glory. Just as God the Father, God the Son and God the Holy Spirit are One, so also we must become one in Him. It is our integrity—spirit, soul and body. This oneness means that we think what He thinks, i.e. we have the Mind of Christ, and we do what He does, i.e. we act out the works of Almighty God. We obey His leadership. *1 John 2:6 states Whoever says he abides in Him ought [as a personal debt] to walk and conduct himself in the same way in which He walked and conducted Himself. AMP He that saith he abideth in him ought himself also so to walk, even as he walked. KJV Whoever claims to live in him must walk as Jesus did. NIV* So we must each look at our own life and ascertain if we have lived as a supernatural god in the earth today. (Did she really write that?) In other words, what miracle have you performed today? What supernatural occurrence did you, by the leading of the Holy Spirit, generate in the now? I don't know about you, but I have not fully arrived at this state in my life. However, I am pressing toward the mark of the high calling of God in Christ Jesus. (Let us be done with fear and compromise and selfish human justification and choose instead to believe Jesus and obey God.)

According to 2 Thessalonians 2:13, 14 there is a three step progression to the glory of God:

4) sanctification by the spirit (NOT necessarily the Holy Spirit), i.e. the rational and immortal soul
5) faith in the truth, i.e. the love of the truth, which includes every true act inspired by faith
6) the glory of the Lord Jesus Christ, i.e. what He thinks and what He does

Yet I have discovered in Scripture two other steps:

1) intercession begun by Jesus Christ and the Holy Spirit of God (for all true things begin in God)
2) justification given by God through Jesus Christ, in the gift of righteousness

These two steps must actually precede the first three listed. In between the first two and the last three is the:

3) Process of Mortification. This is the removal of the veils of the flesh nature, i.e. the death of self, that the life of Christ may be realized. Everything that truly is, begins with God. When all is ended, it will end in God. This process may not even be noticed if one's focus is intent upon the Presence of God Himself. One enraptured with God loses cognizance of himself.

Finally, according to God's present day speaking to me personally, the Bride of Christ must rise up into true worship and relationship with an Holy God:

(7) Sing a New Song to the God of all the earth. Worship God in the beauty of holiness with songs, and hymns and spiritual songs, singing and making melody in one's heart. This true worship is instigated and fulfilled by the Holy Spirit.

Our human spirit is made up of faith, hope, reverence, prayer and worship. Our soul is made up of imagination, conscience, memory, reason and affections. According to Scripture, the love of the truth is paramount in salvation. God is Holy. God is Righteous. God is Truth. God is Love. We must love the truth. We must be honest and sincere and drawn toward the Light of Life. It is this requirement that precedes the infilling of the Holy Spirit within our human spirit. We must receive the love of the truth in order to be saved.

Those who are bound by the Lie or a lie or deception in some form will find it very difficult to rise higher in God. Repent! And be free! Jesus said that in order to take a house one must first bind the Strongman. The Lying Strongman is over every spirit of Religion in any form. *In John 8:44 Jesus said to the Jews—"Ye are of your father the devil.....when he speaketh of the lie, he speaketh of his own; for he is a liar, and the father of it".* The Antichrist is coming whose working is after 'the working of satan' with all 'power' and 'signs' and 'lying wonders', and with all 'deceivableness of unrighteousness' in them that perish. Pastor Sharon Daugherty had a dream or vision in which she was told that the great error of the last days was the spirit of deception. Spirits of Deception or the Lying Spirit is overcome by the Spirit of Truth. Actually there are four strongmen spirits that oppose the Spirit of Truth: error, seduction, lying, and antichrist. Satan's kingdom is religion in any form. Most of us begin in some form of religion but when we progress in the truth we rise up out of religion and into the light of life in Christ Jesus. We must seek out and find every area of deception or lies in our life and be delivered of it. We must repent repeatedly of all darkness, sin, error, deception, lies, etc. that the Holy Spirit shows us in the Word of God or in any other way He chooses. We must love the truth. We must be so in love with truth that we are willing to change—to repent of all lies. Jesus is worth it!

When we are obedient to the truth, we will live by faith. True acts are acts done by faith in God. In God's realm, faith is the medium of exchange or the measure of value as money is the means of payment in the world system. Therefore it is essential that we understand and operate in the faith of God. (We must not compromise and operate in the faith of man. God's faith is the true faith. We must learn about it and learn to operate in it.) Kenneth E. Hagin was especially commissioned by Jesus Christ to "teach His people faith". Therefore his teachings in this area are excellent.

All judgments, woes, hardships and evils that come upon our lives come out from our own selves and the generations who have lived before us. This truth is so untenable, so repugnant to the human mind that it has ceased to be taught or spoken in today's church world. Yet the truth remains. God is only Good. All evil comes from satan and man's compromise and participation with him and our fallen nature from our first father, Adam. Just as faith is never lost when it is exercised in the earth, so evil and sin is not lost but must be brought to fruition in the flesh of man, somewhere, sometime. Sin is transferable, holiness is not. Our lives must be covered by the blood of Jesus Christ to be protected from random evil. God has provided us with the armor of Who Christ Is. We are commanded to be conformed to His image. Just as the five wise virgins did, we must go to those that sell to buy oil for our lamps. We must buy gold tried in the fire.

Revelation 3:17-21 Because thou sayest, I am rich, and increased with goods, and have need of nothing; and knowest not that thou art wretched, and miserable, and poor, and blind, and naked: I counsel thee to buy of me gold tried in the fire, that thou mayest be rich; and white raiment, that thou mayest be clothed, and that the shame of thy nakedness do not appear; and anoint thine eyes with eyesalve, that thou mayest see. As many as I love, I rebuke and chasten: be zealous therefore, and repent. Behold, I stand at the door, and knock: if any man hear my voice, and open the door, I will come in to him, and will sup with him, and he with me. To him that overcometh will I grant to sit with me in my throne, even as I also overcame, and am set down with my Father in his throne. KJV

We must come to truly know and understand that God is outside of our self. He is not small and within us. He is not like some part of us. God is

211

great. He is greater than we are and outside of us. It is we who must change to be like Him. There is only One God. We must develop our trust in an Holy God. It is <u>we</u> who must obey <u>Him</u>. Scripture speaks to many types of people, describing them and their heart motive. Yet God also speaks to types of people within His Kingdom who are in the process of spiritual growth. He classes the best as believers, witnesses and disciples. He also has a hierarchy of leadership: prophets, priests and kings. Jesus Christ, through the Apostle Paul, organized His body as a Church with apostles, prophets, evangelists, pastors and teachers.

Matthew 16:24-28 Then Jesus said to His disciples, "If anyone wishes to come after Me, let him deny himself, and take up his cross, and follow Me. For whoever wishes to save his life shall lose it; but whoever loses his life for My sake shall find it. For what will a man be profited, if he gains the whole world, and forfeits his soul? Or what will a man give in exchange for his soul? For the Son of Man is going to come in the glory of His Father with His angels; and will then recompense every man according to his deeds. Truly I say to you, there are some of those who are standing here who shall not taste death until they see the Son of Man coming in His kingdom." NAS

In the New Testament Jesus Christ, Himself, lists several requirements of one who desires to attain to a place of discipleship in His Kingdom. Three requirements are found in Luke *14:26-27, 33 If anyone comes to Me and does not hate his [own] father and mother [in the sense of indifference to or relative disregard for them in comparison with his attitude toward God] and [likewise] his wife and children and brothers and sisters—[yes] and even his own life also—he cannot be My disciple. Whoever does not persevere and carry his own cross and come after (follow) Me cannot be My disciple...........So then, any of you who does not forsake (renounce, surrender claim to, give up, say good-bye to) all that he has cannot be My disciple. AMP* Another requirement is found in *John 8:31-32 Then said Jesus to those Jews which believed on him, If ye continue in my word, then are ye my disciples indeed; and ye shall know the truth, and the truth shall make you free. KJV* Please read Isaiah 8. *Isa 8:20 …..if they do not speak according to this word, it is because there is no light in them. NKJV* We must be filled with the light of life to live eternally with God. God said, "Go into all the world and make disciples." He did not say, "Go into all the world and make converts." The process of discipleship must include conversion at some point, but it doesn't necessarily begin with conversion. Discipleship can begin far before conversion.

Paul's purpose in ministry was that his hearers might *"obtain the salvation which is in Christ Jesus* **with eternal glory***" 2 Timothy 2:10.* Paul was interested in more than basic salvation. He labored assiduously to lead converts on towards full-grown manhood in Christ Jesus. He wanted those he loved to obtain eternal glory as well. Not all who attain to the eternal, heavenly home will be disciples of Christ. Our goal must be the salvation of our spirit, our soul and our body. Rarely is it stressed that eternal glory is something God desires all believers to acquire. Yet Scripture calls God the Father of lights. Glory will vary from one saint to the next — *"every man in his own order"* — *1 Corinthians 15:23.* The brightness of the glorified will vary. Some will shine like the sun, others like the moon, still others like the stars. We have all known people who seem to be "out to lunch" while others are "full of life". I want to be a 300 watt bulb for Jesus! 1 Corinthians 15:41, 42. Some people may not shine at all, but will make up the large multitude who can only sing about salvation since that's all they experienced Revelation 7:13-15. Rather we should encourage all who are converted to Christ to press on in Christian development, having the fruit of the Spirit fully grown and matured; leading them on toward "the measure of the stature of the fullness

213

of Christ" and urging them to press on toward the goal of the high call of God in Christ Jesus. Those who can only sing about salvation in the heavenly choirs will not rule on the very throne of God like others who were more victorious and whom God calls "overcomers" Revelation 3:21. The full "overcomers" are the ones who enthrone Christ in their hearts, and put the government of their being all on His shoulder, and keep it there. Those servants who are faithful in managing the deposit God made into their lives are rewarded accordingly. They shall be given cities to rule over in the new earth. When the Chief Shepherd appears certain ones will receive crowns of glory that do not fade away. Not all the saints will be crowned, only those who strive lawfully. God has "ways" and we have to do this thing His way. This is why we are warned to seek a "full reward" and "let no man take our crown". *Proverbs 4:23 Keep thy heart with all diligence; for out of it are the issues of life. KJV* If we are able to keep our vessel without allowing anyone to "get inside of us" then we are blessed indeed. Then we shall remain unharmed by another. If not, then Shakespeare's "pound of flesh" may be a reality for us. Satan uses the mouths of men to speak forth his fiery darts. People are not our problem. Yet the unredeemed flesh of man is an open door for satan to come against those who walk in the spirit with God. We must wear the armor of God to withstand him.

There is still much more to the salvation provided by God in Christ Jesus. Our whole lives must be spent in the study and obtaining of this so great salvation. If an individual were to spend every minute of every day seeking and studying this salvation they could not understand all that He IS or all that He has done for us. There are different ways to study and learn about God. Not any one way is the only way. It would be as though a single skin cell decided to obtain all that the man is, upon whom it lived. It simply would be impossible. Salvation provided by Christ Jesus is the original Neverending Story. So it is in our relationship to Almighty God. I believe there are many worlds within many galaxies within the universe God has created. Yet **ALL** lies within God Himself. God's greatness is incomprehensible to man. Yes, He is so great and so mighty! Whatever God says is the truth. If God were to call black, white. Then black would be white. Thus knowing God is greater than the salvation He provides. Knowing God is eternal life. God is Life. His Presence is fullness of joy. His Presence is His glory.

Thank God, He is also Good. In His goodness He has deigned to allow us to know some parts of Himself and to know and understand some parts of the salvation He has provided. For reasons incomprehensible to man, God desires relationship with each individual person. God is Love.

CHAPTER VIII

WHAT IS THE WORK OF THE TRINITY AS SALVATION OCCURS?

Psalm 86:13 Righteousness will go before Him and make His footsteps a way.

**Our Cross is bare, there is no one there.
He is gone, that we all might share, the wonderful Gift He gave us there.**

In the working of the plan of salvation, God has been pleased to reveal Himself to man under a three-fold form, or as three persons, constituting the indissoluble and Holy Trinity. Pastor Dave Roberson teaches there are at least nine attributes that make up the one essence of the three persons of God. Father, Son and Holy Spirit are love, truth, immutable, omnipresent, omniscient, omnipotent, righteous, sovereign, and eternal life. It has been said that God, the Father, creates the plan; Jesus Christ, the Son, executes the plan; and the Holy Spirit, brings the plan to fulfillment.

There are nine baptisms I have found in Scripture thus far. These baptisms are the supernatural power of God Himself worked upon humanity, received by faith and confession, which result in true salvation. Each member of the Trinity is represented in a baptism. Just as the robe the High Priest of Israel wore on the Day of Atonement had gifts and fruit separated by alternating pomegranate and bells [Exodus 39:26], so the baptisms of the Trinity are separated by water and by fire. Yet the alternating of these baptisms is preponderant to God. It is also interesting to note that when enemy contraband was taken in Old Testament warfare, the Law required it be purified either by water or by fire or by both. If the item was strong enough to endure the fire it must be purged by fire. If it was not strong enough it was to be purged by water only. Thus Israel was to be kept holy unto the Lord.

Numbers 31:23 Every thing that may abide the fire, ye shall make it go through the fire, and it shall be clean: nevertheless it shall be purified with the water of separation: and all that abideth not the fire ye shall make go through the water. KJV

Life is in the Blood. It is our faith in the shed Blood of Jesus Christ that saves us. Therefore, study of blood is imperative. Human blood contains the same percentage of salt as the water in the ocean. Jesus told His followers to be careful that their salt retained its savor. Our salt must remain salty. Blood, in its essence, is coagulated light. Jesus Christ is the Light of the world. He is the Word of God. He made all that is.

1 John 5:5-8 Who is he that overcometh the world, but he that believeth that Jesus is the Son of God? This is he that came by water and blood, even Jesus Christ; not by water only, but by water and blood. And it is the Spirit that beareth witness, because the Spirit is truth. For there are three that bear record in heaven, the Father, the Word, and the Holy Ghost: and these three are one. And there are three that bear witness in earth, the spirit, and the water, and the blood: and these three agree in one. KJV God, in three Persons, is spirit in heaven. Man, in three parts, is contained in flesh on earth.

Yet within these three parts of Man are contained, in the natural realm, three fluids: mucus, water and blood. These three fluids must come into unity or, in other words, they must have integrity, to be at peace within the person. Di-vision, or any type of multiple vision, must cease. We must first be emptied of our fleshly self life. One must receive the Holy Spirit WITHIN. Integrity in our spirit, soul and body is required. To be consecrated for ministry we must receive God's Presence and His power. One must receive the Holy Spirit UPON. On the Cross of Calvary Jesus Christ was emptied of spirit, water and blood. Likewise we must be emptied of these three to receive God's resurrection power and His Presence to do His will in ministry. I believe this is salvation brought to its fulness or completion. *Romans 8:9-11 But ye are not in the flesh, but in the Spirit, if so be that the Spirit of God dwell in you. Now if any man have not the Spirit of Christ, he is none of his. And if Christ be in you, the body is dead because of sin; but the Spirit is life because of righteousness. But if the Spirit of him that raised up Jesus from the dead dwell in you, he that raised up Christ from the dead shall also quicken your mortal bodies by his Spirit that dwelleth in you. KJV* Have righteousness and peace kissed one another within you?

THE LORD JESUS CHRIST OF NAZARETH, THE SON OF GOD

The center of this Holy and Sacred Trinity is Christ the Son, yet all three are equal in power and place. Jesus Christ, however, is the Savior of <u>this</u> world. A belief in Christ, as God manifest in the flesh for the sake of the soul's personal redemption, is the real, and we may add, the only, distinctive Christian belief; and that unless the soul exercises this gospel faith in Christ, which includes acceptance of, and surrender to Him, as its Leader and Lord, it is not and cannot be converted in the true sense of that word. Jesus Christ is the ONLY DOOR to eternal salvation from this planet.

As Christ is called the Root of the stem of Jesse and like the mustard seed which is the smallest of seeds, so He, having fallen into the earth and died, grows up into a great tree and bears much fruit — fruit that will remain through eternity; so the Holy Spirit is God's own Power, Life and Light that brings the fullness of this to pass. He is the Power of God unto salvation—the enabling force that creates and gives spiritual life to all mankind. Baptism is linked to justification. There is an intercommunion of justification, inheritance and the reception of the Holy Spirit. It is honest love and esteem of the truth and seeking for spiritual light that opens the heart of man to receive the Holy Spirit of God. Whosoever will let them come! Jesus Christ is the spoken Word of the Father God. Jesus Christ is our Cornerstone. Jesus Christ is the only true Foundation laid by the Father God. We cannot build unless we have the true Foundation. After having walked through the Door that Jesus Christ Is, the new believer must CONTINUE ON. This is a vital truth.

For most of the Christian Church through the last two thousand years, walking through the Door that Jesus Christ Is remains the only truth they have been taught. Yet this is not all there is. The believer must allow God to take them apart and rebuild them. Jesus said He had much to teach His Body but they were not able to bear it at the time He lived upon the earth. Therefore, He gave revelation to the Apostle Paul, who wrote two-thirds of the New Testament about spiritual growth/formation. In the last one hundred years the religious Church has taught that this activity is the work of satan and God only works good in the individual believer's life. Yet this belief is skewed. Satan is a defeated foe. Jesus Christ defeated satan on the Cross of Calvary. The only power he has left to him is to "eat the dust of the earth". Dust is defined as the flesh nature of unredeemed man. Therefore, if all a Christian ever experiences is destruction from satan, then they must realize that they live in the realm of the world, the flesh and the devil. The Apostle Paul taught that we have been seated with Jesus Christ in heavenly places. We must learn to live and operate in the realm of the spirit world. We must keep our minds on heavenly things. We must learn to live in all that Jesus Christ procured for His Body. If we do not, are our lives an affront to the One Who died for us?

Christ has provided that all true believers may, through a vital and unhindered union with Himself in this life, put on His own life, nature, and holiness; and so become one in Him. The believer that yields himself wholly to God, and comes to be filled with the Holy Trinity answers the High Priestly Prayer of Jesus Christ in John 17. A life of unbroken fellowship with the Father, Son and Holy Spirit is possible in this life. Such a life produces joy unspeakable, full of glory! No gloom, sadness, or melancholy can ever have any more place in such a Christian.

Jesus Christ made the way for a believer to operate in the powers of the Age to Come. He made the way for each believer to live this life just as He lived it. 1 John 2:6; 4:17. Are we **doing** it?

BAPTISM

Through the Apostle John, Jesus said that unless one is born again he can not see the kingdom of God and two verses later He said that unless one is born of water and of the Spirit, he cannot enter into the kingdom of God because what is born of the flesh is flesh and that which is born of the Spirit is spirit. We not only want to see the kingdom of God from a distance but we want to enter into it and be fruitful for the glory of God. Thus the necessity of baptisms. There are several baptisms mentioned in Scripture. In "Scripture References for Intercessors" I list scriptural reference for nine different types of baptisms. Each member of the Trinity has a baptism for us to receive. Moses and John the Baptist each ministered baptism to those that followed them. Widely differing interpretations of the act exist among Christians. They have different views on the nature of baptism, who should be baptized, and the appropriate method by which baptism should be administered. They see the major meaning of baptism as purification. Yet our God is One. *Ephesians 4:5 One Lord, one faith, one baptism...*

Spiros Zodhiates, Th.D. in his Hebrew-Greek Key Study Bible defines baptizo as "to be identified with". In 1 Corinthians 10:2 this identification with the work and purposes of Moses describes the Hebrew children who left Egypt with him. He also states that "when the preposition *eis*, "in, into or unto," comes after the verb "baptize" as in Matthew 28:19, "in the name of the Father and the Son and the Holy Spirit," it means "in identification with" that name and all that it stands for. Other Scriptures where the preposition *eis* is used after the verb "baptized" are Acts 8:16; 19:3,5; Romans 6:3; 1 Corinthians 1:13; 12:13; Galatians 3:27.

Christian baptism implies grafting into fellowship or union with the Father, the Son, and the Holy Spirit; for the Greek expresses this (Matthew

28:19): "Go ye, make disciples of all the nations, baptizing them into the name (the revealed person) of the Father, and of the Son, and of the Holy Spirit…" Christian baptism is the seal of gospel doctrine and spiritual renewal. (from Fausset's Bible Dictionary, Electronic Database Copyright (c)1998 by Biblesoft)

God is so vast and so great that a complete understanding of His command to be baptized would take intense study. Scripture teaches there is one baptism. The Holy Spirit is the Agent whereby we are baptized into Christ. This is the "One Baptism" referred to in Ephesians 4. Yet I have listed at least nine baptisms readily found in Scripture. I believe this is the most basic of testimonies to the greatness of God.

Following are three major positions on the nature of baptism which exist among Christian groups:

In **the sacramental view** baptism is a means by which God conveys grace thus receiving remission of sins and regeneration or a new nature and an awakened or strengthened faith. Lutherans emphasize the value of the preaching of the word. Preaching awakens faith in a believer by entering the ear to strike the heart. Baptism enters the eye to reach and move the heart. One Scripture especially important to the advocates of the sacramental view of baptism is John 3:5: "Unless one is born of water and the Spirit, he cannot enter the kingdom of God." They also believe that the act of baptism itself produces a change in the life of the believer.

In **the covenantal view** believers think of baptism not as a means by which salvation is brought about, but as a sign and seal of the COVENANT. The covenant is God's pledge to save man. Because of what He has done and what He has promised, God forgives and regenerates. On the one hand, baptism is a sign of the covenant. On the other, it is the means by which people enter into that covenant. Similarly, baptism also depicts a washing away of sin (Acts 2:38; Titus 3:5) and a spiritual renewal (Romans 6:4; Colossians 2:11-12). In fact, these two procedures are clearly linked in *Colossians 2:11-12: "In Him you were also circumcised with the circumcision made without hands, by putting off the body of the sins of the flesh, by the circumcision of Christ, buried with Him in baptism, in which you also were raised with Him through faith in the working of God, who raised Him from the dead."*

In **the symbolical view** believers stress the symbolic nature of baptism by emphasizing that baptism does not cause an inward change or alter a person's relationship to God in any way. Baptism is a token, or an outward indication, of the inner change which has already occurred in the believer's life. It serves as a public identification of the person with Jesus Christ, and thus also as a public testimony of the change that has occurred. It is an act of initiation. It is baptism into the name of Jesus. According to the symbolic view, baptism is not so much an initiation into the Christian life as into the Christian church. A distinction is drawn between the invisible or universal church, which consists of all believers in Christ, and the visible or local church, a gathering of believers in a specific place. This position explains that the church practices baptism and the believer submits to it because Jesus commanded that this be done and He gave us the example by being baptized Himself. Thus, baptism is an act of obedience, commitment, and proclamation. According to this understanding of baptism, no spiritual benefit occurs because of baptism. Rather than producing REGENERATION of faith, baptism always comes after faith and the salvation that faith produces. The only spiritual value of baptism is that it establishes membership in the church and exposes the believer to the values of this type of fellowship. (from Nelson's Illustrated Bible Dictionary, Copyright (c)1986, Thomas Nelson Publishers)

Hebrews 9:11-18 But [that appointed time came] when Christ (the Messiah) appeared as a High Priest of the better things that have come and are to come. [Then] through the greater and more perfect tabernacle not made with [human] hands, that is, not a part of this material creation,He went once for all into the [Holy of] Holies [of heaven], not by virtue of the blood of goats and calves [by which to make reconciliation between God and man], but His own blood, having found and secured a complete redemption (an everlasting release for us). For if [the mere] sprinkling of unholy and defiled persons with blood of goats and bulls and with the ashes of a burnt heifer is sufficient for the purification of the body, [Lev 16:6,16; Num 19:9,17,18.] How much more surely shall the blood of Christ, Who by virtue of [His] eternal Spirit [His own preexistent divine personality] has offered Himself as an unblemished sacrifice to God, purify our consciences from dead works and lifeless observances to serve the [ever] living God? [Christ, the Messiah] is therefore the Negotiator and Mediator of an [entirely] new agreement (TESTAMENT, covenant), so that those who are called and offered it may receive the fulfillment of the promised everlasting inheritance—since a death has taken place which rescues and delivers and redeems them from the transgressions committed under the [old] first agreement. For where there is a [last] will and TESTAMENT involved, the death of the one who made it must be established, for a will and TESTAMENT is valid and takes effect only at death, since it has no force or legal power as long as the one who made it is alive. So even the [old] first covenant (God's will) was not inaugurated and ratified and put in force without the shedding of blood. AMP

Jesus Christ made the way for all mankind to experience a purified conscience, our everlasting inheritance and eternal life with God. Mankind ate from the Tree of the Knowledge of Good and Evil, i.e. the Tree of Conscience and fell from Oneness with God. Through Christ Jesus' shed blood we are enabled to eat from the Tree of Life and live. Isn't this the true Source of Communion? God desires Oneness again with Man. Every single cell of every part of man must be brought from the darkness to the light. We enter into this covenant with God by faith in the shed blood of Jesus Christ. Jesus commands us to be baptized and to receive communion. These are the two DOCTRINE Jesus Christ initiated and commanded mankind to keep. Just as no person can be changed or conformed to the image of God in Christ Jesus through the will or power of another person, so no doctrine can be initiated or sanctioned by a person. God creates doctrine. What God says is the Truth is the Truth because God is Truth. God alone is God.

We are all growing in the grace and knowledge of the Lord Jesus Christ. The whole of mankind is growing into His fullness. I believe these truths of baptism and communion are real and yet, I believe there is still much more for us to learn and walk in the truth of. I believe this is true for baptism and communion and all the work of the Holy Trinity.

God is eternally great and mighty!

THE HOLY SPIRIT

As faith in Christ Jesus is the Doorway through which we pass into the realm of the spirit, so our ongoing relationship with the Holy Spirit, the Paracletos, enables us to grow up into all the fullness of God. We receive His Person, Who is power. There is no greater force known to man or in nature than the Holy Spirit. He is the muscles of the Godhead. Our knowledge of all the Precious Holy Spirit is to us is fragmentary at best. The Holy Spirit is our Helper, our Assistant, our Representative, our Comforter, our Teacher, our Guide and our Advocate in this life and throughout eternity. He will never leave us or forsake us. He is with us always. God has placed us in the care of the Holy Spirit. God has entrusted our salvation to a member of His Family—not to an angel, a person or a position in a church. Since He lives within us, we can access Him at any given moment. As we follow His leading moment by moment, more and more of our soul is filled with the life and light of Jesus Christ. We are enlightened more and more with the riches of His inheritance in Christ Jesus. We must have knowledge and understanding with insight of the full authority of the Holy Spirit otherwise He is bound in what He can do in us and through us.

"Many times My people come unto Me seeking salvation as 'fire-insurance' against the judgment of hell. Little do they know that they shall receive their judgment also—as to how they have handled My Word, My Body, My Holy Spirit. The Blood of Jesus cleanses away the sin nature but what does transform the soul? If they refuse My Holy Spirit they shall fail to act upon My Word for it is only by the Holy Spirit that My Word can be understood and acted

upon. Without the Holy Spirit the Word of God has no life—it is law and death rather than spirit and life. Therefore, the soul fails to be transformed and the body can not be glorified. Only the Blood, the Word and the Spirit can save a man spirit, soul and body. Many are called— very few are chosen."

Stephen, the first martyr of the Early Church, gave a lengthy defense of his faith to the High Priest and the Sanhedrin before he was stoned to death. In his sermon he gave type and shadow description of the salvation of man by a Holy God. He described three sins common to man that may occur at salvation: a heart that turns back to the world, one who rejoices in the works of their hands rather than God and those who reject the living Presence of God and relationship with Him. These sins reap the following judgments of God: wandering in the wilderness of sin, worship of demons and captivity in religion. We must flee from being stiff-necked and uncircumcised in our hearts and ears and seek God earnestly for His direction, desire and understanding. Our God is the LIVING God! If we do not grow in the grace and the knowledge of the Lord Jesus Christ we founder in aimless religion that leads to the persecution and murder of God's anointed!

The Holy Spirit is the Spirit of Truth. One reason the Holy Spirit has been sent to us is to open our understanding of the truth about Jesus. He desires to speak through us. He works through us to bring conviction of sin. Pentecost is the New Testament outpouring of the Holy Spirit with tongues which enables Christian persons to circumvent and deal with pride. The Day of Pentecost only occurs on Sunday once every eight years. The Holy Spirit has been compared to a dove in Scripture. The Dove has nine feathers on each wing. These nine are flight feathers. The Holy Spirit has nine fruit and nine gifts. Nine is the number of the Holy Spirit. Nine is the number of the latter rain. We may expect as much power as we have fruit—like feathers on a dove. We must have balance between the fruit and the gifts. In the Old Testament the High Priest's garment had bells and fruit alternating around the hem of his garment. The bells symbolize the gifts of the Holy Spirit. The fruit symbolize the fruit of the Holy Spirit. They alternated in order for balance to be maintained. A key to greater power is more fruit of the Spirit. Faith works by love. The truth must be spoken in love. The fruit is love. There are different expressions under different pressures. When the agapeo love of God is shown, the gifts of the Spirit are manifested. The compassion of Christ welling up within my bowels is what the Holy Spirit pours His power upon, just as He did with Jesus, my proto-type.

When the Holy Spirit comes to an unsaved soul He finds it spiritually insensible, paralyzed, and blind. It is dead in trespasses and sins. It is physically and intellectually and emotionally active, with a strong will, but destitute of spiritual life and power. The Holy Spirit first accompanies some word of truth to the mind, some sign or wonder before the eyes, some felt experience in the emotions or any other way of communication between the realm of God and the finite reality of man. Instead of being insensible, the spirit of man begins to be awakened, begins to see and feel and desire. The Spirit continues to press all these new considerations upon it until, confronted with the holiness of His Presence, its past sins loom up like overhanging mountains and threaten to crush it forever. This is the Imminent and Transcendent Presence of God. It then begins to be in agony and cries out to God for mercy, and for the first time is led to pray.

Then having shown the soul its own lost state and led it to realize its sinful state, the Spirit next turns the soul's attention to the remedy, and begins to take of the things of Christ and show them to the soul. This at first only aggravates the distress and the soul's only relief is found in God. Finally, the Holy Spirit begins to give the soul power to believe and to surrender to Christ Jesus. The Holy Spirit continues to use His sword, which is sharp and quick and powerful to the dividing asunder of the soul and spirit, the joint and marrow and the very thought and intent of the heart, i.e. the Word of God, so vigorously that by and by the heart is all cut to pieces and broken up by sharp strokes and rapid blows and seeks for a method of escape but there is only One Way. Then the Spirit applies the Blood of Christ in cleansing.

The real work is to get the soul to surrender itself to Christ, utterly and entirely, and then make it feel that Christ has received and pardoned it and that Christ's righteousness is imputed to it. After which follows peace and pardon and joy, expressed in song and praise and prayer. The soul that gives itself to God in worship with all its heart and mind and strength is truly blessed. It receives a jump-start to the powers of the Age to come via total and complete abandonment to Him. It is the submission of the soul to the Lordship of Christ that brings the greatness of God's power into the individual soul. We are complete in Him because all the fullness of the Godhead dwells bodily in Him.

Continuing on, the work of the Holy Spirit is not yet done. Now He enables the soul to grow in grace and knowledge and helps it resist temptation and overcome sin, within and without. The Spirit helps it pray the effectual fervent prayer that availeth much before God. The Holy Spirit quickens the saved soul enabling it to understand the Scriptures and feed upon them. He gives power to witness to the one filled and baptized with His Presence thus enabling it to work effectively and faithfully for the salvation of others. All the work of sanctification is the Spirit's work. All the Christian graces are His fruits within.

We are <u>sealed</u> by the Holy Spirit unto the fullness of the Father so He can act His divine power in us and enable us to fulfill the duties of our holy calling. **The seal of God is truth.** This sealing gives both us and those to whom we are sent the evidence of our acceptance by God. It assures our preservation unto eternal life. Jesus was sealed by the Holy Spirit. This was evidenced by the Father Himself when He said, "This is My beloved Son in whom I am well pleased." We must be sealed just as He was sealed. This is not conversion but something done upon a converted soul, a kind of crown of consecration put upon the soul. Indeed, the two events stand in marked contrast. In conversion the believer receives the testimony of God and sets *"his seal that God is true" (John 3:33).* In consecration God sets His seal upon the believer that He is true. The last is God's "Amen" to the Christian, verifying the Christian's "Amen" to God. *"Now he which establisheth us with you in Christ, and hath anointed us, is God, who hath also sealed us, and given the earnest of the Spirit in our hearts" (2 Corinthians 1:21, 22).* What is it to which we are committed and separated by this divine action of being sealed by the Holy Spirit? The Apostle Paul has written *"Nevertheless the foundation of God standeth sure, having this seal: the Lord knoweth them that are His and let everyone that nameth the Name of Christ depart from iniquity" (2 Timothy 2:19).* Iniquity is defined as self-will. Therefore, we are to walk in His ownership and His holiness upon us. As a Christian "sealed" by God we no longer "do our own thing". Actually we no longer have our own thing to do. We must have uninterrupted communion with Jesus. The Apostle Paul wrote *"And grieve not the Holy Spirit of God, whereby ye are sealed unto the day of redemption" (Ephesians 4:30).* How can the Holy Spirit quicken us at the rapture of the Church or the advent of the Lord if He does not dwell within us? *"If the Spirit of Him that raised up Jesus from the dead dwell in you" (Romans 8:11)* is the great condition of final quickening. So we are sealed by God when we are free of iniquity (self-will) and walk in obedience and holiness to God in truth.

The Holy Spirit does the work of conviction, enlightenment, subduing, believing, understanding, witnessing, overcoming evil, healing and growth in holiness. He produces conviction in the guilty, illumination in the ignorant, holiness in the defiled, strength and health in the feeble and comfort in the distressed. As the Spirit of Holiness He imparts a pure love; as the Spirit of Glory He throws a radiance over the character; as the Spirit of Life He revives our mortal bodies; as the Spirit of Truth He gives transparency to the understanding; as the Spirit of Prayer (Grace and Supplication) He melts the soul into devotion; and as the Spirit of Power (Might) He covers the face of the earth with works of faith and labors of love. Indispensable Holy Spirit of God!

THE HEAVENLY FATHER WHO IS THE MOST HIGH, ALMIGHTY GOD

Yet the ultimate work of both Jesus and the Holy Spirit is to lead us to Oneness with the Heavenly Father God. It is He Who is Love itself. It is He Who casts out all fear from us that we may live by the faith of the Son of God. It is He Who enables us to speak the Truth as the Holy Spirit gives us the utterance. It is He Who affects varieties of activities and ways throughout the Body of Christ which makes increase of the Body unto the edifying of itself in love. It is He Who brings to pass what we agree upon. It is as we stay in His Love that we are enabled to build our characters upon the foundation of our most holy faith.

Matthew 5:8 Blessed are the pure in heart: for they shall see God.

John 14:23 Jesus answered and said unto him, If a man love me, he will keep my words: and my Father will love him, and we will come unto him, and make our abode with him.

John 17:21-23 That they all may be one; as thou, Father, art in me, and I in thee, that they also may be one in us: that the world may believe that thou hast sent me. And the glory which thou gavest me I have given them; that they may be one, even as we are one: I in them, and thou in me, that they may be made perfect in one; and that the world may know that thou hast sent me, and hast loved them, as thou hast loved me.

1 John 1:3-4 That which we have seen and heard declare we unto you, that ye also may have fellowship with us: and truly our fellowship is with the Father, and with his Son Jesus Christ. And these things write we unto you, that your joy may be full. KJV

The Heavenly Father it is, that determines the times and the seasons and demands that we live and walk in forgiveness as He has given us example. Nothing is impossible to Him. Nothing is impossible to us as we believe Him. He loves His enemies, does good and gives to all. God is Good. God does not judge or condemn us. Rather He forgives us and pardons us and is merciful to us all, willing that we should be saved. He is all goodness, purity and light. God is light, and in Him is no darkness at all. He is the Father of lights, with whom is no variableness, neither shadow of turning. Our God is a consuming fire. He is Omnipotent, Omniscient and Omnipresent. He is Holy. God cannot be tempted with evil, neither tempteth He any man. He is kind to ungrateful and evil men. Yet He reveals His truths to the innocent and to babes. He is revealed to those to whom Jesus Christ chooses to reveal Him. He has been seen by no man at any time, only the Son, Who is very God, has seen Him and reveals Him to whosoever He wills. He seeks people to worship Him in spirit and in truth. This is one of the desires of the Father.

It is His kingdom that is to come upon the earth. He has chosen gladly to give us His kingdom and to add unto us all that we need. We need only ask Him **in prayer in the Name of Jesus Christ. Matthew 6:9-13** *After this manner therefore pray ye: Our Father which art in heaven, Hallowed be thy name. Thy kingdom come. Thy will be done in earth, as it is in heaven. KJV*

The Bible clearly states the work of the Father. The Father is the One Who commands and Who calls and chooses individuals according to His will, plans and purposes. The Father loves those who obey Him. The Father is in us and we are in the Father. He honors those who serve Him. The Father glorifies His Name. The Father, abiding in us, does His works. The Father

233

has Life (Zoe) in Himself. He raises the dead (SPIRIT, SOUL AND/OR BODY) and gives them Life. He draws men unto Himself. The Father appoints and grants salvation to those who are to be saved. *Revelation 22:17 And the Spirit and the bride say, Come. And let him that heareth say, Come. And let him that is athirst come. And whosoever will, let him take the water of life freely. KJV* He calls those things that be not into existence. The "buck stops here" with the Father God!

He puts His Life in His sons. It is by looking at the Father that we understand how to be a son. He shows His sons what to say and what to do. The Father hears the prayers of His sons. He gives His sons' works to do. The Lord disciplines those he loves, and he scourges everyone he accepts as a son. If you are not disciplined (and everyone undergoes discipline), then you are illegitimate children and not true sons. *"But my righteous one will live by faith. And if he shrinks back, I will not be pleased with him."* But we are not of those who shrink back and are destroyed, but of those who believe and are saved. The Father is the Vinedresser or Husbandman. He prunes the branches and takes away those that do not bear fruit. When the disciples bear much fruit the Father is glorified. Agapeo love that is tried and tested in the fires of adversity brings forth Life. The Father does test and try our spiritual Life. Nothing in life is established in truth unless it is first tested and tried. God the Father desires that we pray, fast and give alms in secret that He may reward us openly. He is glorified through the works of His sons. He bears witness of His sons. He sets His seal upon His sons. He gives His sons those who are to be saved. He never leaves His sons alone but is always <u>with</u> them. He glorifies His sons. He gives His sons authority to lay down their lives and authority to take them up again. The Father desires Oneness with His sons.

When we believe in the Light, the Father gives us eyes to see, a perceptive heart and spiritual wholeness and health. The Light of God's knowledge dispels the darkness of deception and ignorance; the Light of Truth destroys the darkness of lies and error. Darkness has no substance. The Father approves those that boldly confess Him. When we behold Jesus, we behold the Father. The Father gives all things into the hands of The Son. All people come to the Father through Jesus Christ. Through Christ we know the Father and in Christ we see Him. We are to believe that Jesus is in the Father and the Father is in Him. When we keep His commandments we truly love Christ and he who loves Christ will be loved by the Father and Christ will disclose Himself to him. The Father will love us, come to us and make His abode with us. We are to keep Christ's commandments, abide in His love and in the Love of the Father. Christ's commandment is that we love one another. Love works no ill to any man. Christ makes known to us the plans and purposes of the Father. Whatever we ask the Father in the Name of Christ He gives us. All things that the Father has are Christ's.

The Holy Spirit takes what Christ has and discloses it to us. The Father is the One Who gives us the Holy Spirit that He may be with us forever throughout eternity. The wonderful Holy Spirit is called, by Jesus Christ, the 'Promise of the Father'. The Father sends the Holy Spirit to teach us all things and bring to our remembrance all that Christ said to us. The Holy Spirit empowers the will, plan and purposes of the Father God. He seeks that that is of the Father that He might return it unto Him.

The Father is greater than Christ. To know the Father is Eternal Life. It is the Father's will that must be accomplished, not only the will of the Holy Spirit. The doing of the Father's will is what brings about the Kingdom of God upon the earth. Jesus Christ's relationship with the Church is likened to the reciprocal obligations found in the marriage relationship between man and woman. *"And they two shall be one flesh..."* The doing of The Truth of the Word of God brings about the manifest glory of the Holy Spirit. The King must rule His Kingdom. The Gospel of the Kingdom of God has not been truly preached or received on this earth yet. The Church Age shall result in the Kingdom of God. It is the restoration of Mankind in the image of Jesus Christ.

Salvation is a matter of Truth not a matter of intellect, feelings or willpower. In other words, salvation is first of all spiritual, not of the soul of man. Jesus is our way, our truth and our life. We enter into The Truth that is Christ. We do not enter into mere knowledge of facts. We do not enter into the knowledge of the truth. We enter into He Who is The Truth. However, as the veils of the world, the flesh and the devil are removed we understand Who Christ Is. We become One with God. We conform our life and our mind to His Life and The Mind of Christ. Self falls away. We train ourselves to think of ourselves as the Word of God describes us. We think the Word of God. Christ remains. This must be a literal experience in real time not something we give mental assent to.

It is very important that we not be presumptuous in our relationship with the Trinity of God. Being able to "see" the things of God and/or being able to understand revelations of the Word of God does not automatically denote the reality of any given truth in one's life. Has God spoken to you that you have attained such and such? Have other people experienced the fruit of it? Are you only associating with someone who walks in a given anointing or do you walk in that anointing?

To see our soul saved we must go through the fire, go through the flood, be turned from side to side, experience the judgments of our blindside and allow the Holy Spirit to thoroughly purge our floor. The flesh (self) must be overcome.

"I want My children to know that these years on earth are not Life. They are merely the ante-chamber—the waiting room—of Life. These years are to be spent in preparation."

236

CHAPTER IX

HOW DOES THE INTERCESSOR CONFORM TO GOD'S WAYS?

"The Holy Spirit rests only on someone whose heart is happy."
Jerusalem Talmud Sukkah 5:1

*F*ruitful praying brings to mind the symbol of the Cross. Jesus prayed in John, Chapter 17, that we would be one, even as He and the Father were One. This is a vertical Oneness with God. Being in right relationship to man is a horizontal oneness as we reach out to others. Being in right relationship to God and to man causes the individual intercessor's life to be fixed at the point where the two lines meet, thus enabling the intercessor to be effective in both the realm of the natural and the spiritual. The fixed point is the place where Jesus' Heart rested against the Cross. Pastor Kenneth W. Hagin has said many times that the natural and the spiritual, working together, make an explosive force for God. *Romans 14:17-19 For the kingdom of God is not meat and drink; but righteousness, and peace, and joy in the Holy Ghost. For he that in these things serveth Christ is **acceptable to God, and approved of men.** Let us therefore follow after the things which make for peace, and things wherewith one may edify another.*

KJV It is this positioning at the fixed point of God's Heart of Love that causes the prayers of intercession to produce fruit that remains unto eternity. The fruitful prayers referred to are the fruits of the spirit mentioned in Galatians 5:22, 23, and the fruit that grows in the Father's vineyard—the lost souls of this world system.

God created man to both BE and to DO. God created us in His image with a spirit, soul and body. Our soul is made up of our mind, our emotions and our will. God gave us our human will to keep our being and doing in balance. Just as God is both Transcendent and Imminent, we are created in His image to DO and to BE. We are both separate and belonging in our persons. Our salvation must be worked out through the entirety of our person. As healthy and whole individuals we must have both "roots" and "wings". We can not be saved in our minds only. We must be doers of the gospel of Jesus Christ. We participate in the divine nature through our knowledge of Him when we meet the conditions of the promises of God by doing them. We must win favor and a good name in the sight of God and man. *Luke 2:52 And Jesus increased in wisdom and stature, and in favour with God and man. KJV* Ultimately God had to decide whether or not He was to be alone or whether He would have relationship with another. He chose to have relationship. God chose to have a family. This is why salvation—true Biblical salvation—has Godly relationship with man and with God. God is a social being and we, in His image, must be social too. Note the contradiction between the following two Scriptures: *Jude 19 These be they who separate themselves, sensual, having not the Spirit VS . Romans 14:18 For he that in these things serveth Christ is acceptable to God, and approved of men. KJV*

The failure of our work is due to the fact that we are eager to preach the Cross without that Cross being within us. Is the Cross of Christ of none effect within you? The Cross of Jesus Christ is the power of God. The Cross of Calvary which Jesus

238

Christ hung upon is the source of God's power in this Dispensation of Grace. It is the Gospel. The Cross we preach to others should first crucify us. We cannot give what we do not have. In short, crucifixion spells death. The crucifixion of our old nature will be expressed in helplessness, weakness, fear, and trembling. Frequently, in our attempt to achieve Pentecost, we bypass Calvary. This was the third temptation of Jesus Christ by satan in Luke 4:9-11. Jesus was tempted by satan to enter into His Kingdom without first dying or suffering. This is the same temptation many preachers in the worldly Church have succumbed to. It is the wisdom of God that saves man not the wisdom of the world. We do not realize that without our being crucified — thus shedding all the trappings of the natural man — the Holy Spirit cannot work through us to gain many people. Here, then, is the spiritual principle: die, and then bring forth life. With real death there comes real resurrection. This is what satan hates the most, because he has no foothold on those who have died. Imagine sitting a corpse in a chair. No matter what you parade in front of a corpse there will be no response. Gold, power, position, sex, beauty, houses, lands, possessions—nothing affects that corpse. It is really dead!

If all we have is thoughts, we can only give thoughts. However, what people lack are not thoughts or intellectual facts about God, but spiritual life that is tangible! If the Holy Spirit is not working with His authority and power behind the words we speak, the hearers or those we pray for will not undergo any change in their lives. To be fully saved a person must undergo a supernatural metamorphosis. The "do" of the Scriptures is not the doing with our own strength; it is instead allowing the Holy Spirit to live out the Word of the Lord through us. True prayer occurs when the Trinity prays through a sanctified vessel for the glory of God. This is one reason we worship God before entering His Presence. It prepares us to receive His power flowing through us.

The Lord has appointed the way to victory for us: it is the Cross (1 Thessalonians 3:3). The defeat of satan is at the Cross. Therefore, he is most fearful of people going to the Cross and obtaining the victory of Calvary in their daily lives. Victory is not due to our depending on self. On the contrary, victory is due to our standing in the finished work of Calvary by Jesus Christ, the Father and the Holy Spirit. We receive His victory/strength by faith. The most beautiful thing in the world is to learn obedience and how to be subject to others. The thirty silent years of Jesus' life were when He learned obedience. It was the one thing He had to learn. We must sever our private life from our public ministry and be one as He is One. Realize that if God is going to use you to save others **you cannot save yourself.**

What is the Cross of Calvary in reality? It is the death of our fleshly self life. The wisdom of Christ is that we, our <u>self</u>, are reduced to nothing. In this world we have nothing, we are nothing. There is nothing for satan or any worldly person to grab hold of. We let go of everything and everyone for the Supremacy of Christ Jesus! Having found the Pearl of great price we go and sell all to obtain it. As with everything in God's Kingdom—having nothing—all things become ours. (In other words, God's Kingdom is diametrically opposed to satan's kingdom.) Therefore, once we have died to self, our power, possessions and produce (fruit) become unlimited. This is what the world seeks after but is unable to attain to because it refuses God's ways of faith and has chosen fear instead. The surest way to have unlimited resources is to give it all away while in the Presence of God— under His anointing. This must be done in faith and initiated by the Holy Spirit with a proper heart motive of love toward God. Even after obedience rest assured that God and/or satan will test your faith. We must have the wisdom of God (vs. the wisdom of the world) + revelation knowledge of Jesus Christ to attain to = the power of the Holy Spirit. Philippians 3:17-21. This is a matter of the heart and of faith that results in action. Jesus only died on the Cross once and God only requires this once in our life unless we resurrect our dead flesh and become spiritual zombies.

When God becomes more real than the natural realm we die to self and our soul is shut down. The Presence of God stills the soul. The Presence of God produces holy silence. The deeper your prayer the more powerful it is. Quietness is more powerful than words. Your spirit prays with perfection. Madame Jeanne Guyon (1648-1717) describes this as "going within yourself". The flesh is cancelled. There is a place in prayer where the flesh is cancelled and Jesus becomes the reality. You lose your reality. You go into a deep place of the spirit and there is absolute stillness. If it doesn't come from the spirit it is rejected. Tears are the only language. This is the secret place of the Most High. What are the qualifications of entering into the shadow/secret place of the Most High? *Zephaniah 2:3 3 Seek the LORD, all you meek of the earth, who have upheld His justice. Seek righteousness, seek humility. It may be that you will be hidden in the day of the LORD's anger. NKJV* True prayer enables you to enter this worship. Only worship enables you to enter this place.

Hearing the Voice of God.

The first requirement for true prayer then, is that we learn to listen to the Voice of God. We must learn the difference between mental energy and God's Voice. Never forget that you serve the Living God. To accomplish this we must learn to wait upon the Presence of the Lord. Psalm 46:10 It is as we enter into His rest that His Presence will abide upon us. Hebrews 4:7 Abiding in Christ brings us into the abiding Presence of the Father God. The Presence of God is what sustains you, keeps you holy, nourishes you, strengthens you and enables you to walk with the Lord. He keeps you from falling. All is well. His Presence is salt and light.

In John 15:1-11 Jesus explains to us how our prayers become fruitful. We must abide in Him; that is, to continue in Him. We must remain in His perfect will at all cost. This speaks of that positioning and right relationship. Second, His words are to abide in us; they are to become a vital part of our life. We are to be filled with and guided by His words for they are the path of life to us, showing us the ways of the Father. The Lord Jesus has taught us that our soul life, or natural life, like a grain of wheat, should fall into the ground and die (John 12:24). The mortification of the flesh is not changing the flesh but always following the dictates of the spirit rather than the flesh. True mortification is to choose the direction of the spirit rather than the flesh. If we always maintain an attitude of uncompromisingly hating our soul life, we will learn experientially how to depend on the power of the spirit life and thus bear fruit to the glory of God. As we continue to be spiritually minded, the power of eternal life, or Zoë, works through us to effect change in us. Our focus must be on God as we fall more and more in love with Him. We want to abide in the place where He guides us with His Eye and we have eyes that hear Him.

God created man in His image, male and female He created them. God created man spirit, soul and body in His image. Within the human body there are three fluids: mucus, water and blood. In heaven there is unity: the Father God, Jesus Christ and the Holy Spirit all agree as One. To become one with God, man must first be one, or have integrity, within his own self. When there is unity within a person and unity in heaven then oneness occurs. This is not a matter of physical location for there is no distance in the realm of the spirit. Under the Old Testament the spirit and the flesh were in unity against the mind. Under the New Testament the spirit and the mind must be in unity against the flesh. The battle is in the mind, i.e. the soul of man. This is our spiritual warfare. The flesh of man must lose all power and authority and find complete subservience to the Spirit of God within the human spirit. God desires Oneness with man. We must become spiritually minded, i.e. have the Mind of Christ. We must think the Word of God in the first person.

God says His answers to our prayers are Yes! and Amen! In Psalm 50:17 the Spirit of the Lord through the psalmist equates wickedness as those who hate discipline or instruction and those who hate God's words. Proverbs 10:17 teaches, *"He who heeds instruction and correction is [not only himself] in the way of life [but also] is a way of life for others. And he who neglects or refuses reproof [not only himself] goes astray [but also] causes to err and is a path toward ruin for others."*AMP Therefore it behooves us to willingly submit to God's instruction and discipline through His Word and to practice obedience. Who are we to obey? We are to obey the Holy Spirit, the Word of God and those in spiritual authority over us which are responsible to God for us AS they obey the Holy Spirit and the Word of God. What disciplines are we to practice? Prayer. Fasting. Study. Simplicity. Solitude. Submission. Service. Confession. Thanksgiving. Praise. Worship. Guidance. Celebration. Some of these disciplines are inward, some are outward and some are corporate. To practice them effectually we must first recognize that God created man in His image with a spirit, a soul and a body. Thus we have an inward man and an outward man. Psychology has named these the Id, the Super Id, the Ego and the Conscience. Each of the Christian disciplines mentioned above is vital to produce spiritual growth and maturity.

Stability and balance are pivotal to success in our spiritual growth. We must grow into the fullness of both sides of Godly wisdom. In the natural realm wine is not good unless it has been "turned upon its lees", for example Scripture states in Hosea 7:8 "Ephraim is a cake not turned". Ephraim was, in many respects, untouched by Divine grace, though there was partial obedience there was very much rebellion left. Charles Spurgeon has noted that a cake not turned is soon burned on the side nearest the fire, and although no man can have too much faith, there are some who are burned black with bigoted zeal and religion for that part of truth which they have received, or are charred to a cinder with that "vainglorious Pharisaic ostentation of those religious performances which suit their humor." God created the physical body of man with two eyes, two ears, two nostrils, two sides of the brain, two lungs, two kidneys, two arms, two hands, two legs and two feet. Two denotes difference. If two different persons agree in testimony it is conclusive. Otherwise two implies opposition, enmity, and division, as was the work of the Second Day of God's creation. Compare the use of the word "double" applied to "heart", "tongue", "mind", etc. The significance of the number *two* is seen in the New Testament. Wherever there are two Epistles by the same name, the second has some special reference to the enemy. *Psalms 86:11 Teach me thy way, O LORD; I will walk in thy truth: unite my heart to fear thy name. KJV Psalms 86:11 Teach me your way, O LORD, and I will walk in your truth; give me an undivided heart, that I may fear your name. NIV* Mankind has been given one heart (although it possesses four parts), one stomach, one spleen, one gallbladder, one liver, one neck and one mouth. Man and woman together in holy matrimony, were given one penis and one womb denoting unity and oneness to bring multiplication.

Our very own hearts, minds and bodies must come into agreement and peace to be enabled to receive the goodness of God. To be complete or full in our knowledge of God and His ways we must be turned from side to side. We must experience wisdom in each of our two sides and come into its fullness. To open the Gate of Wisdom we must hold up the blood of Jesus and forgive all done to us by others realizing that nothing and no one can damage us when we are "in Christ". God will restore all. In all this we must still manifest stability and balance! **In order to come into Oneness with God, man must first come into oneness or integrity within his own self.** We must let go of the differences within our own self and find the oneness of who we truly are in Christ Jesus. Therefore, we understand from observing our own body that spiritual growth is necessary for wholeness. Balance is imperative to be able to "walk" and to "run". Walking is defined as two same legs moving in opposite directions to go forward in the same direction. There is a difference between spirit-led ministry and flowing in the Love of God. Spiritual balance is achieved when the Love of God is proved by sincerity of action. Love compels to action. *"God so loved that He gave…" Amos 3:3 Do two walk together except they make an appointment and have agreed? AMP* God has called us to be overcomers. In each of the four gospels Jesus Christ went to "the other side". In the gospel of Matthew He went to the other side four times. In the gospel of Mark He went to the other side four times. In the gospel of Luke He went to the other side three times. In the gospel of John He went to the other side two times. Have you ever been to the other side of your own person? There are many called to be apostles who have falsely professed they are, without actually possessing the other side of their own person.

Rev. Ron McIntosh teaches that the intercessor and each Christian must have formed within them a system of belief that will facilitate the meeting of their needs and the occurrence of spiritual life and liberty. In Roman 10:13-15 the Apostle Paul clearly gives the progression of ministry used to teach an individual to believe. The scriptures are written that we might believe that Jesus is The Christ, The Son of God; and that believing we might have life in His Name. This is why we go to church and to meetings. We are having our belief system developed. When we wait upon God in prayer and in quiet adoration, He is able to develop our system of belief. When we pray in tongues quietly and read the Word of God, book by book, revelation knowledge and understanding are birthed within us. Rev. Dave Roberson and Pastor Benny Hinn both teach that it is the manifold repetition of our reading of a book of the Bible while praying in tongues that brings God's truth to us through revelation by the Holy Spirit. When we pray in the spirit and allow the Holy Spirit to give us the interpretation of our prayers and to prophecy to us, through us, we shall receive more and more revelation. It is important to journal our spiritual life and pray back to God His directives to us, exercising faith in His plan. We must **do** His will for us personally. As we meditate upon the Word of God and confess it, our system of belief is developed. Jesus taught by subject. Where a subject begins and where it ends has nothing to do with the chapter and verse numerics that were added much later. Each scripture is a piece of the puzzle. We must see the whole puzzle to understand the point. This is why we meditate God's Word. It is the verses that go unnoticed that bring the understandings and revelations of God, according to Pastor Dave Roberson. Knowing who we are and what we believe is pivotal to Christian maturity. If you know it, you can stand upon the truth of it and nothing in hell or on earth can change you. The Holy Spirit is our Teacher. He lives in our heart and speaks to our own mind through our own spirit.

In verse 2 of John 15, Jesus discusses the purging, cleansing or washing that comes as a result of the living, eternal Word of God Almighty at work within us. In order to produce fruit we must be free of every dead, non-productive part of our lives. God's Word is alive! It is like a sharp sword that is quick and powerful to the dividing asunder of soul and spirit, joint and marrow and the very thought, motive and intent of the heart. God uses His Word to prune those of us who are branches abiding in the vine of Jesus Christ. We are *"made clean because of the word which I have spoken to you"*. The washing of the water of the Word of God makes us clean and the pruning of the sharp sword of the spirit keeps us clean that we may bear more fruit. It is God's desire that we *"bear much fruit and prove to be His disciples"*.

This process of putting off the old man and putting on the new man moves us from being outwardly ruled or governed by our senses to being inwardly ruled or governed by the Holy Spirit within our human spirit. Putting off and putting on has to do with the renewing of our minds. Our ability to walk through this life governed by the Holy Spirit within our human spirit and Bible-formed beliefs, convictions and persuasions rather than being governed by our senses will determine whether or not we are the conduit for God's purposes being fulfilled in the earth today. Our belief system is the armor of God for our life. Psalm 91:4 LB *"His faithful promises are your armor."* It is our ability to be conformed to the image of Christ. Jesus is the Word of God. His promises describe His character. As the Holy Spirit gives each individual a particular promise of the Word of God, that promise becomes part of their individual armor. What we believe, think, say and do in Christ Jesus is the protection of God that keeps us spiritually strong as we allow the Word of God to become part of the fiber of our being and thereby to influence our words and actions. A spiritual person's words and actions are the result of their beliefs. We are to think the Word of God and do it. No one can wear another person's armor effectively. For example: David could not wear King Saul's armor when he fought the giant, Goliath. We must each wait upon God to be personally fitted with our very own armor. The promises of God in His Word are the spiritual Truth He gives each of us personally to keep us strong and enable us to do His will.

2 Peter 1:3, 4 we know that God has given us everything we need *"pertaining to life and godliness"* by the knowledge we have of Christ and that through His great and precious promises we become partakers of His divine nature. The peace of God in

our hearts and minds is another avenue whereby we partake of God's Divine nature. Jesus Christ was our peace offering unto the Father. He is our Prince of Peace. He has given unto us His peace, not the peace that the world has, but His very own peace has He given unto us. As far as it lies within our power we should live in peace with every man. There is a path of peace and a way of peace for God's children to walk upon. We must ask God to set our feet upon that path of peace. It is an ancient way and a good way. When walking upon it we shall find rest for our souls. *James 3:17-18 But the wisdom that is from above is first pure, then peaceable, gentle, and easy to be intreated, full of mercy and good fruits, without partiality, and without hypocrisy. And the fruit of righteousness is sown in peace of them that make peace. Matthew 11:27-30 All things are delivered unto me of my Father: and no man knoweth the Son, but the Father; neither knoweth any man the Father, save the Son, and he to whomsoever the Son will reveal him. Come unto me, all ye that labour and are heavy laden, and I will give you rest. Take my yoke upon you, and learn of me; for I am meek and lowly in heart: and ye shall find rest unto your souls. For my yoke is easy, and my burden is light. KJV*

We appropriate the promises of God's Word by faith. In Mark 11:11-26 Jesus teaches us by example and word to speak to the mountains of difficulty and to that part of our own selves which is capable of bearing fruit for the Father and believe that what we say will come to pass. He again stresses right relationships and forgiveness of others. Every one of God's promises to us demands a response. The realm from which you respond to the promise determines the outcome of the promise in your life. Are you responding from the natural realm or the spiritual realm?

There are two ways to be clean, fruitful branches according to the Word of God. *Psalm 12:6 says, "The words of the Lord are pure words; as silver tried in a furnace on the earth, refined seven times."* We

Human beings are created for relationship. To have healthy relationship, a human being (Dr. Henry Cloud)

can receive the Word of God as it is quickened to us by the power of the Holy Spirit and repent of our own sins in private or we can go through the purging fires of God and man and be made clean. Joyce Meyer has said that we either choose to be accountable by our actions or we are forced to be accountable by our circumstances. It <u>will</u> finally catch up to you! To get out of a pit of your own creation you must do the same thing you did to get into the pit in reverse. You must do the right thing over and over again. You must be a lifetime learner — educate yourself as a believer. This is a responsibility you have in order to have victory in your life. Worship God. Be accountable for your actions. Be led from within. It is spiritual truth that we cannot obtain something outwardly if it first is not birthed within us inwardly. In other words, it is wrong to use the power of God for selfish ends. Go after the will of God for you personally every single day of your life. In Romans 2 the Apostle Paul teaches us that those things we see and hate in others are within us. In reality, it is our own sinful self that we hate. God, in His mercy, has given us our life on this earth to change so that we may live in an eternity of peace and blessing with Him.

Mike Murdock teaches that a Master Key to radically change your life is your daily routine. The secret of your future is hidden in your daily routine. The difference between champions and losers are their habits. "Jesus, as was his custom...." David prayed seven times a day. Daniel prayed three times a day. You cannot change until you change your daily habit. Rev. Murdock calls this the Law of Eventuality. Do what you hate to create what you love. Jesus said, "Let this cup pass from Me." Habits create experiences. He also said that when you want something you have never had you have got to do something you have never done. **Logic produces order. Obedience produces miracles.**

I "heard" two things when I was young in the Lord that were very inconvenient to my flesh nature

249

but I felt compelled to do them. I did not want to incorporate these two "ways" into my daily practices because, first of all, they seemed too hard to do and, secondly, and quite frankly, far beyond my personal ability to accomplish, and thirdly, because I was too selfish and lazy to do them. Rev. Kenneth E. Hagin, my spiritual father, often spoke of this little formula: "If you only spend time in the Word you will dry up. If you only spend time with the Holy Spirit you will blow up. If you spend your time in the Word and with the Holy Spirit you will grow up." Since my natural tendency was to the things of the Holy Spirit I had to train my flesh nature to spend time in the Word of God. I <u>made</u> myself read the Word. I would have rather prayed all the time in tongues. The second instruction came through Rev. Marilyn Hickey. She taught that eventually one must study the Word of God to continue to grow in the grace and knowledge of the Lord Jesus Christ. I didn't know how to study! It seemed totally overwhelming to me. Besides, I thought, who cared if some little, inconsequential woman studied the Word of God? Yet I knew I had to do this. Then I attended Bible School and a minister I respected very much, Rev. Cooper Beatty, taught a class on the study of God's Word. He taught us the laws of interpretation of Scripture. He said we must understand the cultural and spiritual context from which Scripture was spoken. Finally, the Holy Spirit moved our family to Rev. Dave Roberson's church. It was there I learned in depth that the Holy Spirit is my Teacher. Both Rev. Dave Roberson and Pastor Benny Hinn have taught me I must read whole books of the Bible while praying quietly in tongues to receive revelation and understanding of the Word of God. Each of these spiritual imperatives made a deep impression on me. They changed the way I knew God. They changed the amount of time I spent with God. They changed my ability to trust Scripture as the real truth. If we really desire to spend our eternity with God we must DO what He says.

Isaiah 6:5-7 and James 3:5, 6 contrast fire and the tongue. If we allow the fire of God to cleanse our tongue we are made pure and holy. If we allow our tongue to be set on fire by hell it will, in turn, set on fire the course of our life. Remember, our God is a consuming fire! 1 Corinthians 11:31 instructs us that *"if we judged ourselves rightly, we should not be judged"*. Also in Matthew 7 Jesus teaches us not to be hypocrites by judging others but first to take the log out of our own eye before we attend to the speck in our brother's eye. In the Book of James, chapter Three, the Holy Spirit teaches us that our tongue must be tamed. This is a crucial requirement in your spiritual life. Our lips, mouth and tongue must go through the purging and sanctifying fires of God or else we shall become an accuser of the brethren. We must pray to God for this. We must pray that the salt water of sin be removed from the fountain of our life that the Water of Life may flow forth from us to give life to others. This is a primary prerequisite of being used by God in His family business.

There are three breastplates mentioned in Scripture: the breastplate of righteousness, the breastplate of faith and love, and the breastplate of judgment. The breastplate of righteousness is a free gift from the Father God as, ultimately, it was His Blood flowing through His Son on the Cross of Calvary. The breastplate of faith and love is ours as a result of our own self control as we grow in the graces and fruit of the Holy Spirit. The breastplate of judgment is owned by an individual when they judge their own hearts and lives, putting off their self as Jesus Christ did and putting on God's beauty, lights, glories and perfections as Christ did in His resurrection. The mere fact that there are three breastplates mentioned denotes spiritual growth. We grow into God's fullness as our relationship with each member of the Trinity is developed. We are changed from glory to glory in His image. Romans 12:2

251

The power of fasting.

Fasting is God's atomic power in the life of the intercessor. Fasting is the real and physical means to remove self from the equation of spiritual warfare. Fasting is a spiritual circumcision. Therefore, the intercessor must grow in spiritual strength and personal ability to fast—either food, water, sleep, sexuality, or entertainment/society—as this gives them God's power to overcome satan and his schemes. Fasting must be done in faith and in obedience to the leading of the Holy Spirit within. The Holy Spirit's leading in the Word of God, prayer and worship must be followed diligently during one's fast. Spiritual battles occur at the end of a fast—when the fast is over. Therefore, humility and sensitivity are vital as the intercessor carefully follows the leading of the Holy Spirit in agreement with the Word of God. There are times in the life of the intercessor that the **only** way to make it through a situation, obeying the leading of the Father God and yet still walking in love with our brothers and sisters in Christ and our fellow men, is to fast. Common sense and wisdom are vital at the end of the fast to enable one to accurately follow the will of God and focus the power and anointing previously gained during the fast to accomplish God's purposes. Jesus taught by word and example that certain evil powers cannot be cast out except by prayer and fasting. Therefore, our experiential knowledge and understanding of this spiritual tool is invaluable. Fasting is like a muscle that must be exercised and used, to grow and be strong. No one is exempt from this spiritual discipline. All Christians are commanded to fast. For the intercessor it is an imperative that **must** be practiced.

Intercessors must learn that we, as humans, do not exist and draw breath because of food, water, sleep, pleasure or outward stimulation. We are intrinsically a spirit, soul and body alive on this earth by God Himself. Every thing put into our vessel will be brought <u>out</u> of it. By this I mean that what we have ingested or inherited physically or spiritually will be brought out of us during our fasts until nothing is within us but God. This is a major way that God purges our person of everything but Himself. To grow in our personal ability to fast we must deal with both our positive and negative attributes. Before we can overcome forces without our self or others, we must first overcome what is within. God deals with individuals as whole beings. (Remember Ezekiel's vision of the wheel within the wheel.) We are both simple and complex. We are both positive and nega-tive. We are spirit, soul and body. Each part of us is a world within itself. Yet God is greater than all. The salvation that God has provided (sozo) is defined as wholeness, soundness, health, deliver-ance and freedom. God's salvation provides us with *1 Peter 3:21 the answer of a good and clear conscience (inward cleanness and peace) before God.* AMP Fasting is a spiritual tool that accomplishes this purpose of God within a person. It is a tool of sanctifica-tion and a source of power and anointing. Fasting helps us fasten on the Breastplate of Faith and Love with all self control. Therefore, it is something which must be sought after and mastered. Mankind fell from the grace of God when he ATE from the Tree of the Knowledge of Good and Evil. Let us refrain from eating for a time that we may find life.

It is best to start small when fasting, realizing that one must overcome battles with self, flesh and the devils both inherited and surrounding one. The intercessor must learn to master fear. Fear is to the enemy what faith is to God and the Christian. The devil, as a roaring lion, eats fear and worry for breakfast. Fear is the doorway that every other spirit must enter through. When overcoming sickness, lack, a character flaw or any other thing, one must first master the fear of it. Begin fasting with one meal or with a fast of television or any conversa-tion. You may then be led to progress on to fast one day per week. Fasting is defined by time and method.

Examples of various times and methods are in both the Old and New Testaments. For example, series fasting over time will break life-long strongholds. Fasting must be done with humility of heart and a repentant attitude, never from religious ritual. The Bible commands that those who are married be in agreement about the fast before one or both begin. Another definition of the word "fast" is to keep what you have, to remain stable, fixed and immovable. When we fast our physical needs met, we are holding onto God, Who is immovable and fixed, looking to Him to meet our need. Fasting causes the growth of self-control. Self-control enables us to be protected in our hearts and lives. Scripture gives us three breastplates: righteousness, self-control and judgment. This second breastplate of self-control causes personal growth enabling a person to overcome the enemy within and receive God's peace of heart and mind. Self-control produces good character. To successfully fast one must focus on God, not on one's body, self or circumstances. One's motive of heart is of primary importance in fasting. All time formerly spent in the thought, preparation and partaking of nourishment, sleep or entertainment or worldly society is most profitably spent with God in His Word, prayer and worship. Fasting, if done properly, is not easy. However, it is extremely beneficial.

Jeremiah 14:10-12 Thus saith the LORD unto this people, Thus have they loved to wander, they have not refrained their feet, therefore the LORD doth not accept them; he will now remember their iniquity, and visit their sins. Then said the LORD unto me, Pray not for this people for their good. When they fast, I will not hear their cry; and when they offer burnt offering and an oblation, I will not accept them: but I will consume them by the sword, and by the famine, and by the pestilence. KJV If a person loves to wander they are out of the way of understanding and have loved the wages of unrighteousness. Wandering stars are cast into outer darkness. A wandering star is one that does not have covenant with the Living God. They have removed themselves from God's covenant. Whether we eat and drink or do not, all should be done unto the Lord our God.

Zechariah 7:9-10 Thus speaketh the LORD of hosts, saying, Execute true judgment, and shew mercy and compassions every man to his brother: And oppress not the widow, nor the fatherless, the stranger, nor the poor; and let none of you imagine evil against his brother in your heart. KJV This should be our attitude and the motivation of our actions whether fasting or not.

Over time our ability to enter upon a longer fast grows. We are strengthened to encounter higher truths. As our time is refocused upon God, physical consciousness of the things of the world, the flesh and the devil are removed from us. We begin to be "other worldly". We see the waste involved with the physical processes of eating, sleeping and pleasure. Our ability to hear God is magnified. A new realm of peace is entered upon. The flesh is quieted and made still. Hunger ceases. God becomes all to us. The Bible comes alive and our understanding is quickened. Perspective rises to an eternal plane. This life is put into its proper place in our eternal existence. Knowledge of and experience with God's supernatural power becomes easy and ordinary. We enter into the Mind of Christ. We enter into God's Light and become One with Him. The harassments of darkness fall away and are no longer experienced. How beautiful is God's Presence! When ordained by God these precious times of separation unto Him are unequalled in sublime experience. They must be highly treasured and protected. These are hidden times, alone with God. Sharing them with others is usually done on a need to know basis. God Himself will quicken us as to what to share and with whom to share our experiences.

Historically, whole denominations receive their power from God via fasting sleep upon occasion. They minister as they are led by the Holy Spirit during the day and pray in tongues and with the understanding all night, forsaking the body's need of sleep. Other ministries depend on fasting food to receive power from God. They spend seasons of time waiting upon God, seeking Him in prayer and through the study of His Word, as they fast all physical sustenance. In Medieval times, monasteries and convents were established as places of safety and protection from the dark forces in the world. Within the walls of these establishments men and women spent their lives in contemplation, prayer and study of God. They fasted their sexuality and social interaction taking upon themselves mantles of celibacy in imitation of Christ. They did not speak. These all are means of separation from the world and the receiving of God's power. Some individuals may even combine these various methods of fasting to enable them to walk in the supernatural power of the Holy Spirit.

Fasting food, water, sleep, sexuality, social interaction and entertainment upon occasion; praying in tongues; confessing the Word of God aloud; praising and worshipping the Lord God; and the study of the Word of God are all methods of obtaining God's power. Separating oneself from the ways of the world and the development of Christian virtues prepare one to practice God's Presence and receive His Power. These are valuable habits for an intercessor to form and to practice. Again, the Apostle Peter teaches in his letters that growth in grace and the knowledge of God must be <u>built</u> into a person. We learn to establish God's ways and truths in our lives and then we add a new way and truth as we establish the practice of it on a consistent basis. It is in these ways that we are conformed to the image of Jesus Christ. To be a powerful tool in the Hand of God we must be exercised in these ways through a Godly life style and **consistent practice.** We learn to live Jesus Christ's life as He lived it when upon the earth. We are saved not only by the death of Christ on the Cross of Calvary but also by His life as we are conformed to the image of God as a son of God, through the development of our Godly character. The result of a true God-given fast should be justice. This is God's delight. His throne is founded upon justice and judgment. God is always on the look-out for a person who walks in justice and judgment. David walked in this and it is one reason that he was a man after God's own heart. This is God's Heart.

Fasting must never be done to exert power or control over another. This is especially true in marriage. Ahab and Jezebel did this to steal land from Naboth. God, Himself, sent His prophet to judge the situation. They died because of their spiritual manipulation of another. Fasting must be done from a pure heart, with a right motive, or not at all. God is Omniscient. He knows everything—not only what we do, but our motives and the thoughts of our hearts. He even knows what we are going to think before we think it. Generally, when He asks you a question, it is not because He desires to know your answer. He already knows your answer. He wants you to think new thoughts about the matter. (God can take care of Himself.) Since we have our very existence within Him, it behooves us to do things His way. I, personally, am so very thankful that God is truly GOOD. He is a Good God. Therefore, my obedience to Him is the happiest and best thing I can do for myself and for others.

Prayer is Warfare.

Those who are active in intercession know that prayer truly is warfare. The three greatest intercessors in the Old Testament were Job, Noah and Daniel. Each was well acquainted with warfare. Each was thoroughly tried in their faith. As in any war, there is contraband taken from the enemy. In the Old Testament God instructed Israel that all things taken in war had to be either washed with water or purged with fire. Water and fire, as two of the four basic elements of creation, run throughout scripture speaking of purification, sanctification and holiness. Thus we see in John 15 that it is always God's intention that we go from glory to glory, bearing more and more fruit for His Glory. Every bit of the soil of this earth, dust or ground, which comprises the individual person, must eventually be cleansed with fire and/or water and receive the wind of the Holy Spirit.

We do bear much fruit and prove to be Jesus' disciples by asking. Jesus instructs us to ask, seek and knock that it may be opened unto us. God promises to give good things to those who ask Him. Jesus goes on to discuss different types of fruit and says in verse 19 of Matthew 7 that every tree that does not bear good fruit is cut down and thrown into the fire. He then discusses relationship and positioning and the peril of lawlessness. Jesus says, *"Everyone who hears these words of Mine and does not act upon them will be like a foolish man"*. In Ezekiel 15 worthless branches that are thrown into the fire are to be consumed because they are good for nothing else.

When we ask in prayer it has nothing to do with our own desires and fleshly lusts. The Word of God has been given to show you God's intent and purpose so that you may know what to do to bring it to pass. This takes prayer. The Word in itself does nothing to bring your desires to fruition. You will not be able to gratify your own desires and lusts when you delight in God. In other words, all power and ministry are God's power and ministry. All glory belongs to God. This is all about Jesus!

Just as the student is not greater than the teacher so we, who belong to Christ, must follow in His footsteps and allow our self-life to be washed and/or purged that we are able to give the Father a good return on His investment in our lives. We do not need to die as Christ did. However, death to self is prerequisite to the bringing forth of fruit. *Heb 2:10 For it was an act worthy [of God] and fitting [to the divine nature] that He, for Whose sake and by Whom all things have their existence, in bringing many sons into glory, should make the Pioneer of their salvation perfect [should bring to maturity the human experience necessary to be perfectly equipped for His office as High Priest] through suffering.* AMP His death provided our salvation eternally but we do need to be changed from the glory of this earth unto the heavenly glory of eternity that we might bear fruit that remains—lost souls saved eternally. We will not be able to pray with power for others if we do not own and have not experienced what we are praying for. That is why Jesus counseled us to buy gold tried in the fire, to anoint our eyes with eye salve that we might see and to wash our garments in His blood that they would be white.

In 1 John 5:14, 15 the apostle John instructs us to ask according to the will of God and we know that the will of God is the Word of God. If He hears our prayer then the answer is Yes! and Amen! We know He hears our prayer when we pray His Word. Praying the Scriptures at the instigation and unction of the Holy Spirit is truly efficacious. God calls us to work together with Him to accomplish His will. God's purpose is for us to be so filled with His will that we forget our own interests. Prayer sets heaven in motion and brings Jesus on the scene. Prayer is meeting with God. When you are totally in agreement with God, you will be in agreement with yourself.

Praying the Word of God takes guts. It can be the scariest thing you have ever done but it is well worth it. Actually, walking in the Spirit with God is the most exciting, frightening and awesome experience a human being can have on this earth. In her book, Hinds Feet On High Places, Hannah Hurnard tells the story of little Miss Much Afraid. In it she also discusses the life of one who travels the whole world without leaving her room. I believe true nuns in convents in the Middle Ages did much the same thing. I have learned of such a one—Julian of Norwich, the Anchoress. Once appointed to her position as Anchoress, she never again left the room in which she lived, prayed and ministered. Spiritual life and spiritual growth most often take place without the observance of the human eye or any knowledge of the world. Only God sees the one thus engaged.

God's Power of Forgiveness.

All of Scripture is about forgiveness. Though unspoken this has been God's main experience with mankind. What is spiritual maturity? To understand spiritual maturity we must understand forgiveness. Mankind has been like a very young, rebellious child that depends upon the goodness of its Father for everything in life and yet fights every instruction and discipline given by Him. As intercessors for the lost we must learn to truly love the lost (walking dead) of this world system as the Father loves them. This involves our walking in forgiveness with them. Just as Jesus Christ our Lord forgave us from the Cross saying, *"Father, forgive them for they know not what they do."* So must we forgive. Just as the first martyr of the Church, Stephen, forgave those who stoned him to death, so must we forgive. Stephen's forgiveness was the primary impetus for the salvation of Saul of Tarsus. The other primary impetus was the life and death of Judas Iscariot. Just as satan stole Judas Iscariot from Jesus' ministry, so God was given legal right to steal Saul from satan's kingdom. Judas Iscariot was a man like you and like me. He had like passions. He felt, he thought, he spoke, and he did. He was the friend of Jesus Christ. And he betrayed Jesus. Why? One reason was that he sought for self rather than seeking God's will. Beware of that desire. Secondly, he knew the plan of God when the other disciples didn't. He understood that Jesus was to lay down His life. However, he did not understand that Jesus was to suffer and descend into hell and that Jesus had to overpower death and hell. Jesus saw Judas in hell. What do you think that meeting was like? All the training and understanding of God's ways developed in Saul over his lifetime was turned from satan's kingdom of dead religion to the use of the Lord. Stephen's forgiveness gave the Father God the legal right to send Jesus Christ to Saul on the road to Damascus that he might be saved. Because Stephen forgave Saul, who participated in his death, millions of individuals have been saved over the last two thousand years. Stephen's life counted. His blood counted. It was not in vain. His life was not in vain. His ministry is true ministry and it is ongoing. He imitated Jesus Christ. He was conformed to His death.

What did Paul have to say about these events in his life? *1 Timothy 1:12-17 I give thanks to Him Who has granted me [the needed] strength and made me able [for this], Christ Jesus our Lord, because He has judged and counted me faithful and trustworthy, appointing me to [this stewardship of] the ministry. Though I formerly blasphemed and persecuted and was shamefully and outrageously and aggressively insulting [to Him], nevertheless, I obtained mercy because I had acted out of ignorance in unbelief. And the grace (unmerited favor and blessing) of our Lord [actually] flowed out superabundantly and beyond measure for me, accompanied by faith and love that are [to be realized] in Christ Jesus. The saying is sure and true and worthy of full and universal acceptance, that Christ Jesus (the Messiah) came into the world to save sinners, of whom I am foremost. But I obtained mercy for the reason that in me, as the foremost [of sinners], Jesus Christ might show forth and display all His perfect long-suffering and patience for an example to [encourage] those who would thereafter believe on Him for [the gaining of] eternal life. Now to the King of eternity, incorruptible and immortal, invisible, the only God, be honor and glory forever and ever (to the ages of ages). Amen (so be it). AMP*

Am I calling you to martyrdom? No! However I am calling you to forgive. *Matthew 5:38-48 Ye have heard that it hath been said, An eye for an eye, and a tooth for a tooth: But I say unto you, That **ye resist not evil:** but whosoever shall smite thee on thy right*

cheek, turn to him the other also. And if any man
will sue thee at the law, and take away thy coat, let
him have thy cloke also. And whosoever shall compel
thee to go a mile, go with him twain. Give to him that
asketh thee, and from him that would borrow of thee
turn not thou away. Ye have heard that it hath been
said, Thou shalt love thy neighbour, and hate thine
enemy. But I say unto you, **Love your enemies, bless**
them that curse you, **do good** to them that hate you,
and **pray** for them which despitefully use you, and
persecute you; <u>that ye may be the children of your
Father</u> which is in heaven: for he maketh his sun to
rise on the evil and on the good, and sendeth rain
on the just and on the unjust. For if ye love them
which love you, what reward have ye? do not even the
publicans the same? And if ye salute your brethren
only, what do ye more than others? do not even the
publicans so? Be ye therefore perfect, even as your
Father which is in heaven is perfect. *KJV* Please read
Luke 6:27-36 AMP. Obviously, this cannot be entered
into lightly. However the Church must grow up. We
must mature. The Lord said that in the same way that
we judged, we ourselves would be judged. In the way
that we forgive, we loose the power of God into the
lives of those who sin against us.

"There is coming a day of reckoning for the Body of
Christ. It is a day when those in the Body of Christ
shall go forth through the fires of God that those
that remain should come forth as gold tried in the
fire. Very, very few have ever even 'seen' this day in
the spirit. Most see this time as the work of satan
but it is not. Through the Ages there has been very
little gold produced in the Body of Christ. Most has
been wood, hay and stubble. But there must be gold!
I will have gold and precious gems in My Body! My
Hand is bringing this time forth for it is of God."

When we, because we love God, pour out our love
and forgiveness on sinners and they, as the agents of
satan, steal, kill and destroy us, then God promises
that He shall give back to us pressed down, shaken
together and running over shall men give unto our

bosoms! We cannot out give God! This is the true meaning of the verses in Luke 6. This is one way to overcome evil with good.

*Romans 15:1-3 We then that are strong ought to bear the infirmities of the weak, and not to please ourselves. Let every one of us please his neighbour for **his** good to edification. For even Christ pleased not himself; but, as it is written, The reproaches of them that reproached thee fell on me. KJV* Romans 12:17-21 teach us to let go and let God care for all done to us. We are to only be involved with doing good and forgiving those who have sinned against us. We are to be wise in that which is good and simple concerning evil. We must take especial care of this if we are called to positions of authority where we must adjudicate righteousness. Our forgiveness will be in the way and in the measure we forgive others. Unredeemed flesh, by nature, will sin. It is only doing what "comes natural"!

Spiritual maturity is where love lives. This is where light overcomes the darkness. Darkness has no substance. This is where good overcomes evil. Love is the essence of the gospel. Forgiveness is the essence of the action of love. Sometimes we must choose to lose when we can win. For example: Abraham chose to give Lot the fertile valley rather than take it himself. As mentioned previously this is achieved by the consistent growth of character in an individual. The English poet William Blake, 1757-1827, in his book, The Gates Of Paradise, wrote, "Mutual forgiveness of each vice, such are the Gates of Paradise."

How are we filled with The Trinity of God? We come to God by faith in the shed blood of Jesus Christ. By faith we receive Jesus into our heart. We ask God to baptize us with and in the Holy Spirit in Jesus Name. Then we ask Jesus Christ and the Holy Spirit to fill us with the Presence of the Father God, Who is Love. Thus we are filled with and baptized into the Divine Trinity. *John 14:23 Jesus answered and said to him, "If anyone loves Me, he will keep My word; and My Father will love him, and We will come to him and make Our abode with him. NASU*

2 Peter 3:8, 9 declares to us that God is not willing that any should perish but that all should come to repentance. It is up to us to ask Him to save the lost. We must appropriate what Jesus has already accomplished on the Cross with His shed blood. As we are led by the Holy Spirit to claim the promises of God by believing in our hearts and releasing the faith of God with our tongues tremendous power flows into the lives of those for whom we pray. The corresponding works that accompany our faith are most often evidenced and exercised by our tongues and the words they produce. However, God, upon occasion, does require forgiveness of great evil for great good to occur. God is released in all His love, light and purity to set the lost (walking dead) free!

Being conformed to Christ's death on the Cross while living, walking in love and forgiveness and praying the scripture and in tongues as the Holy Spirit gives utterance are the most powerful and efficient means of causing the lost to be saved. *The effectual, fervent prayer of a righteous person availeth much. James 5:16* It is of pivotal importance that we are righteous. When we release our faith in God's own Word and agree with it, we conform ourselves and those for whom we pray to His image, and give God legal right to move in our behalf. God's Word is eternal. It never changes and neither does He. He is the Living Word, the Lord Jesus Christ. When we pray His words we are opening up the situation to eternity. Eternal results shall occur. Bypassing the fleshly human intellect is to enter upon the threshold of eternity. We open those for whom we pray to the infinite and supernatural results shall be theirs. Why be content with only what our senses perceive? God has so much more for us!

Hearing the Voice of God and allowing the Holy Spirit to impart acutely accurate revelation knowledge of the specific need releases awesome power into the lives of those for whom you pray. Deuteronomy

5:24 And ye said, *"Behold, the Lord our God hath shewed us His glory and His greatness, and we have heard His Voice out of the midst of the fire: we have seen this day that God doth talk with man, and he liveth."* To be an open door for the lost to touch the Hand, Face and Heart of God we must learn to walk in the Spirit of God. We begin by becoming still and peaceful (not passive) and knowing that He is God. (Psalm 46:10) There are many voices in the world and none of them is without signification but only one Voice is the Truth. Our personal relationship with the Lord Jesus Christ will bring many unto salvation as we walk with Him in the supernatural power of the Holy Spirit.

One who really prays not only is a person who often approaches God, but also is a person whose will frequently enters into God's will — that is to say, his thought often enters into God's thought. He walks in the spirit, in love and in forgiveness. He has the Mind of Christ. He is One with God. This is God's goal for relationship with each individual. When we are in right relationship to God and man and His Presence is with us, tremendous power is instantly released. Answers to prayers are realized faster than the speed of light. There is no need for hours, days and years of prayer.

Thanksgiving, praise and worship is the means of entering into this door of oneness with God. Psalm 100. God seeks those who will worship Him in spirit and in truth. Oneness is achieved in secret. God has taught mankind this truth through the example of marriage. This is the new song we sing unto Him. The Holy Spirit's song is much greater than the mere edification of the human soul. A whole new realm of existence opens before the one so exercised. Just as night and day have flow and flux and yet live in harmony so must we. The goal is not to eliminate but to assimilate.

Compassion is defined as sorrow for suffering with the urge to help. Pity, on the other hand, is defined as sorrow with no desire to help. Compassion will

265

take you out of your comfort zone. Compassion is a key ingredient for mankind to be saved. GOD IS LOVE. There are very few individuals who cannot or will not receive when they feel true compassion coming to them from a minister. If you have a low tolerance for mankind you have no business in the ministry. The intercessor is a sower and a reaper, a weeper and a rejoicer. The intercessor is a forgiver and a lover. The intercessor is a person of the heart and the condition of that heart is a primary ingredient for success in the work of intercession. A mean-spirited intercessor is an oxymoron. Selfish motivations will find shipwreck in the work of intercession.

All success in intercession and answered prayer are the result of God, by the power of the Holy Spirit, flowing through the intercessor to meet the need of a hurting and lost humanity. Who is Jesus Christ to you? How well do we know the Lord Jesus Christ, the Holy Spirit and God, the Father? What is our revelation of the Trinity? What is the condition of our heart? What do we know of the Cross? What did God accomplish at the Cross of Calvary for you? The focus of the true intercessor is God and those that are lost and separated from Him—never on self. A compassionate heart of love, humility, self-sac-rifice, forgiveness and obedience to the Holy Spirit and sensitivity to His leadings are key qualities in the work of intercession. To be spiritually sen-sitive is a blessing. Our perspective must be an eternal one and our vision a heavenly one. The things of the earth and the visions of this world system must be allowed to fade away. We must forever leave the world and the affections and lusts thereof.

The ministry of Jesus Christ is not about rules and whether an individual or their actions are right or wrong but rather it is about love. Faith and prayer lead to power but the end of Holy Scripture is not about power it is about love. God is Love! **It is better to love than to be right.** God does not need your sacrifice or your works as much as He does need your love, your tears and your prayers. Do you love those for whom you pray? We must eat from the tree of life not the tree of the knowledge of good and evil. There are fifty-eight kinds of blessings in the Bible. Look for and focus on God's miracles rather than on enemies and problems. Conversely, the most selfish and egotistical bigot that kneels and prays is of more service to their heavenly Father than the purest saint who never begins. The best and most powerful way to learn the heavenly art of intercession is simple—just do it! Be a Nike individual. Always stand firm on the teachings of Romans 6:11 by reckoning yourself to be dead to sin and alive to God. In this way, you can triumph today and reign in the age to come.

Take your place of authority in Christ and use it against the Enemy. Do not look at yourself to see if you are fit or not; just take your place and pray that the Holy Spirit will do His convicting work. Do not pray in the spirit of fear and worry, pray in faith! Remember, *"With God all things are possible." Mark 10:27* God has done everything necessary for the salvation of mankind. He accomplished it through Jesus Christ and His work on the Cross of Calvary. The Holy Spirit is now present in this Age of Grace to implement the salvation that Jesus Christ accomplished. You are not begging God to save the lost—you are warring against the devil to loose the captives. You are praying for the eyes of their understanding to be enlightened that they may see Christ Jesus.

Being strong in the Lord and the power of His Might is not so much about supernatural experiences, though these are wonderful and a great encouragement to our faith. Rather, I believe those who are great in God's Kingdom are those who can take a lickin' and keep on tickin'! It is about endurance. It is about loving Jesus so much that you would rather live a short time for Him in obedience to His will than live a long time for your self. Greatness in the Kingdom of God is about obedience. It is about laying your life down for a mean-spirited sinner whose only hope of eternity is your ability to walk with them in love and forgiveness as they stab you, once again, in the back. I have unending respect for those I see about me who do these things quietly on a daily basis with no fanfare and no "seen" reward. Those who care enough to remove some dark room of sin buried in the depths of another person's character by listening to and obeying the Voice of God to them, as the result of hours of prayer and days of fasting, are truly great and magnificent individuals. Triple Wow!!! They deserve God's best!

Your destiny in God is before you. When you choose obedience to God you choose to fulfill destiny. Nothing and no one can stop you. No devil in hell, no pastor on earth, no parent, no spouse, child, or enemy can keep you from fulfilling your destiny in God. You alone are your worst enemy. To accomplish our destiny we must run from pride, unbelief, fear and hardness of heart. Only two who left Egypt entered the Promised Land. Most fell due to lust, idolatry, immorality, rebellion and complaining. However, if we avoid these areas of sin we can enter our Promised Land. For years it looked gloomy for David, as with Noah, as with Job, as with Daniel, as with Joseph, as with Moses, as with Joshua, as with Hannah, as with Esther, as with the rest of the patriarchs. But remember, there is a hall of fame for those who fulfilled their destiny, and those listed above made it. God is looking for men and women in these last days to add to the list of the patriarchs to be honored at the judgment seat of Christ. I pray we can be among those who fulfill the commission to bring glory to our wonderful Lord!

A man's prayer is only answered if he takes his heart into his hand. Babylonian Talmud Taanit 8a

CHAPTER X

WHAT IS THE WORK OF THE INTERCESSOR?

My dear children, for whom I am again in the pains of childbirth until
Christ is formed in you
Galatians 4:19

"Why [does Yohanan say that one may pray all day long]? Because
prayer never loses its value."
Jerusalem Talmud Berakhot 4:4

He prayeth well, who loveth well
He prayeth best, who loveth best
Both man and bird and beast.
All things both great and small.
'The Rime of the Ancient Mariner' (1798)

A life of prayer is a call to the highest work
with the Lord — the work of intercession that
Jesus is doing. Intercession is the greatest ministry
of all. We're praying the mysteries of God—Christ
in you the hope of glory—and these mysteries have
been hidden deep in the Heart of God. God desires
each generation to have a full revelation of Him and
His Word. It is about the ministry of Jesus Christ
right <u>now</u>. The ministry of the intercessor empowers

the five-fold ministry giftings when the wind of the Holy Spirit blows through them. Real intercession is about praying for the Kingdom—God's Kingdom to come—God's will to be done. Intercession is the result of intimate fellowship with Jesus. Prayer is love melted into worship. Jesus Christ and the Holy Spirit of God are the only true intercessors mentioned in Scripture. Therefore, to truly intercede is to become the vessel through which God prays His will into the earth. The ministry of the intercessor is to work by the will and power of the Holy Spirit the empowering of the groanings to bring about the perfect will of God. It is the ministry of justice and judgment. To serve in the sanctuary is something seldom seen by men. Except for God, no one sees those who serve. They receive neither glory nor praise from men. They shut the door and pray in secret. They are rewarded in secret. In a place unknown to men, they see God's Face, hear His Voice, and walk with Him. They serve in that dark and lonely place within the veil. Intercessors are called to work in the ground of men's hearts, cultivating the soil of repentance and faith toward God. As an intercessor are you called according to God's will, God's plan or God's purpose? Intercessors are the most important people on the earth when they are connected to the right purpose. One utterance in the spirit connected to God's purpose can change the face of the earth. Just never quit! Do not stop in your pursuit of God!

Scripture speaks of numerous veils and these veils are associated with the flesh nature of man, the world system and demonic deceptions. Intercessors have power to remove veils and break the coverings over nations. In Scripture this is referred to as breaking the covering over mountains. Intercession births ministries. By faith in the shed blood of Jesus Christ intercessors remove the veils from man. The flesh nature of man hides the glory of God and causes the life of God to be bound inoperable. It is the work of the intercessor to remove those veils. The veils must be removed from the hearts and minds of God's people that they would be sanctified sons of God before the second coming of the Lord Jesus Christ. *Leviticus 4:6 And the priest shall dip his finger in the blood, and **sprinkle of the blood seven times** before the LORD, **before the vail** of the sanctuary. Song of Solomon 5:7 The watchmen that went about the city found me, they smote me, they wounded me; **the keepers of the walls took away my veil from me**. Ezekiel 13:20-21 "Therefore this is what the Sovereign LORD says: I am against your magic charms with which you ensnare people like birds and I will tear them from your arms; I will set free the people that you ensnare like birds. **I will tear off your veils** and save my people from your hands, and they will no longer fall prey to your power. Then you will know that I am the LORD. Hebrews 10:20-22 By a new and living way, which he hath consecrated for us, **through the veil, that is to say, his flesh;** and having an high priest over the house of God; let us draw near with a true heart in full assurance of faith, having our hearts sprinkled from an evil conscience, and our bodies washed with pure water.*

Rev. Mike Murdock teaches that those who unlock your compassion are those to whom you are assigned. Your worth is determined by the problems you solve. You are a creator, just as your Heavenly Father is The Creator. You were created in His image. Every time you initiate changes you are solving a problem. Your rewards are determined by the problems you solve. Your assignment is always attached to a person. Whose problems are you solving? Total focus determines success. Broken focus determines failure. If you fail with your life it is because you did not solve somebody's problem. Your significance, rewards and worth are attached to your ability to solve others' problems. You sow, then you reap. The problem that infuriates you the most is the problem God has assigned you to solve. It is also a clue to the anointing and timing of God.

In <u>The Handbook For Spiritual Warfare</u> Dr. Ed Murphy writes, "Our task is to help the believer know who he is in Christ, to help him take his position as an heir of God and joint heir with Christ. It is also to help him identify any grounds of sin yet remaining in his life: to confess them, to break with them, to repent, and to receive God's cleansing and forgiveness. Finally, our task is to help the believer break the hold of any demons still hanging on in his life. This is more truth encounter than power encounter."

"Sometimes the believer is not aware of all the evil done to him in his past. He is not even fully aware of certain dimensions of his personal life which provide sin handles, or soul-bruising handles, (or open doors) to which demons often attach themselves. When this state exists we ask the Holy Spirit to reveal anything which gives the oppressing spirits grounds to continue afflicting the believer's life. Amazing things occur in this prayer process."

We can pray with our understanding as much as possible. We must use every avenue at our disposal to pray with power. As we continue in our pursuit of true intercession—we must present the individual, the family, the city, the people group or the nation to God and claim them for His Kingdom because it is God's will that all men be saved and come unto the knowledge of the truth. It is God's will that all men's names be written in the Lamb's Book of Life. Play until you win! It is not given unto man to save himself. An individual person must be presented to the Lord daily and prayer made that that one is saved and brought forward—brought from the darkness to the light.

In 1 Corinthians 4:3, 4 the Word of God says that the god of this world, satan, has blinded the minds of those who are lost, keeping them from hearing the truth. In the Name of Jesus Christ and by faith in His shed blood and in the power of the Holy Spirit we break the power of satan and all powers of darkness that have kept the individual's mind from the glorious gospel of Christ Jesus. The devil no longer has power to blind this person. When we pray as we ought to, our prayer will shake up hell and affect satan. For this reason, satan will rise up to hinder such prayer. All prayers that come from God touch the powers of darkness. Nothing of the will of God is ever released without passing through man. Moreover, the will of God, when released through man, is never free from an encounter with satan. However, he and his entire demonic hierarchy are defeated foes. Our wrestling is not against flesh and blood (Ephesians 6:12). Therefore, we should be inwardly exercised and have spiritual insight so that we gain a knowledge of the spiritual realm and can observe much of satan's "hidden" work. Since the weapons of our warfare are not carnal (of the flesh), we should not employ any earthly means against the fleshly, earthly instruments used by satan. (2 Corinthians 10:4) Rather we must walk in forgiveness toward those who persecute us. Realize it is never the world that persecutes those who operate from the Holy of Holies. It is those who live spiritually in the Inner Courts of God who persecute those who operate from the Holy of Holies. We must hold in honor those of God's children who live in the Inner Courts of God. They truly are His children. They do His works as much as they are able. We are bound by love to honor them and pray for them and forgive whatever comes to hurt us through them. The Father does this for us. We must do so for them.

Prayer in tongues by the power and unction of the Holy Spirit is very effective. It is far, far more powerful than has been taught by the Church. We don't always know how to pray as we should, therefore, we can ask the Holy Spirit to take hold with us and give us the utterance with groanings that cannot be uttered. It is the groanings of the Holy Spirit through us that move us from glory to glory. When we pray according to this kind of burden, we will have a sense that we are divulging the very will of God. Whatever the will or burden that the Lord puts in us, whenever it is reproduced in a person's heart, that person is able to make the Lord's will his own will and pray it out accordingly.

Pray that the works of the Enemy will be torn down in the individual life. *"For the weapons of our warfare are not carnal, but mighty through God to the pulling down of strongholds; casting down imaginations (speculations) and every high thing that exalteth itself against the knowledge of God and bring into captivity every thought to the obedience of Christ." 2 Corinthians 10:4, 5* This shows the mighty power of our spiritual weapons. Pray that all of this will be accomplished in the individual. By faith pray that the person's will be made one with the will of God for their life. Pray their mind be made one with the Mind of Christ. Pray the love of their heart be made one with the Heart of God, Who is Love. Loose the enemy from his assignment in the person's life.

The solid foundation for our prayers is the basis of redemption. In reality, Christ's redemption purchased all mankind, so that we may say that each one is actually God's purchased possession, although he is still held by the Enemy. We must, through the prayer of faith, claim and take for God in the name of the Lord Jesus Christ that which is rightfully His. This can be done only on the basis of redemption. This is not meant to imply that, because God has purchased all persons through redemption, they are automatically saved. They must believe and accept the gospel for themselves; our intercession enables them to do this. The Positional Truth of what Jesus Christ accomplished for us must be made Experiential Truth in each individual's life for the reality and fruit of salvation to occur. This brings about "change" in the individual. It is important to God that we have fruit that remains. Consequently, we must pray that God accomplish an eternal work in those for whom we intercede.

To pray in the name of the Lord Jesus is to ask for, or to claim, the things that the blood of Christ has secured. Therefore, each individual for whom prayer is made should be claimed by name as God's purchased possession, in the name of the Lord Jesus and on the basis of His shed blood. Prayer is the union of the believer's thoughts with the will of God. It is simply the believer speaking out, through his mouth, the will of God. Rev. LaDonna Osborn has written, "When Christians understand that all prayer is rooted in the realities of Christ, His death and resurrection, and when we learn to pray according to what has already been provided, rather than what we want Christ to do, it changes everything!"

Claim the tearing down of all the works of satan, such as false doctrine, unbelief, atheistic teaching and hatred, which the enemy may have built up in their thinking. Pray that their very thoughts will be brought into captivity to the obedience of Christ. Command the Hand of the Lord Jesus Christ to remove from them all hindering spirits and everything not of God. Pray for life, light and the blessings of God's love to be manifested in every area and relation of the individual life. Ask the Father God in the Name of Jesus Christ that you be enabled to see clearly and penetratingly into the individual's heart of hearts by the power of the Holy Spirit and that the Father's Love and Grace be supernaturally imparted unto them — that they would be established and ennobled and strengthened in Christ, that God's peace would be theirs. With the authority of the name of the Lord Jesus Christ, claim their deliverance from the power and persuasion of the evil one and from the love of the world and the lust of the flesh. Claim their deliverance from blindness and darkness of the enemy's kingdom. Command the Hand of the Lord Jesus Christ to loose them from satan's blindness and darkness and bring them to the Kingdom of Light, Life and God's Glory. Pray that their conscience will be convicted, that God may bring them to the point of repentance and that they may listen and believe as they hear or read the Word of God. Pray that God's will and purposes may be accomplished in and through them.

275

Break the powers of darkness and all demons that would hinder the person from the truth. Come against all powers of darkness that have been assigned to take the individual to hell. Loose them from their assignment. Command them to loose the individual and let him go. Quote the Word of God as the Holy Spirit unctions it. If this fails to remove the darkness, then mock and laugh at the devil. He cannot bear ridicule and mocking. Stand in the gap for the individual and be willing to give your life for theirs. Pray for their promotion and favor.

It is our duty to fight for the souls for whom Christ died. Get a personal vision of hell and a revelation that each soul lives eternally. Where will the eternal soul of each individual live—heaven or hell? Intercession must be persistent because of the Enemy. If there were no devil then why did the Holy Spirit lead Jesus to the wilderness, why was He tempted time and time again and why did Christ have to shed His life's blood to overcome him and the sin of mankind? Satan yields only what and when he must, and he renews his attacks in subtle ways. Therefore, prayer must be definite and persistent, even long after definite results are seen. We must pray for the new Christian even after he begins to be established in the faith. Paul said, *"I travail in prayer for you until Christ be formed in you fully." Galatians 4:19 AMP*

As intercession is made, the Holy Spirit will give revelation knowledge and understanding of the individual and their situation. As you wait upon Him, He will give rhema words both by God's Holy Bible and the voice of the Holy Spirit and a myriad of ways as to the specific need of the individual. Pray what God speaks to you back to the Father in the name of Jesus Christ. This releases power in behalf of the individual in the realm of the spirit.

Our God is mighty to the pulling down of all strongholds. He has given us His holy angels, ministering spirits, to minister for us as heirs of salvation. Loose and send forth warring angels to do battle with the demonic forces that have been hindering the person's salvation. Loose and send forth ministering spirits to minister to him. Singing the "new song" in the realm of the spirit releases angels to do battle in behalf of those for whom you pray. Ask God to hasten His Word to perform it as it is written in *Jeremiah 1:12 Then said the LORD unto me, Thou hast well seen: for I will hasten my word to perform it. KJV*

For example: "One time I was interceding for a soul and began to feel that my prayers were largely ineffective, when the Holy Spirit inspired me to begin presenting that person to God in the name of the Lord Jesus. Romans 12:1 instructs us to present our bodies to God which is our spiritual service of worship. As we stand in the gap for those in need we can perform this ministry for them until they are able to do it themselves. As I obeyed this leading, praying, 'I present so-and-so to God in the name of the Lord Jesus,' I felt that my prayers were gradually becoming more effective. It seemed that I was drawing that person from deep within the very camp of the Enemy. Then I was able to proceed as usual claiming every detail of that life for God, using the power of the blood against the Enemy." (from The Handbook for Spiritual Warfare by Dr. Ed Murphy) When strategies of the enemy or negative information are revealed it is crucial that evil is overcome with good. Turn that situation around through identificational repentance for the individual and the release of positive faith in their behalf. This is true warfare in the spiritual realm. Nehemiah, Ezra and Daniel prayed prayers of identificational repentance for their fellowman and their nation, thus changing the judgments of God and history. This is a high call of God.

The Bible says in *Romans 15:1, "Now we who are strong ought to bear the weaknesses or infirmities of those without strength and not just please ourselves."* As an intercessor that stands in the gap for those who are far from God we carry the weaknesses of

277

those for whom we pray. The outworking of this truth has many different facets. For example, as we pray and intercede for more than one individual we have to walk very sensitively in the realm of the spirit that we are able to ascertain whose particular need we are experiencing. Just as the Apostle Paul in Holy Scripture commands us to put on the whole armor of God we are also commanded to put on Christ. By faith we may put on the glory of God. When we walk in the Holy Spirit, in Christ Jesus, the supernatural power of the Father (Almighty God) flows through us. I also believe we can "put on" those for whom we intercede by faith. As we do this we know where their weaknesses and darkness lie. We are better able to pray and exercise faith and the power of God to bring them the change needed to be conformed to the image of Christ Jesus.

When we carry another's soul it may involve carrying their physical symptoms. These symptoms are not to be retained as one's own but they are to be presented or given unto the Father that He may deal with them. A prerequisite to walking in this ability is forgiveness of our enemies, those who hate us and those who hate us without a cause. This enables us to be clean conduits of God's power. We command the Hand of the Lord Jesus Christ to remove that symptom, weakness or darkness and stand on the rhema word of God given to us by the Holy Spirit as we pray. If we deal with issues in the realm of the spirit we can prevent their manifesting in the natural, fleshly realm. In their place we receive even more of His Presence and His Holy Spirit. We, ourselves, continue to walk in the divine life that Jesus Christ purchased for us with His shed blood.

For some we become aware of a particular sin or stronghold that they are unable to overcome or may even be unaware of. The same process still applies. We present the sin to the Father that He may deal with it. We forgive them their sin. We command the Hand of the Lord Jesus Christ to remove the sin, weakness or whatever as we present the individual to the Father. We speak forth the rhema word of God that the Holy Spirit quickens to us and we praise the Father for His mercy and grace. Call forth the resurrection power of God by the action of His Right Hand and His Arm that awakened and quickened the faculties of Jesus Christ in His resurrection from the dead. This is particularly effective when done with the Holy Spirit upon one standing in ministry position as an Agent of Authority. Hallelujah! We continue to stand in the righteousness that Jesus Christ died to obtain for us. In this way we give God the legal right to enter into the individual's life to bring the experiential reality of the supernatural presence of God. As this is practiced over and over again the individual is brought from the darkness to the light. They are changed or transformed into His image and saved from hell and brought to heaven. We remain hidden behind the veil of the Holy Spirit and His anointing which is efficacious to the breaking of every yoke and the destruction of every stronghold. It is the power of God that distributes every grace and glory that already belongs to each child of God in their position at the right of God in Christ Jesus in heavenly places.

Why is this so? Everything that exists IS. It cannot be lost. Faith is not lost. Fear is not lost. They must come to fruition somewhere, sometime, in someone. There are great evils and bad things in this earth. Yet by faith, intercessors have the ability before God to cause the thing to be diffused and to pass away. When they, who have been judged, and who have died to self, take sin upon themselves, that sin has no place in them and it must pass away. Satan had nothing "in" Jesus Christ. He is innocent. He is Pure. Therefore when sin is put upon Him it must pass away. The same must be true of each intercessor. Everything in us will be tried by the light, the fire and the glory of God. Is your eye selfish? Do you own or possess something you cannot give away? Do you love things more than people? Do you love pleasure more than the work of God? Is there some part of your life that no one else has a right to, even God? Do you have an area of your life behind a closed door? Is there a NO TRESPASSING sign on a part of your life?

True intercessors are not brought lower or destroyed by their association with the sin in others. True intercessors continue to be transformed from glory to glory into His image. The revelation knowledge of the Holy Spirit is not given to spread gossip or to bring judgment upon others but it is given that those prayed for will come from the darkness to the light. Are we willing to work in the Father's vineyard? Do we want to work in the family business? If we want to work for the Father we must be willing to learn His ways. Spiritual things are dealt with in the spirit. We do not deal with the things of the spirit in the flesh. We must walk in forgiveness. We have to do things secretly and be able to keep a secret. We have to lay down the very human desire for recognition. God requires that all glory be given to Him.

Why is this? For one thing, it is for our protection. When someone stands out from the crowd they are an easy target for the marksman. The enemy goes about as a roaring lion seeking whom he may devour. I pray it won't be you or me! Let us remain hidden in the secret place of the Most High, which is prayer, abiding under the shadow of the Almighty. Another reason for God's working as He does is that in His goodness, kindness and gentleness He is about the business of saving and building us up, not of destroying us. We are to be wise in what is good, and innocent in what is evil that the God of peace will soon crush satan under our feet. Another reason for the necessity of absolute control of one's words is that continuing on with God in obedience to His will shall ultimately lead to His power filling and producing your every word. We must speak His Words and they must be holy words. Only the words of God Almighty bring Life in a 360° radius, above and beneath.

Each individual has the potential to attain to the fullness of God in Christ Jesus. Although the reality

of the matter reveals that there are 30-fold, 60-fold
and 100-fold Christians, yet each babe in Christ is
as yet unformed and malleable in the Master's Hand.
The potential to have Christ fully formed in an individual life is a possibility for all. The desire
must be present in the heart of the individual but
it is the Lord who shall will and do all His good
pleasure. Persistent endurance and unfailing long-
suffering shall prevail. Our part is to pray and
not to give up. Our part is to love those for whom
Christ Jesus died. If you don't love those for whom
you pray, your prayers may not be very effectual. God
is Love. The highest goal of this life is love. Our
faith works by love. We must speak forth the truth
in love. Judgment is not the goal of the intercessor.
Love is the goal of the intercessor.

Thank God that our spiritual weapons are mighty
and that our authority in Christ is far above all the
authority of the rulers, powers and forces of darkness, so that the enemy must yield. It takes faith
and patience and persistence.

What does one do to bring salvation to the lost
humanity of this earth? No man can save, unless he
understands the sinner. Why were the Apostle Peter
and the Apostle Paul so mightily used of God in the
foundation of the early church? God used the Apostle
Peter to found the Church of the Lord Jesus Christ
as the second son of God, conformed to the image of
Christ. Jesus loved Peter. He was the first member
of fallen mankind to experience the process of salvation. He was used as a great power for God as a
natural born leader. Peter could never have been the
after power he was, had he not first learned his own
weakness. His passion for Christ had to be based on
reality. Peter denied knowing Christ three times.
His denial of Christ was the actual equipping that
enabled him to be a door of entrance to eternal life
for so many. Satan came and sifted him like wheat,
devouring his flesh life and destroying his natural
pride, leadership and strength. Then and only then
could the love of God begin to grow in him. All

miracle work is not the work of a moment as so often men imagine. As the Apostle Peter experienced first-hand the forgiveness of God in his moment of abject remorse, his foundation was secure on the rock of God's love. Peter tested the forgiveness of God in his own person and was, therefore, the best quali-fied to minister Jesus Christ as Savior. He was Jesus' first convert after His resurrection. The other apos-tles followed. He was the second son of God brought forth by the Father. It was God's love that Jesus Christ spoke to him about in His post resurrection appearance on the beach. Jesus called Peter to tend His lambs, feed His sheep and guide His flock. He grew in the divine love of God from a beginning of true humility. Jesus provoked Peter by asking him about the quality of his love for the Master. Just as Peter had denied knowing Christ three times, just so Jesus asked Peter if he loved Him three times. When he experienced the "phileo" of God, the deep, instinctive, companionship and friendship of the Lord that is deep and personal, as for a close friend; then he could begin to grow into the "agapeo", the reasoning, intentional, spiritual devotion, as one loves the Father, the Most High. This must be the goal of each Christian. Our growth in love is the path of spiritual victory. Yet that growth in love must be the truth within us. In other words, if it is really real love in us it will go through the fires of testing and come forth as pure gold. As most of us are, when tried by the fires of satan in our flesh, Peter was knocked back to his foundational phileo love of Jesus. It was only then that true growth in real love could occur. Peter was the second son of God and the first man, born in the sin of Adam, to receive the "new nature" of Christ on earth. Peter was called as an apostle to the Jews and was a leader of the Jerusalem church. God used an unlearned fish-erman as leader of a people who were experts in His Word. God used the Apostle Peter to remove the spir-itual uncleanness of the Gentile nations through the vision given him at Simon the tanner's house. He was the first man used to bring the Baptism of the Holy Spirit to the Gentiles with the evidence of speaking in other tongues. He admitted the first Gentiles into the church by baptism.

Matthew 16:15-20 He saith unto them, But whom say ye that I am? And Simon Peter answered and said, Thou art the Christ, the Son of the living God. And Jesus answered and said unto him, Blessed art thou, Simon Barjona: for flesh and blood hath not revealed it unto thee, but my Father which is in heaven. And I say also unto thee, That thou art Peter, and upon this rock I will build my church; and the gates of hell shall not prevail against it. And I will give unto thee the keys of the kingdom of heaven: and whatsoever thou shalt bind on earth shall be bound in heaven: and whatsoever thou shalt loose on earth shall be loosed in heaven. Then charged he his disciples that they should tell no man that he was Jesus the Christ. KJV

Genesis 22:2 And he said, Take now thy son, thine only son Isaac, whom thou lovest, and get thee into the land of Moriah; and offer him there for a burnt offering upon one of the mountains which I will tell thee of. KJV

John 21:15-18 So when they had dined, Jesus saith to Simon Peter, Simon, son of Jonas, lovest (agapeo) thou me more than these? He saith unto him, Yea, Lord; thou knowest that I love (phileo) thee. He saith unto him, Feed my lambs. He saith to him again the second time, Simon, son of Jonas, lovest (agapeo) thou me? He saith unto him, Yea, Lord; thou knowest that I love (phileo) thee. He saith unto him, Feed my sheep. He smith unto him the third time, Simon, son of Jonas, lovest (phileo) thou me? Peter was grieved because he said unto him the third time, Lovest (phileo) thou me? And he said unto him, Lord, thou knowest all things; thou knowest that I love (phileo) thee. Jesus saith unto him, Feed my sheep. Verily, verily, I say unto thee, When thou wast young, thou girdedst thyself, and walkedst whither thou wouldest: but when thou shalt be old, thou shalt stretch forth thy hands, and another shall gird thee, and carry thee whither thou wouldest not. KJV

The Apostle Paul, taught by Rabbi Gamileil, grew up in privilege and relationship with the spiritual leadership of his day. He was the epitome of all man knew of God through religion before Christ came. His knowledge resulted in ignorance and blindness when confronted by the reality of Christ Jesus. He wrote from personal experience when writing to the Ephesian church, *"Ephesians 4:18 ...Having the understanding darkened, being alienated from the life of God through the ignorance that is in them, because of the blindness of their heart KJV* After having truly met Christ he counted all his attainments as dung for the excellency of knowing Christ. He was the apostle chosen by God, Himself, to replace Judas Iscariot. He was the author of two-thirds of the New Testament, having spent his entire life prior to salvation in the study of Scripture. The Apostle Paul was used of God as the first missionary to establish over 300 New Testament churches among Gentile nations. Jesus told His disciples He had much more to tell them but they were not able to bear it when He was with them. God used the Apostle Paul to expound the Mind of Christ to His people. Thus he was used of God, via the Mind of Christ, to establish the foundations of truth in spiritual growth for all who belong to the universal Church of Jesus Christ. Yet, because of his lack of love, his religious zeal, his murder and torture of the early Christians, his entire life after salvation in Christ Jesus was one of suffering and hardship. As a missionary he took the gospel to the Gentile nations and founded the Church as we know it today. After conversion he epitomized the Mind of Christ. From studying his introductions in each epistle we can readily ascertain that Paul grew in the grace and truth of Jesus Christ into his apostleship. He received many revelations and had supernatural experiences in God. His calling as an apostle of God involved personal spiritual growth even though he had been called of God before his birth. Christ Jesus was first presented to the Gentiles when the Magi attended his birth in Bethlehem and gave Him gifts. The Apostle Paul was the missionary of the Gentiles.

To bring salvation to a lost person we must literally and spiritually carry the blood of Jesus Christ to that person. It is the blood of Jesus that sets the captives free. It is faith in the shed blood of Jesus Christ that is the spontaneous combustion causing salvation to occur. What is the blood of Jesus Christ? The Bible says that the life is in the blood. Jesus is our way, our truth, our life. Jesus is the light of mankind. Blood is literally coagulated light. Life and light make up the blood of Christ. When we speak forth the Word of God under the anointing as we have experienced it and it has been worked out in our own personal life, we release spiritual life and spiritual light. A spiritually dead person receiving this light and life by faith, as they receive Jesus Christ into their heart, is spontaneously ignited by the power of the Holy Spirit and salvation occurs. Life, light, love, laughter — these forces are the spiritual power that sets the captives free through faith in the shed blood of Jesus Christ. It is the combination of received faith in the human heart and God's power by the Person of the Holy Spirit resident in His delegated Agent of Authority that ignites the spark of eternal life in His Seed.

Light expels and judges darkness. Sin and darkness are equal. The flesh nature is darkness. Sin is separation from God. Yet darkness has no substance. God is light. When God is present sin is judged instantly. One meaning of "If we walk in the light" means if we walk in fellowship with God. What is in Christ cannot sin; what is in Adam can sin and will sin whenever satan is given a chance to exert his power over it. When a born-again, Spirit-filled believer who has experienced the Cross of Christ allows his flesh to predominate and exert itself, the devil has a heyday if allowed to. We must take up our Cross daily. Our walk in the Spirit and in love is a moment by moment experience with God. A person can be reconciled and forgiven and satan can still have a foothold in his life. When a person is forgiven, the devil can still harass the person because the seed of sin is in the life. When a person is sanctified, the devil can't touch him. Satan can harass a reconciled child but cannot touch a sanctified child. They are most holy unto God. You cannot be sanctified and backslide. You can be reconciled and backslide. Once sanctified it is impossible to walk away. You become holy as God is holy. Without holiness no man shall see the Lord.

Pastor Benny Hinn teaches that the Apostle Paul attained to the removal of the seed of sin. The power of sin was removed from his life. When death to flesh takes place we are cleansed by the blood of Christ. When this happens we receive absolute authority over the devil. It is written in Romans, chapter 6, that he that is dead is free from sin. The strength of sin is the Law. Darkness is Satan's grip on the soul. When a person is sanctified all darkness goes and God's light enters them. I once personally experienced the light of a sanctified prophet of God within my spirit and will never forget it. I have also experienced the bright, bright golden light in the spirit of a true apostle of God!

When we honor the blood of Jesus Christ, God honors us. The blood of Jesus is His life. When the blood is understood and applied, the power of God is released. The blood of Jesus not only forgives but brings cleansing. The blood of Jesus cleanses our soul, removing the old man, and cleanses our old life. Jesus Christ's blood purges our conscious-ness of sin. Christ's blood sanctifies our new man and brings us into union with God. Cleansing by the blood of Jesus comes as a result of crying unto God for it. The moment you are cleansed you receive the power of God to be sanctified. To understand sanc-tification we must understand the holiness of God. Sanctification is obtained when we become one with the Holy One. Oneness with God Almighty is a vast subject. All veils are removed. When this occurs we enter into His rest. Jesus died that we may be sanctified. A dedicated vessel will never be forsaken.

There is a three-fold cord in the spirit — the Love of God, the Power of God and the Word of God: the Trinity of GOD. This is THE three-fold cord that cannot and will not be broken. All three must be in operation for proper balance to be maintained. Each and every part is vital for the full expression of truth, power and love to occur. Only God Himself can bring this to pass in the individual's life. Those He calls He also equips.

The New Testament Epistles contain several imperative commands. We must be doers of these commands in the "continuing present". We must trust God specifically. These are not holy suggestions. Our obedience to these commands is crucial to the success of our spiritual life. We must <u>abide</u> in Him. To abide means to obey, realizing it is not what we know. It is what we <u>do</u>! God does not save people and fill them with His Holy Spirit to abandon them to the world, the flesh and the devil. God has an abundant provision of supernatural protection for believers in Christ Jesus. It is freely spoken of in the Word of God. However, it is up to each believer to find this protection and to put it into practice personally. You must be a doer of the protection of God to be protected. Otherwise, you and those you hold dear will be sitting ducks for satan and his demonic forces of evil. The choice is yours. We must not seek the world's wisdom for knowledge to get through this life responsibly. The Church of the Lord Jesus Christ is responsible before God to preach and teach the whole truth of the counsel of God. It is important to note that you are only held accountable for the light you walk in. In other words, if you know and understand a truth of God then He holds you accountable to do it. If there is something you don't understand or don't know about, then God does not hold you accountable for it. God is not unjust. Yet we are commanded in Scripture to grow in the grace and in the knowledge of the Lord Jesus Christ. We must make listening to God a moment-by-moment habit. Joyfully and thankfully receive His correction and truly repent, keeping your heart and mind clean before Him.

Some imperative commands that keep us in right relationship to God and man and help build our character as we are conformed to the image of God in Christ Jesus are:

1. Be born-again.	John 3:3-7
2. Receive the Holy Spirit.	John 20:22
3. Love the Lord your God with all your heart, mind, soul & strength.	Mark 12:30
4. Be still, and know that I AM God.	Psalm 46:10
5. My people shall not say, "I am sick".	Isaiah 33:24
6. If you are sick: pray.	James 5:13
7. If you are happy: sing praises.	James 5:14
8. In God we trust.	2 Samuel 22:3
9. Jesus Christ did not receive honor from men.	John 5:41
10. Present your body to God as a living sacrifice.	Romans 12:1
11. Be renewed in the spirit of your mind.	Romans 12:2
12. Put off the old man with its weakness, failure and fear.	Ephesians 4:22
13. Put on the new man, created in Christ Jesus in righteousness and true holiness.	Ephesians 4:24
14. Put on the whole armor of God.	Ephesians 6:10-17
15. Put on the armor of light.	Romans 13:12
16. Do not have a spirit of fear.	2 Timothy 1:7
17. Do not call any man father.	Matthew 23:9
18. Do not call any man teacher.	Matthew 23:8
19. Do not put your trust in man.	Psalm 118:8, 9
20. Do not put your trust in princes.	Psalm 146:3
21. Love one another. Remain in My love.	John 13:34
22. Walk in love with your fellow man.	Ephesians 5:2
23. As far as possible, live in peace with every man.	2 Corinthians 13:11
24. Be kindly affectioned one to another.	Romans 12:10
25. Do not lay hands suddenly on any man.	1 Timothy 5:22
26. Pray for those who persecute you.	Matthew 5:44

27.	Forgive all.	Mark 11:25
28.	Judge not.	Matthew 7:1
29.	Ask God for wisdom in faith believing.	James 1:5
30.	Speak the truth in love.	Ephesians 4:15
31.	Worship God in spirit and in truth.	John 4:23, 24
32.	Worship God, making melody in your heart, with psalms, hymns and spiritual songs.	Ephesians 5:19
33.	Give God ALL the glory.	Psalm 29:2
34.	Enter into God's rest.	Hebrews 4:4
35.	Fret not. (Do not worry.)	Psalm 37:1-9
36.	Abide in Me.	John 15:4
37.	Obey My commandments.	Deuteronomy 27:10

✝

CHAPTER XI

THE ARMOR OF GOD

*W*e have been seated at the right hand of God in Christ Jesus by the operation of the faith of God. We are being conformed to the image of Christ as we are changed from glory to glory. Psalm 91:4 in the Living Bible says *He will shield you with his wings! They will shelter you. His faithful promises are your armor.* In Ephesians 6:10-18 the Apostle Paul charges us: *In conclusion, be strong in the Lord — be empowered through your union with Him; draw your strength from Him — that strength which His boundless might provides. Put on God's whole armor — the armor of a heavy-armed soldier, which God supplies—that you may be able successfully to stand up against all the strategies and the deceits of the devil. For we are not wrestling with flesh and blood — contending only with physical opponents — but against the despotisms, against the powers, against the master spirits who are the world rulers of this present darkness, against the spirit forces of wickedness in the heavenly supernatural sphere. Therefore put on God's complete armor, that you may be able to resist and stand your ground on the evil day of danger, and having done all the crisis demands, to stand firmly in your place. Stand therefore — hold your ground — having tightened the belt of truth around your loins,*

*and having put on the breastplate of integrity and
of moral rectitude and right standing with God; and
having shod your feet in preparation to face the
enemy with the firm-footed stability, the prompt-
ness and the readiness produced by the good news of
the Gospel of peace. Lift up over all the covering
shield of saving faith, upon which you can quench
all the flaming missiles of the wicked one. And take
the helmet of salvation and the sword the Spirit
wields, which is the Word of God. Pray at all times
— on every occasion, in every season — in the Spirit,
with all manner of prayer and entreaty. To that end
keep alert and watch with strong purpose and perseverance, interceding in behalf of all the saints —
God's consecrated people. Amplified Bible*

Each element of the armor mentioned in Ephesians 6
is an attribute of Jesus Christ when studied out in
the Word of God. Truth, Righteousness, Peace, Faith,
the spoken Word, and the Mind of Christ all refer to
the character of Jesus Christ personally. As we put
off our old, unredeemed nature and put on the character of Christ Jesus we become invulnerable to the
slings and arrows of satan through unredeemed men.
We are hidden in the "secret place" of the Most High,
safe from the strife of tongues.

We must also add to our confession those scriptural promises quickened to us by the Holy Spirit as
personal rhema words from our Heavenly Father. These
are the personal attributes that fit our armor to us
alone for the work we are called of God to accomplish.

It is as we take the literal Person of Jesus
Christ into our spirit, soul and body, by faith that
we are able to stand against the enemy. We do this
as we conform our belief system to the belief system
of God as presented in the example of the person of
Jesus Christ in the Scriptures. Roy Hicks teaches
that there are five ways to enter into the realm of
the spirit: The Sacrament of Communion; Confession
of the Word of God; Thanksgiving; Praise and Worship
of God; and Praying in Tongues by the Unction of
the Holy Spirit. When we receive the elements of

communion personally or in a corporate setting we are receiving the blood and body of Christ by faith. Supernatural life, truth and healing come to us as we partake. The confession of the Word of God and the exercise of faith is one of the ways to enter in. Confession must be made of the Word of God. If you confess the Word of God as it is written in Scripture your confession will be primarily about God and you shall be conformed to His image. As we vocalize who we are in Christ Jesus we mount up with wings of eagles in the realm of the spirit. We take our place in the heavenlies in Christ Jesus at the right hand of the Father God. We are then ready to exercise the dominion of God in the earth today. We are ready, as intercessors, to stand in the gap for a hurting humanity and see them changed in like manner into the image of Christ Jesus. We are ready to serve a hurting humanity and see needs met in a real way. Our goal must be to see the will of the Father God performed and His Kingdom come, not the will of man, even one of His children. In Psalm 100 the Lord has shown us clearly the proper way to enter His Presence by thanksgiving, praise and worship. As we pray in tongues, unctioned by the Holy Spirit, God will speak to us and reveal His strategies. We can also pray in tongues without God revealing anything to us. God is God and great things occur when we pray!

The first piece of armor listed in Scripture is the Belt of Truth. This is because all other pieces of armor are dependent upon the Truth of God. Jesus Christ is the Way, the Truth and the Life. Jesus Christ is the Light of the world. He is all honesty and truth. Those who love what is honest and good and true come to Him when He is lifted up among them. Liberty is a result of the truth. Liberty and freedom are a result of honesty and truth. Loving what is true, honest and good is one of the prerequisites of being Baptized in the Holy Spirit. As God, He is a Speaking Spirit. He is the Word of God.

You can never put the Breastplate of Righteousness on unless you have already put on the Belt of Truth so that your righteousness is based on the Word of God. The four requirements of righteousness are to 1) know Who God is: Heavenly Father, Jesus Christ His Son and the Holy Spirit, 2) know who you are, 3) know who your enemy is, and 4) know how to worship God. You will receive experiential righteousness by God's grace. Once you have the Breastplate of Righteousness on you have peace with God—the Shoes of the Preparation of the Gospel of Peace. Jesus Christ was not raised from the dead until the full price of sin had been paid and when He was raised mankind was justified (when each individual receives justification by faith). We are justified by faith and through our faith we have peace with God. Peace with God and man brings about experiential righteousness. It is that right positioning at the place where Jesus' Heart rested upon the Cross of Calvary.

Of particular note are the breastplates. Three are mentioned in Scripture. I personally believe there is a progressive growth in grace with regard to our hearts. We first appropriate Jesus' own righteousness. It is a free gift. Then, as we exercise the fruit of the Holy Spirit in self-control, we grow in faith and love. This gives us strength to relate to others. Thirdly, as we grow in our love of the Father and adoration of the Holy Spirit we consecrate ourselves unto Him by judging our own selves and repenting, receiving Jesus' cleansing blood and the Father's restoration and empowerment. Thus our hearts and lungs are changed into the image of Christ and we receive strength to do the will of God in works of service. We receive, by faith, the Heart of God and the Breath of His Holy Spirit, the Ruwach (in Hebrew). "His own arm delivered Him and His own justice strengthened Him.....faithfulness is the breastplate that arms Him, that saving power the helmet that guards His Head; vengeance the garment He wears, jealous love the mantle that wraps Him round." "...love of right the helmet He wears, faithfulness the strength that girds Him." "His own faithfulness is the breastplate He will put on, unswerving justice the helmet He wears, a right cause His shield unfailing."

What is the Gospel of Peace? *All is well! Thy God has claimed His throne! Isaiah 52:7.* Our enthroned Savior gives us His confidence. The will of the Father has come to pass concerning His Promise. God's confidence is our preparation to walk. Shoes are something we wear to walk in. In order to walk we must first be balanced and stable. We must have use of both our two legs. Walking denotes movement in opposition.

Mentioned together in Ephesians 6:17 are the Helmet of Salvation and the Sword of the Spirit, which is the Word of God. This bespeaks of eye/hand coordination. It is the combination of thought and the spoken word as it is unctioned by the Holy Spirit that dispels the darkness with the Light of the Glory of God in the Face of Jesus Christ. The Mind of Christ expressed by the Speaking Spirit of God creates life and good and brings the will of the Father to pass in the earth. 2 Corinthians 4:6; Isaiah 11:5; 59:17; Wisdom 5:19 and 1 Thessalonians 5:8 give us clues and a greater understanding of Ephesians 6:17.

God's kingdom is opposite and upside down of the world's kingdom. We go to battle by humbling ourselves under the mighty hand of God. We increase by giving away our goods. We are strong in the Lord by allowing our self-life to become weak. We receive the life of God by allowing our self-life to die. We overcome hate and persecution with love, forgiveness, and kindness. In order to prepare for battle we do not exercise our bodies, we use faith in the spoken Word of God. Our faith comes by hearing and hearing by the Word of God. We are exalted when we become the servant of all. Whoever finds his lower life will lose the higher life, and whoever loses his lower life on Jesus Christ's account will find the higher life. Therefore, every one who acknowledges Jesus Christ before men and confesses Him out of a state of Oneness with Him, He will also acknowledge that one before His Father Who is in heaven, and confess abiding in him. Jesus Christ did not come to bring peace but to bring a sword. We must take up our cross and follow Him, conforming wholly to His example in living, and if need be, in dying also.

Do you realize that what you know from the Word of God will save your life? In his book, <u>My Utmost For His Highest</u>, Oswald Chambers writes that character determines how a man interprets God's will. *Psalm 18:23-26 I was also upright before him, and I kept myself from mine iniquity. Therefore hath the LORD recompensed me according to my righteousness, according to the cleanness of my hands in his eyesight. With the merciful thou wilt shew thyself merciful; with an upright man thou wilt shew thyself upright; with the pure thou wilt shew thyself pure; and with the froward thou wilt shew thyself froward. KJV* Character + Discipline = Protection. This is crucial to your existence so it is worth your time to understand. Godly character = integrity = being the same in your thoughts, words and actions. Every choice of obedience to that still, small voice inside us strengthens our character in our inner man. Character is the issue. It is the difference between life and death. This is in direct relation to the Mind of Christ, a crucial part of the armor of God. We must be the same, i.e. to have integrity or be one, to be strong and have the power of God flow through us. Multiple vision, division or multiple personalities are sources of our defeat and destruction. We must be one. We must understand and know who we are and why we are. What is our purpose? What is the Call of God upon us? Why are we on the planet at this time in history? Who have we been sent to? Where is our provision? What gift is within us to help another?

During the 911 crisis our country faced in 2001, Rev. Kenneth Copeland was a bulwark of understanding and peace to the Body of Christ. He taught several crucial truths: "Now I want to communicate something to you that is vital to your life and to your protection. Heads up! This is important! How does the enemy get through a believer's line of protection? If a believer is confessing the Word of God over their lives and is walking in obedience to the instruction and leading of the Holy Spirit and yet the enemy still gains entrance to their lives to steal, kill and destroy, how did it happen? It can happen if a person is <u>violating a higher law</u> than the promises he or she is confessing. This is a crucial truth. Can you see how this relates to the issue of character? The Apostle Paul tells us exactly what that violation is in *Romans 13:9, 10 For this, Thou shalt not commit adultery, Thou shalt not kill, Thou shalt not steal, Thou shalt not bear false witness, Thou shalt not covet; and if there be any other commandment, it is briefly comprehended in this saying, namely, Thou shalt love thy neighbour as thyself. Love worketh no ill to his neighbour: therefore love is the fulfilling of the law.* It is easy to see how character and love are God's prerequisites to walking in Divine protection". Both Rev. Kenneth Copeland and Rev. Gloria Copeland have excellent teachings on protection.

As you read, out loud, the following confessions of the Word of God exercise your faith in the person and the power of Jesus Christ. As much as possible quote Scripture exactly. I believe it is an open door to error when people too freely paraphrase the Word of God. If there are words you don't understand look them up in a dictionary. Public Libraries have many dictionaries and you may look at them for free. Add those promises and scripture passages that the Holy Spirit has quickened to you personally over time for the call of God upon your life, believing God to conform you to your confession.

I believe in my heart and confess with my mouth that
Jesus Christ is my Savior and my Lord by faith in His
shed blood, in His virgin birth, sacrificial death
and resurrection.

I PUT OFF THE OLD MAN, with all its weakness,
failure and fear. I put off all PREJUDICE, whether
racial, moral, economic or gender. I put off all
UNBELIEF, all darkness, hardness of heart, ignorance,
disobedience, rebellion and stubbornness. I put off
all covetousness and greed, which is idolatry. I put
off all IDOLATRY, which leads to deception. I put off
all DECEPTION, refusal to love the truth, adherence
to the Law rather than grace, self-exaltation and
pride, false signs, wonders, miracles and offense.
I put off all instability and imbalance which leads
to ERROR. I lay aside my old self and all lusts of
deceit. I put off all lying and stealing, all bitterness, wrath, anger, clamor, slander, malice and
Unforgiveness. I put off all RELIGION, all wickedness
and twistedness. I put off all forms of godliness
without the substance thereof. I put off all hypocrisy
and compromise. I am a doer of the Word of God. I do
not deceive my own self by apathy, passivity, pride,
selfishness or disobedience to God or His authority.

I PRESENT MY BODY TO GOD, a living sacrifice, holy,
which is my reasonable service of worship. I am not
conformed to this world but only to the image of God
in Christ Jesus. I RENEW MY MIND in spirit and in
truth, proving what is the good and well-pleasing
and perfect will of God. I ask for the ancient paths,
wherein is the good way, that I might find rest for my
soul. I STAND still and see the salvation of the Lord.
I WAIT upon Him in stillness as He fights my battles.
I thank and praise the Lord, removing the precious
from the vile, as I consider His wondrous works. With
Him there is mercy and plenteous redemption.

I PUT ON THE NEW MAN, created in Christ Jesus, in
righteousness and true holiness. I put on the armor
of the light on the right hand and on the left. I put
on Christ. I put on lovingkindness, tender-hearted-
ness, goodness, gentleness, kindness, meekness, and

humility of mind. I put on the same attitude of mind that was in Christ Jesus. He did not regard equality with God a thing to be grasped but humbled Himself before God, emptied Himself and took upon Himself the form of a servant and became obedient. I put on all longsuffering, all forbearance, all patience and all steadfastness. I put on THE ARMOR OF LIGHT for I am a child of the light. I put on incorruption. I put on immortality.

Upon my loins I put the GIRDLE OF TRUTH for You, Lord Jesus Christ, are my Way, my Truth and my Life and I come to You, Father God, by Christ Jesus. I continue in Your Word and I am Your disciple indeed for I know the truth and the truth sets me free. Wherever the Spirit of the Lord is, there is liberty. I am judged by no law, but the Law of Liberty for whom the Lord sets free is free indeed. Through me today, Lord, You open blinded eyes, open deaf ears, heal the broken-hearted, cause the lame to leap and walk, proclaim the acceptable year of the Lord and set the captives free for Your glory. I give You all the glory. I pray I, and all true Christians, would be of the same mind, the same spirit and the same purpose in Christ Jesus. Knit our hearts together in love and let us seek to outdo one another in honor. Deliver me from evil. Deliver me from the Evil One. Deliver me from wicked and perverse men for not all have faith. Deliver me from the traditions and vain philosophies of men. Deliver me from all self-deception and self-delusion. Thank You, Father, that You have filled me with Your Holy Spirit of Truth. Holy Spirit, You teach me the Word of God. You lead me and guide me into all the Truth. You disclose to me the things of the Father and of Jesus Christ. You remind me of the words of Jesus Christ. You show me things to come. You do the greater works through me. You raise the dead through me. You quicken my mortal body by Your power according to the Word of God in which it is written that by Jesus stripes I was healed. You strengthen me with might in my inner man so that I may be strong in the Lord, and in the

power of Your might. I thank You that You strengthen
me according to the riches of Your glory, to be
strengthened with might by Your Spirit in my inner
man. Thank You, Heavenly Father, that You enable me
to speak the truth in love for Your glory.

Over my heart I put on the BREASTPLATE OF
RIGHTEOUSNESS, the BREASTPLATE OF FAITH AND LOVE
with all self-control, the BREASTPLATE OF JUDGMENT
whereby I consecrate myself to God with His beauty,
lights, glories and perfections. My heart is strong
in the Lord and in the power of Your might. I sanctify my heart unto You, Father God, as Your throne.
Your throne is based on righteousness, justice and
judgment. Your Kingdom is righteousness, peace and
joy in the Holy Ghost. For Jesus Christ is made unto
me wisdom, righteousness, sanctification and redemption. God show me the secrets of wisdom. I pray for
understanding and insight into both sides of sound
wisdom. I pray I would be skillful in wisdom. By
faith in the shed blood of Jesus Christ I am made the
righteousness of God in Christ Jesus. By the abundance of grace and the gift of righteousness I rule
and reign in this life by Christ Jesus. No weapon
formed against me shall prosper and every tongue
that rises against me in judgment, I condemn, and it
shall be proved to be in the wrong, for this is my
inheritance in Christ Jesus and my righteousness is
of God. I abide in Christ and the Word of God abides
in me, therefore I can ask what I will and God will
do it. The Father, Son and Holy Spirit live, abide
and have their being in me and I live, abide and
have my being in them, therefore we are one and I am
come into all Your fullness.

Thank You, Father, for Your love, joy, peace,
patience, goodness, kindness, gentleness, meekness,
faithfulness, and self-control. Grant me favor with
You, Heavenly Father, and with all those with whom I
come in contact today. I pray I will be a blessing
to each one. Thank You that I grow in wisdom, stature
and favor with You, God, and with man. Thank You,
that through me You evidence Your ministry in signs,

wonders, miracles and works of power through tongues, interpretation of tongues, prophecy, word of wisdom, word of knowledge, gifts of healings, working of miracles, the gift of faith, discerning of spirits, the ministry of the Word or howsoever You will. I give You all the glory for each thing You do. Thank You, Father, that You put Your robe of righteousness upon me today. You put Your separation, dedication, commitment, justification, sanctification, consecration, and holiness upon me that Your will, plan and purpose be fulfilled in the earth today for Your glory, and I give You all the glory.

Upon my feet I put the SHOES OF THE PREPARATION OF THE GOSPEL OF PEACE. I seek peace and I pursue it. As far as it lies within my power I live at peace with every person for Jesus Christ was made my Peace Offering to the Father and He is now become my Prince of Peace. Jesus Christ is my peace. Jesus gives unto me His peace, not the peace that the world gives, but His very own peace He gives unto me. I thank You, Heavenly Father, that You keep my heart and my mind in Christ Jesus because I have the peace that passes all understanding. You set my feet upon the path of peace and in the way of peace. Your peace is the arbiter of my soul. My heart is not troubled, neither is it afraid. I do not turn to the right hand or the left but I hear a word in my ear saying, "This is the way, walk ye in it." Thank You, Heavenly Father, that You turn my weaknesses into strength. The joy of the Lord is my strength. I am strong in the Lord and in the power of Your might. Thank You for joy unspeakable and full of glory. Thank You for Christ in me, the hope of Glory. Thank You for Your glory within me and a wall of fire around about me. God is my balance and my stability so that I am well able to walk in love and in the spirit.

Thank You, Lord that You have placed all things beneath Your feet and I am seated at Your right Hand in Christ Jesus. Thank You that all serpents, scorpions, dragons, lions, young lions, adders, poison, sickness, disease, infirmity, pestilence, plague, lies, judgments, accusations, insinuations, temptations, slanders, gossip, maligning of character, persecutions, inferiority and insecurity, poverty, lack, want, need, insufficiency and debt are beneath my feet.

Thank You that all DIVINATION, sorcery, witchcraft, shamanism, voodoo, hexes, vexes, curses, incantations, evil speaking, FAMILIAR spirits, passivity, sensationalism, false prophecy, magic, false signs & wonders, FAMILIAL spirits, PRIDE, arrogance, haughtiness, conceit, vanity, self-exaltation, selfishness, ego, JEALOUSY and selfish ambition, envy, all forms of malice, rebellion and stubbornness, division, strife, spite, cruelty, contention, competition, enmity, variance, emulations, BITTERNESS, anger, wrath, rage, hatred, hatred without a cause, murder, revenge, retaliation, resentment, PERVERSE spirits, lust, uncleanness, concupiscence, lasciviousness, immorality, adultery, fornication, pedophilia, bestiality, worry, WHOREDOMS, love of the world (spirit, soul or body), gluttony, dissatisfaction, DUMB AND DEAF spirits, suicide, Epilepsy, seizures, allergies, Asthma, insanity, Paranoia, Schizophrenia, blindness, dimness, Macular Degeneration, Glaucoma, Cataracts, spirit of INFIRMITY, Stroke, impotence, Heart Attacks, high blood pressure, Acid Reflux Disease, digestive problems, lameness, Cancer, weakness, Arthritis, Diabetes, AIDS, HIV, Anorexia, Bulimia, Alzheimer's, Tuberculosis, issues of blood, Swine Flu, Heart disease, all infection, HEAVINESS, rejection, depression, self-pity, sorrow, grief, despair, discouragement, deception, delusion, destruction, demons, obesity, gluttony, BONDAGE, control, manipulation, oppression, addictions, DOUBT, self-doubt, FEAR, all types of fears, fear of death, fear of man, terror, horror, torment, Heart Attacks, UNBELIEF, darkness, hardness of heart, ignorance, disobedience, rebellion, stubbornness, harassing spirits, instability and imbalance which leads to error, ERROR, contentiousness, unsubmissiveness, unteachablesness, SEDUCING spirits, hypocritical lies, enticement, false comfort, enchantments, passivity, LYING spirits, deceptions, flattery, superstitions, accusations, false prophecy, religious bondage, slander, gossip, spirits of ANTICHRIST, against God, against the people of God, the kingdom of God, the Church of God, wrong thoughts and thinking patterns, negative thinking, HERESY, deception, humanism, lawlessness, DESTRUCTION, the Accuser of the Brethren, the spirit of the Queen of Heaven, Apollyon spirits, Jezebel spirits, SUICIDE and DEATH, that which would kill, destroy, steal, or hurt: all are beneath my feet in Jesus Christ's Name.

For I AM SEATED at the right Hand of God Almighty in Christ Jesus, far above all principalities, all powers, all rulers of darkness, all wickedness in high places, all thrones, all dominions, and every name that can be named in heaven and on earth. All these things are beneath my feet in Jesus Christ's Name. Thank You, Father, that You have quickened me together with Christ and that I am seated at Your right hand in Christ Jesus until You make my enemies my footstool, that in the ages to come You might show the exceeding riches of Your grace in Your kindness toward me through Christ Jesus.

In my left hand, and over all, I take the SHIELD OF FAITH. Right now my faith is the substance of things hoped for, the evidence of things unseen. I live by faith. I walk by faith. I obtain Your promises by faith. I obtain a good report by faith. I please You, Father God, by faith. I have favor with God and man by faith. I grow by faith. I overcome the world, the flesh and the devil by faith. I walk in love by faith in Jesus Name. I am caught up in the rapture by faith in Jesus Name.

On my head I put the HELMET OF SALVATION, for I have the mind of Christ. I cast down all vain imaginations, all speculations, all reasonings, I pull down all fortresses and strongholds and every high and lofty thing that would exalt itself against the knowledge of God in Christ Jesus. I bring every thought into submission and obedience to the will of

God. Whatsoever is good, true, pure, honest, just, lovely, and excellent and of a good report; if there be any virtue, if there be any praise; I think on these things. I resist all doubt, fear, unbelief and worry. I have not a spirit of fear but I have power, love, a sound mind and right thinking. I keep asking that the God of my Lord Jesus Christ, the glorious Father will give me the spirit of wisdom and revelation so that I may know Him better. I pray also that the eyes of my heart may be enlightened in order that I may know the hope to which He has called me, the riches of His glorious inheritance in the saints, and His incomparably great power for us who believe. I pray that out of His glorious riches He may strengthen me with power through His Spirit in my inner being, so that Christ may dwell in my heart through faith. And I pray that I, being rooted and established in love, may have power, together with all the saints, to grasp how wide and long and high and deep is the love of Christ, and to know this love that surpasses knowledge — that I may be filled to the measure of all the fullness of God. I walk in the light even as God is in the Light and I have fellowship with the Body of Christ.

In my right hand I take the SWORD OF THE SPIRIT, which is the Word of God. It is sharp, quick, powerful, sharper than a two-edged sword; dividing asunder soul and spirit, joint and marrow and the very thoughts and intents of the heart of man. Thank You, Heavenly Father that You give unto me unlimited end-time discernment, revelation knowledge, understanding with insight, wisdom, prudence, discretion and the spirit of counsel. Thank You for Your spirits of Counsel and Might with me today. I do not meditate before what I shall answer, for God gives me a mouth, utterance and wisdom, which all my adversaries shall not be able to gainsay nor resist, deny or refute.

I PRAY that I may be invigorated and strengthened with all power, according to the might of God's glory, to exercise every kind of endurance and patience (perseverance and forbearance) with joy, giving thanks to the Father, Who has qualified and made me fit to share the portion which is the inheritance of the saints in the Light. I thank You, Father that the Law of the Spirit of Life in Christ Jesus has made me free from the Law of Sin and Death. I put on all graciousness and grace seasoned with salt, that I would know how to answer every man of the hope that is within me in Christ Jesus. I put on a heart of gratitude. I put on a thankful heart and all thanksgiving. I put on the spirit of Mastery. In Christ Jesus I have all eloquence and knowledge of every sort, especially in my ability to teach and my ability to preach so that I have all of the gifts of the Holy Spirit as He wills and with complete ability

to communicate the gospel for the glory of the Father God Almighty. I put on the spirit of seeing and knowing.

I PRAY that my love may abound yet more and more and extend to its fullest development in knowledge and all keen insight — that is, that my love may display itself in greater depth of acquaintance and more comprehensive discernment; so that I may surely learn to sense what is vital, and approve and prize what is excellent and of real value — recognizing the highest and the best, and distinguishing the moral differences; and that I may be untainted and pure and unerring and blameless, that — with a heart sincere and certain and unsullied — I may approach the day of Christ, not stumbling nor causing other to stumble. May I abound in and be filled with the fruits of righteousness (of right standing with God and right doing) which comes through Jesus Christ, the Anointed One, to the honor and praise of God — that His glory may be both manifested and recognized. God's love edifies me and others.

Love endures long and is patient and kind; love never is envious nor boils over with jealousy; is not boastful or vainglorious, does not display itself haughtily. It is not conceited — arrogant and inflated with pride; it is not rude or unmannerly and does not act unbecomingly. God's love in us does not insist on its own rights or its own way, for it is not self-seeking; it is not touchy or fretful or resentful; it takes no account of the evil done to it — pays no attention to a suffered wrong. It does not rejoice at injustice and unrighteousness, but rejoices when right and truth prevail. Love bears up under anything and everything that comes, is ever ready to believe the best of every person, its hopes are fadeless under all circumstances and it endures everything without weakening. Love never fails. God is LOVE. Because we have been begotten of God and are coming progressively to know and understand Him, we love others.

I PRAY I may be filled with the full, deep and clear knowledge of His will in all spiritual wisdom, in comprehensive insight into the ways and purposes of God and in understanding and discernment of spiritual things; that I may walk, live and conduct myself in a manner worthy of the Lord, fully pleasing to Him and desiring to please Him in all things, bearing fruit in every good work and steadily growing and increasing in and by the knowledge of God — with fuller, deeper and clearer insight, acquaintance and recognition. May God deem and count me worthy of my calling and His every gracious purpose of good-ness, and with power complete in every particular my work of faith. Thus may the name of our Lord Jesus Christ be glorified and become more glorious through and in me, and may I also be glorified in Him accord-ding to the grace, favor and blessing of our God and the Lord Jesus Christ, the Messiah, the Anointed One.

I HUMBLE MYSELF before You, Father God. I submit my will to Your will. I pray that Your will, plan and purpose would be fulfilled. I give my life to You, Father God, without reservation. I give all I have and all I am. I give You my past, present and my future. I abandon all to You. I give You today. I submit to the godly leadership You have placed over me. My focus is upon Christ Jesus each moment of my life. Thy will be done, Thy kingdom come on earth as it is in heaven.

FATHER, I FORGIVE ALL those who have sinned against me, if I have ought against any. I forgive all my debtors. I forgive those who have despitefully used me, offended me, rejected me and persecuted me. I forgive those who have hated me and those who have hated me without a cause. I forgive them because you have forgiven me for Christ's sake and in His Name. I release them now in the Name of Jesus Christ. I pray each one will come to know You in all Your fullness. God bless each one. I thank You that the love of God is shed abroad in each one's heart. I am not afraid of men or the sons of men. For if God be for me what can man do against me? If God be with me, what can man do to me? Jesus said, "Father forgive them for they know not what they do." I ask You to forgive my enemies Heavenly Father.

SATAN, I RESIST YOU now in the Name of the Lord Jesus Christ. I resist your kingdom, your strategies, plans and purposes. I resist your social, religious, financial and governmental systems in the earth today. I resist your fear, doubt, unbelief, accusation, lies, guilt and condemnation. I resist all that would steal, kill and destroy. I resist all sickness, disease, infirmity, pestilence and plague. I resist all poverty, lack, want, need, debt and insufficiency. Every knee must bow and every tongue must confess that Jesus Christ is Lord to the glory of God the Father.

May the God of peace Himself sanctify me through and through — that is, separate me from profane things, make me pure and wholly consecrated to God — and may my spirit and soul and body be preserved sound and complete and found blameless at the coming of our Lord Jesus Christ, the Messiah. And now, Lord, take note of their threats and grant unto me that with all boldness and freedom of utterance, courage and confidence, I may speak Your

Word by Your stretching forth Your Hand to heal and that signs, wonders and miracles take place through me by the power, authority and Name of Jesus Christ. And for me, that a door of utterance may be given unto me, that I may open my mouth boldly and may boldly and freely make known the mystery of the Gospel. I pray that I may speak fearlessly as I ought. This is the day that the Lord has made. I rejoice and am glad in it. Joy unspeakable and full of glory! Blessed be the Name of the Lord Who lives and reigns forever more!

HEAVENLY FATHER GOD, I WORSHIP YOU!!! You alone are God. You alone are the Creator of the Universe. There is no other god before You. You are worthy of all praise, honor and glory. All might, power and wisdom belong to You. You are beautiful beyond description. You are holy, pure and absolute light! By Your knowledge of Yourself, Jesus, which You understand and impart to all of mankind do You justify and make us righteous. You exist outside of time in pure light. You are Love. All glory and majesty belong to You.

I PRAY for the blessing of Abraham, the forgiveness of Joseph, the spirit and heart of David, the wisdom of Solomon, the miracles of Elijah, the judgment of Daniel and the mind of Christ to be my portion today.

Anything and everything we have need of shall come to us today according to God's will and according to His Word so that we walk in divine health, divine wealth and divine stealth. May the power of God direct us in every area of our lives.

I PRAY FOR THE PEACE OF JERUSALEM and the peace of Israel, God's chosen people. Build the walls of Jerusalem. I PRAY the salvation of Israel will come through Zion. I PRAY our country's leaders will love and support Israel.

I offer petitions, prayers, intercessions and thanksgivings on behalf of all men, for kings and all who are in positions of authority or high responsibility, that outwardly we may pass a quiet and undisturbed life and inwardly a peaceable one in all godliness and reverence and seriousness in every way. For God wishes all men to be saved and increasingly to perceive and know precisely and correctly the divine Truth: that there is only one mediator between God and men, the Man Christ Jesus.

I WALK IN THE SPIRIT giving full expression to the fruit of God's love, crucifying my flesh with its affections and lusts. I WALK IN THE LIGHT as a child of God, in all goodness and righteousness and truth, proving what is well-pleasing to the Lord, forsaking the love of money, idolatry, pride and haughtiness. I WALK IN WISDOM toward them that are without buying up the time, because the days are evil. I understand what the will of the Lord is. I WALK IN LOVE toward all men, just as Christ also loved me, an offering and a sacrifice to God. May the Lord make me increase and abound in love toward other Christians and toward all men so that my heart may be strong and fault-lessly pure, unblameable in holiness before our God and Father in the Presence of Jesus Christ. I trust You, Father, to help me learn to walk in love.

I RUN THE RACE set before me with humility, gentleness, patience and temperance, keeping my body in subjection, for the joy set before me enduring the contradiction of sinners. Father God, I give you ALL the glory!!!

CHAPTER XII

HOW DO WE WORSHIP GOD?

"What is the chief end of man?
To glorify God and to enjoy Him for ever".
The Shorter Catechism (1647)

God desires Oneness with mankind just as He has Oneness in the Trinity. This is not achieved by a gradual breaking down of the barriers in an individual's heart but conversely it is achieved by a growth in wholeness with a progression from strength to strength in Truth and Light by the grace of Jesus Christ and our individual growth in our ability to walk in love with our fellow man. We must be one within our own self in integrity to come into His Oneness. We must become beautiful with His holiness to be His sanctuary—a living Temple—built upon the knowledge of His Truth. What do we do? We offer up to Him true worship—that **new song** sung in the beauty of holiness that He Is.

His abundance of grace and the free gift of His Righteousness has given us boldness to enter into His Presence. Boldness is the result of faithfulness, wisdom, knowledge, mature love and the power of a supernatural God. What are we to know? We must know Who God is, Who Jesus Christ is, Who the Holy Spirit is, who we are, i.e. man, who our enemy is and, ultimately, we must know how to worship our Heavenly Father. What will the result be? Righteousness. The free gift of our positional righteousness in Christ Jesus shall become our experiential righteousness. It is who we ARE.

The degree of revelation and anointing an individual has is in direct relation to the accuracy of their vision and understanding of Who God is. It is crucial to have as great and as high a revelation of God as possible. A. W. Tozer said in his classic work The Knowledge of the Holy, "Worship is pure or base as one entertains high or low thoughts of God." He also said that "we tend, by some secret law of the soul, to move toward our mental image of God." What you think about God will directly affect how you live as well as how you worship. Tozer continued, "An inadequate view of God is actually idolatry. To worship God or to worship anything less than what God has revealed Himself to be is idolatry." Warped and twisted ideologies emanate from theologies that begin with man and then seek to define God. Jesus Christ did not come to teach us only who we are in relation to Himself but also who we are in relation to our Heavenly Father. The Almighty Heavenly Father God is the object of the worship of mankind. Jesus said so.

Many Christians today judge God. They only receive from God what they consider to be good. They have perceived God to be the same as sinful man. God does separate the good from evil in man. God separates the flesh nature in man from the spirit of man that is indwelt by the Holy Spirit. However we, the Church, must not separate (or judge) what we consider to be "good" from "evil" in God. God is only Good. Jesus said so. Am I preaching that you should accept sickness and disease, poverty and lack as the will of God? No, I am not! I believe mankind makes these judgments because they are unwilling to acknowledge their own sinfulness. Man is not the Creator or center of this Universe. God is Immutable. God is. There is a fine line in this truth and to receive it

310

the Body of Christ must come up higher in the Light of Who God Is. We must receive all that God is. We must seek God on His terms and study what He has revealed to man about Himself in His written Word, the Bible. If change must occur it is not God Who will change. What has God revealed to mankind about His nature and His character? Each book of the Bible reveals some hidden truth about God and how we can know Him. Six is defined as the number of man. There are sixty-six books in the Bible. God has made a way for man to know Him that is eleven times greater than man is. The true worshippers are those who are of the <u>same</u> spirit —— who worship God in the <u>same</u> spirit and the <u>same</u> truth......that Jesus has ......that God the Father has.....that the Holy Spirit has...... It is not God AND me. It is only God. God IS. Mankind has been called to Oneness with the Trinity.

Our walk with our Heavenly Father enables us to walk in Divine Life—perfect health and wholeness—and with every need met—as we walk in His Purpose being fulfilled in the earth in the now. Unafraid and unashamed, we must walk with our Heavenly Father in His Fire and Light! When God gave Moses the Ten Commandments man came to learn that God desired man to conform to attitudes and actions in relation to God, Himself, and to his fellowman. Our attitude and action toward God is to be one of total submission and surrender. We are not to have expectations of our fellow man. Neither are we to take action against our fellow man. God desires peace with man. We must walk in peace with our fellow man.

God is looking for the worship we give Him when we are absolutely alone in privacy, when we have no known need and when we have chosen His Presence rather than genuine earthly delights. When we are utterly alone and could easily choose other activities, do we ever choose God first? Is He our delight? Do we worship God when alone? God is looking for our worship in the community of the saints, in public assembly, that lifts up Jesus Christ and gives God all the glory. Do we worship God in public? Or do we care more for what the people about us think of us? God looks for true worship from the heart of an individual that stems from an overflow of life and love for God within them. God is All. He must be our All in All.

God is not combing the earth for traditional-ized ritual. That is easy to find. It is also of not much value for there is little life within it. God isn't looking for something pretty or nice. He isn't interested in how much we know <u>about</u> Him. He is not vain. He doesn't need us to tell Him what He already knows. God is looking for our fiery passion of love that is genuine and true. What gold, tried in the fire, have we purchased from Him? God combs the earth and searches for those who come from His Heart. He searches for those who are bone of His Bone, life of His Life. He looks for those who contain that which is most precious unto Him. He looks for that that is strong and clean, full of faith believing, and joy, peace and love. God longs for that which He took from within His own self to return unto Him that we might join together and become One. In Scripture the defi-nition of the noun "glory" (Greek: *doxa*) is recog-nition. The Holy Spirit is combing the earth seeking what He recognizes of God. All that is of the Holy Spirit shall be retained, strengthened and blessed. This shall bring the fulfillment of God's plan. This is the good plan of God.

Matthew 22:36-40 Master, which is the great com-mandment in the law? Jesus said unto him, Thou shalt love the Lord thy God with all thy heart, and with all thy soul, and with all thy mind. This is the first and great commandment. And the second is like unto it, Thou shalt love thy neighbour as thyself. On these two commandments hang all the law and the prophets. KJV

Mark 12:28-34 And one of the scribes came, and having heard them reasoning together, and perceiving that he had answered them well, asked him, Which is the first commandment of all? And Jesus answered him, The first of all the commandments is, **Hear, O**

Israel; The Lord our God is one Lord: And thou shalt love the Lord thy God with all thy heart, and with all thy soul, and with all thy mind, and with all thy strength: this is the first commandment. And the second is like, namely this, Thou shalt love thy neighbour as thyself. There is none other commandment greater than these. And the scribe said unto him, Well, Master, thou hast said the truth: for there is one God; and there is none other but he: And to love him with all the heart, and with all the understanding, and with all the soul, and with all the strength, and to love his neighbour as himself, is more than all whole burnt offerings and sacrifices. And when Jesus saw that he answered discreetly, he said unto him, Thou art not far from the kingdom of God. And no man after that durst ask him any question. KJV

John 13:34-35 A new commandment I give unto you, That ye love one another; as I have loved you, that ye also love one another. By this shall all men know that ye are my disciples, if ye have love one to another. KJV

To give real love to our Heavenly Father we must first receive His love. *1 John 4:10-11, 19 Herein is love, not that we loved God, but that he loved us, and sent his Son to be the propitiation for our sins. Beloved, if God so loved us, we ought also to love one another...............We love him, because he first loved us. KJV*

Worship that is in spirit and in truth comes with complete abandon and trust. We worship with the whole heart (spirit), the whole soul (mind, emotions, will), and our whole body (leaping, running, dancing, singing and rejoicing). God is everything to us! He is our Life! He is the joy and rejoicing of our hearts! Nothing in life or in eternity compares with the Presence of the Living God! Yet only God can truly bring forth real worship through us. Before this worship can come forth restoration must come to an individual. The resoration that God brings comes to a vessel that is purged of self. When one's focus

313

is firmly fixed upon Jesus Christ, the Holy Spirit and the Heavenly Father God from an obedient heart of love, God is enabled to remove self without anguish of soul. This is a positive experience in real time. We become One with God and enter into His glory.

WHAT IS SONG?

Jesus is the Song of the Father God

The Hebrew Chumash or Torah are the first five books of our Bible: Genesis, Exodus, Leviticus, Numbers, Deuteronomy. In the Commentary of Exodus 15, The Song of the Sea (what we have termed The Song of Moses) is written, "In the Torah's definition, a 'song' is a profound and unusual spiritual phenomenon; according to *Mechilta* 15:1, there were only ten songs from the beginning of Creation to the end of the Scriptural period. Even the sublime 'poetry' of David and Isaiah, as well as that of the other prophets, is not among the ten songs. What then constitutes the Torah's concept of song? In the normal course of events we fail to perceive the hand of God at work, and we often wonder how most of the daily, seemingly unrelated phenomena surrounding us could be part of a Divine, coherent plan. We see suffering and evil, and we wonder how they can be the handiwork of a Merciful God. Rarely, however—very rarely—there is a flash of insight that makes people realize how all the pieces of the puzzle fall into place. At such times, we can understand how every note, instrument, and participant in God's symphony of Creation plays its role. The result is song, for the Torah's concept of song is the condition in which all the apparently unrelated and contradictory phenomena do indeed meld into a coherent, merciful, comprehensible whole." Because we believe, we can sing. Song is a choice that is often borne of faith in the supernatural power of God. In Torah there is a Midrashic allusion to the principle that God will bring the dead back to life in Messianic times—and then they will sing God's praises once more. Is this the New Song? Is the New Song a song of salvation through faith in Christ Jesus?

We must come boldly to the throne of the Most High God, the Heavenly Father, who is all Grace and Mercy and Love itself, in the Name of the Lord Jesus Christ.

Psalm 100:1-5
Shout joyfully to the LORD, all the earth.
Serve the LORD with gladness;
Come before Him with joyful singing.
Know that the LORD Himself is God;
It is He who has made us, and not we ourselves;
We are His people and the sheep of His pasture.
Enter His gates with thanksgiving
And His courts with praise.
Give thanks to Him, bless His name.
For the LORD is good;
His lovingkindness is everlasting
And His faithfulness to all generations. NASU

1 Corinthians 14:14 "I will pray with the spirit, and I will pray with the understanding also: I will sing with the spirit, and I will sing with the under-standing also." Psalm 47:7 "God is the King of all the earth. Sing your praises with understanding." Many intercessors don't miss it in prayer but they miss it because they are not thankful and don't offer God their praises and joyful worship. They are not happy, joyful people. Our God is a God of joy and rejoicing. We are to rejoice to do His will. We enter into the very Presence of the Most High God in heaven with worship. Allow the Lord to fill you with His spirit of joy and rejoicing, with heavenly laughter, songs and dancing, running and leaping. Arise in the light and the life of Jesus Christ. Resist the tra-ditional rigidity and separation of formal religion and cut loose in the spirit of life in Christ Jesus! Be raised from the dead!

I believe that God experiences and expresses the full spectrum of life through His Person, His

315

character, mind, emotions and will. Just as there is a time and a season for everything under heaven so is there also a time and a season for all that God is, does and will do. We need not limit God. Each individual life has its own times and seasons just as the existence of God Himself has times and seasons but these are called dispensations. The Scriptures teach that God does not change. That does not mean that God is rigid and limited. He is Life! Scripture teaches us to fear God. What does that mean? There are both positive and negative sides to the word "fear". God would have us reverence Him for all power is His and He is truly great. God's Presence is not to be taken lightly. The most important thing to know about the Times and Seasons is that God uses them—uses the "change"—to bring us to Himself. Just as flour and yeast is kneaded to change the mixture into dough so we are changed and turned in the course of our lives. It is the changing which allows God entrance to work in our souls. This is how He saves us.

Lately, the Holy Spirit has been showing me an amazing thing in the Body of Christ. Music is the language of the spirit. Beautiful music is the spirit speaking to the heavens without use of the intellect and tongue. When we listen our heart and soul are lifted higher. Our mind is freed from oppression. Certain tones, whether they are brought forth from the human throat or through a musical instrument, affect us spiritually at our core. Certain sounds release the angels to battle the darkness. Myriad bondages may be broken on many levels through anointed music and worship. Just as words are containers for power; so our anointed worship of the Father changes the heavenlies, changes peoples lives, changes nations! It's a scientific fact that music powerfully affects the human brain. People are set free by music when they can not be free in any other way. Healing is ministered to the maimed through music therapy. Singing in the spirit is a very, very powerful tool of God. It is another avenue of the ministry of the Holy Spirit.

Yet, currently, in the Church world, worship is given to God using worldly songs: music, melodies and words. Religion will condemn the current styles of music in the world and yet in ten to fifty years will adopt that same melody, rhythm and style of music and call it Most Holy to God, using it to approach His Divine Presence. For example, several ancient and revered hymns of the Church are set to the music of the popular bar song of the day, i.e. Amazing Grace! Yes, the music of the church has always been the expression of our communal heart toward God. We, as the Church, no longer sing the medieval songs sung in monasteries and convents in the Middle Ages. We have also progressed beyond the "hymn sandwich" common in the last century. Certainly God's Presence has come into our places of worship when we come into an oneness of adoration of His Spirit. However, I believe God is calling the Church higher in our adoration and experience of Him.

The singers of the current styles of worship music have been, themselves, deified. Their ministries emulate the careers of worldly musicians and singers. I know most all of these worship leaders love the Lord. I know that they live for the Lord. I know they are worshipping God to the best of their ability. They reach up to God with all they know to do. I do not judge or reject them or their love of the Lord. Yet I believe God has shown me that it is all of the world as far as He is concerned. It has caused me to wonder if we are truly worshipping God, Himself, or one another? Does God listen to our worship?

Malachi 2:1-3

AND NOW, O you priests, this commandment is for you. If you will not hear and if you will not lay it to heart to give glory to My name, says the Lord of hosts, then I will send the curse upon you, and I will curse your blessings; yes, I have already turned them to curses because you do not lay it to heart. Behold, I will rebuke your seed [grain—which will prevent due harvest], and I will spread the dung from the festival offerings upon your faces, and you shall be taken away with it. AMP

Amos 5:21-24
*I hate all your show and pretense—the hypocrisy of your religious festivals and solemn assemblies. I will not accept your burnt offerings and grain offerings. I won't even notice all your choice peace offerings. Away with your hymns of praise! They are only noise to My ears. I will not listen to your music, no matter how lovely it is. Instead I want to see a mighty flood of justice, a river of **righteous living** that will never run dry. NLT*

God has given us the ability, by the power of the Holy Spirit, to sing Him songs of the Spirit, i.e. singing in tongues as the Holy Spirit Himself leads us, allowing the Holy Spirit to use instruments or we, ourselves, as instruments, in His orchestra. This is pleasing to God as a soothing aroma. However, it is not practiced in the Church of America as a whole. I do not know of many or any places in the world where it is practiced. I do not know of any place in the world where the Holy Spirit has been set free to develop true spiritual worship of God through music, song and dance; in freedom and in love. Nowhere is this spiritual worship practiced freely. Nowhere has it been developed by the Holy Spirit as a soothing aroma to the Heavenly Father. How shameful for we, who call ourselves Christians, to oppress the true worship of God! Who will allow the Holy Spirit freedom to worship the Father? Some teach that singing in the spirit is only the soul of man comforting itself but in reality this gift of God is far, far greater. Be free Church! Worship God in spirit and in truth!

God wants His Bride to come up higher. In recent years prophets of God have said that in this last hour the darkness will become darker and the light will become brighter. Separation between God's People and the people of the world system will become greater. God desires true spiritual worship from the realm He has created not from the realm of the world system. How dare we compromise our worship of the Most Holy God with the ways of the world! God desires our worship to be the free, alive worship of the Holy Spirit. He desires worship initiated and instigated by the Holy Spirit—not old worldly songs or songs birthed in the same style as the world's songs. If Lucifer was the leader of the heavenly worship of God before he lost his place in heaven, why are we using the same styles he currently uses in his kingdom of the world? Remember, he was cast out of heaven. He lost his job because his heart and his motives were not right. Furthermore, if Lucifer, a created cherubim led worship, how much better would worship be if a member of the Godhead led it? Why do we not allow the Holy Spirit to lead the worship of the Father? God does not allow our salvation to be brought about by angels or by men. Why would He allow His worship to be led by angels or men? The Holy Spirit knows what will please the Father better than anyone else ever could. I believe He desires to work this true worship—worship in Spirit and in truth—through the Bride of Christ for the glory of the Father. I believe it is this worship that shall usher in the true revival of the last hour.

Song 2:10-13 My beloved spake, and said unto me, Rise up, my love, my fair one, and come away. For, lo, the winter is past, the rain is over and gone; the flowers appear on the earth; the time of the singing of birds is come, and the voice of the turtle is heard in our land; the fig tree putteth forth her green figs, and the vines with the tender grape give a good smell. Arise, my love, my fair one, and come away. KJV

Let's come up higher Church! Let's come up higher!!! Let us no longer look at man in worship, for worship or to worship. Let us affix our spiritual eyes on our Most High Heavenly Father and release

319

the Holy Spirit in freedom to worship Him! Let us allow the Holy Spirit to use the Body of Christ as holy instruments of worship in adoration. The Holy Spirit is the expression of God in the earth today. Do you not think He knows what real worship is? I believe He does. I believe the Holy Spirit has something entirely new and wonderful to work through us, bringing us up higher in realms of God's glory, to express our love to our Heavenly Father.

Song 2:4; 7:13 He brought me to the banqueting house, and his banner over me was love. . . . . The mandrakes give a smell, and at our gates are all manner of pleasant fruits, new and old, which I have laid up for thee, O my beloved. KJV

In August 1977 the Lord God gave me an open vision of the nations of the earth. It was the last night of Kenneth E. Hagin's Campmeeting in Tulsa, Oklahoma. Kenneth Hagin stood on the platform and said that God was pouring out gifts unto men that night. I stood on a folding chair in an upper level of the Convention Center in Tulsa, Oklahoma, as a 25 year-old young woman and asked God to use my life and give me His gift. A fiery meteor fell from heaven into the top of my head and I began to sing in tongues operatically. Before that I sounded like a frog in a bucket! People were slain in the spirit in a ten foot diameter around me. In an open, full-color vision, I saw masses of people in various nations of the earth in darkness, huddled together, longing for God, with the names of the nations above them in lights. I saw the people of the nations of the earth, standing in the darkness—their hearts hungry, longing for God. Since that time I sing in the spirit very frequently. Many portions of Scripture are pertinent to this practice.

Psalms 149

*PRAISE THE Lord! Sing to the Lord a **new song**, praise Him in the assembly of His saints! Let Israel rejoice in Him, their Maker; let Zion's children* *triumph and be joyful in their King! Let them praise His name in chorus and choir and with the [single or group] dance; let them sing praises to Him with the tambourine and lyre! For the Lord takes pleasure in His people; He will beautify the humble with salvation and adorn the wretched with victory. Let the saints be joyful in the glory and beauty [which God confers upon them]; let them **sing for joy** upon their beds. Let **the high praises of God** be in their throats and a two-edged sword in their hands, to wreak vengeance upon the nations and chastisement upon the peoples, to bind their kings with chains, and their nobles with fetters of iron, to execute upon them the judgment written. He [the Lord] is the honor of all His saints. Praise the Lord! (Hallelujah!) AMP*

The Holy Spirit may choose to express Himself in any myriad of ways. I have personally experienced the Spirit of the Lord leading a congregation into absolute silence for an extended period of time as He, Himself, ministered to the people. This is very powerful! Actually I have experienced this several times. Once a visiting lady minister, Rev. Rosalind Rinker, led the congregation into this. Other times, in different congregations, the Holy Spirit brought this to pass sovereignly. This is the way the Quakers of old used to worship. Therefore, let us let go of fear and allow the Lord to change His Body from being a mass of spectators who observe a few performers, to being His instruments of worship, that God be glorified! Many in the Body of Christ have experienced holy laughter poured out upon the entire assembly. Great healing has come to the Body of Christ through His joy.

God has risen up highly anointed soloists who often lead the way into His Presence. There is a time and a place for the highly anointed soloist but the masses of lay people in the Church need to be set free to develop their own abilities to worship their Heavenly Father. This is not about observing one another or being spectators of one another. Rather it is about spiritual freedom and the holiness of

God's Presence. Three choruses and a hymn just don't cut it. God desires His Bride to sing Him a new song! Are you a part of His Bride?

One way to begin spiritual worship is by singing in the spirit, or tongues, and allowing the Holy Spirit to orchestrate the entire assemblage. He will do a better job than any one person or persons could. Whether He chooses to use individual people as His instruments or musical instruments or both, He will direct proceedings. He may choose to use the entire congregation. It is imperative that each singer <u>and</u> each instrument personally follow the leadership of the Holy Spirit and not a common tune. There can only be ONE orchestra leader and that leader must be God!

Where will all this lead? I believe it will lead to Oneness with the Trinity. I imagine the very thought of all this will be quite frightening to those bound by religion who only feel secure and peaceful when they are in control of the situation. Their focus on the ways of tradition has them bound. Focusing on the "way" worship is conducted takes the focus off of **Who** is being worshipped. The focus should not be on we, the worshippers, or on how we worship. We don't worship people — we worship God. Our focus must be on God, Who is so great! Yes, our worship must <u>result</u> in lives of integrity that meter out true justice, judgment and righteousness. However, Peter walked on the water and it's time for the Body of Christ to get out of the boat and start walking! We must grow in our ability to love God and to be loved by Him. Love is the way believers experience eternity within time. Worship is pivotal to our relationship with our Heavenly Father. The end result or point of our worship is to know God and to be One with Him.

It is of the utmost importance that all people know and understand that this Oneness which we enter into with God does not mean that we, ourselves, become the Most High God. There is only One God and we, as individuals, are not Him. *1 Corinthians 8:4c-6* **...there is none other God but one.** *For though there be that are called gods, whether in heaven or in* *earth, (as there be gods many, and lords many,) But to us there is but* **one God,** *the Father, of whom are all things, and we* **in** *him; and one Lord Jesus Christ, by whom are all things, and we* **by** *him. Ephesians 4:5-6 One Lord, one faith, one baptism, One God and Father of all, who is* **above** *all, and* **through** *all, and* **in** *you all. Colossians 1:16-17 For by him were all things created, that are in heaven, and that are in earth, visible and invisible, whether they be thrones, or dominions, or principalities, or powers: all things were created* **by** *him, and* **for** *him: And he is* **before** *all things, and* **by** *him all things consist. KJV* The exercise of God's power does not mean that we become God. God's Oneness means that we enter into His works. This truth is crucial. We must not allow satan to so obsess us with the power of God that we lose our self. Yes, the fleshly nature or self nature must "die" in this world but God, Himself, shall resurrect our true self. This true self must be maintained with boundaries. We must not allow our border lines of personal identity to be erased. We are created beings. We have a beginning. Though we come forth from God's Heart and return to His Heart, yet we, individually, are not the totality of God. This truth is so crucial! This fine line must not be crossed. *Deuteronomy 6:4-5 Hear, O Israel: the Lord our* **God is one Lord [the only Lord].** *And you shall love the Lord your God with all your [mind and] heart and with your entire being and with all your might. AMP* We must never, never allow anyone to give us His worship. The glory must be given to God, not to man. I AM NOT GOD! YOU ARE NOT GOD! Being One with God and entering into His power does not mean that we are Omnipotent. In Revelation 22, the last chapter of the last book of the Bible, the Apostle John, caught up into the very throne of God, received the revelation of Jesus Christ to the Church of the Living God. In verses 8 and 9 is a great example of our above discussed Oneness with the Father: *Revelation 22:8-9 And I, John, am he who heard and witnessed these things. And when I heard and saw them, I fell*

323

glorified human

prostrate before the feet of the messenger (angel) who showed them to me, to worship him. But he said to me, Refrain! [You must not do that!] I am [only] a fellow servant along with yourself and with your brethren the prophets and with those who are mindful of and practice [the truths contained in] the messages of this book. **Worship God!**

Entering into Oneness with God via worship in spirit and in truth by the **new song** is to experience the Presence of God, Himself. What do we experience? We experience His righteousness, His faithfulness, His salvation, His lovingkindness and His truth. His lovingkindness and His truth continually preserve us. In this experience His Name is as Perfume Poured Forth. See John 12, esp. verse 3: *John 12:1-8 Then Jesus six days before the Passover came to Bethany, where Lazarus was which had been dead, whom he raised from the dead. There they made him a supper; and Martha served: but Lazarus was one of them that sat at the table with him. Mary took a pound of ointment of pure liquid nard [a rare perfume] that was very expensive, and she poured it on Jesus' feet and wiped them with her hair. And the whole house was filled with the fragrance of the perfume. Then saith one of his disciples, Judas Iscariot, Simon's son, which should betray him, Why was not this ointment sold for three hundred pence, and given to the poor? This he said, not that he cared for the poor; but because he was a thief, and had the bag, and bare what was put therein. Then said Jesus, Let her alone: against the day of my burying hath she kept this. For the poor always ye have with you; but me ye have not always. Matthew 26:6-13 Now when Jesus was in Bethany, in the house of Simon the leper, there came unto him a woman having an alabaster box of very precious ointment, and poured it on his head, as he sat at meat. But when his disciples saw it, they had indignation, saying, To what purpose is this waste? For this ointment might have been sold for much, and given*

*to the poor. When Jesus understood it, he said unto
them, Why trouble ye the woman? for she hath wrought
a good work upon me. For ye have the poor always
with you; but me ye have not always. For in that
she hath poured this ointment on my body, she did
it for my burial. Verily I say unto you, Wheresoever
this gospel shall be preached in the whole world,
there shall also this, that this woman hath done, be
told for a memorial of her. Mark 14:3-9 And being
in Bethany in the house of Simon the leper, as he
sat at meat, there came a woman having an alabaster
box of ointment of spikenard very precious; and she
brake the box, and poured it on his head. And there
were some that had indignation within themselves,
and said, Why was this waste of the ointment made?
For it might have been sold for more than three hundred pence, and have been given to the poor. And
they murmured against her. And Jesus said, Let her
alone; why trouble ye her? she hath wrought a good
work on me. For ye have the poor with you always, and
whensoever ye will ye may do them good: but me ye
have not always. She hath done what she could: she
is come aforehand to anoint my body to the burying.
Verily I say unto you, Wheresoever this gospel shall
be preached throughout the whole world, this also
that she hath done shall be spoken of for a memorial of her. KJV* He is Flowing & Purified Oil; that
is, oil that has been poured from vessel to vessel.
It is this pouring forth from vessel to vessel that
change the taste and the scent and causes one to be
armed. Whatever touched the holy anointing oil of
the sanctuary became holy. It was this oil that sanctified the altar, the High Priest and the offerings
upon the altar. This "oil" is mentioned 193 times
in Scripture. It is the crown upon, the oil of joy,
the garment of praise and the unity of the brethren.
This is the path of the true love of God. In the
Song of Songs there is much about various beautiful
scents and tastes. Myrrh, Spikenard, and Camphire
are associated with the Father, the Holy Spirit and
with Jesus at His birth and death. Strong's OT:1736

duwday (doo-dah'-ee); a basket; also the mandrake (as an aphrodisiac): KJV—basket, mandrake. *Song 7:13 The mandrakes send out their fragrance, and at our door is every delicacy, both new and old, that I have stored up for you, my lover. NIV* We experience His scents and tastes spirit, soul and body when we enter into His Oneness. Oneness with God necessitates operation of supernatural power, love, joy, good and beauty. It is the ability to rise above religion into the true love of God and worship Him. It is the supernatural realm of the passionate and fiery love of God where there is perfect peace and calm. Again, LOVE, not power, is the way believers experience eternity within time.

2 Corinthians 2:14-17 But thanks be to God, Who in Christ always leads us in triumph [as trophies of Christ's victory] and through us spreads and makes evident the <u>fragrance of the knowledge</u> of God everywhere, for <u>we are the sweet fragrance of Christ</u> [which exhales] unto God, [discernible alike] among those who are being saved and among those who are perishing: To the latter it is an aroma [wafted] from death to death [a fatal odor, the smell of doom]; to the former it is an aroma from life to life [a vital fragrance, living and fresh]. And who is qualified (fit and sufficient) for these things? [Who is able for such a ministry? We?] For we are not, like so many, [like hucksters making a trade of] peddling God's Word [shortchanging and adulterating the divine message]; but like [men] of sincerity and the purest motive, as [commissioned and sent] by God, we speak [His message] in Christ (the Messiah), in the [very] sight and presence of God. AMP

The English word oil is translated from the Hebrew word *shemen*, which is taken from the Hebrew root word *shaman* (Strong's 8080). By definition this means grease, especially liquid as from the olive, often perfumed; richness, anointing, fruitful, to shine, to wax fat. It is very interesting to note that in animistic societies the position of the shaman was that of the witch doctor. That person was known as

one able to contact good and evil spirits; who operated in supernatural power and one who met needs.

In Scripture who is it that sings the **new song**
unto God? Scripture teaches in Revelation 14:4, 5; 2
Corinthians 11:2, 3 that the virgins are those who
have been given the right to be with Jesus Christ
continually. Scripturally, what is a virgin? It is
a person who has not been defiled by the systems of
religion in the world. That defilement would prevent
the ability to love God properly. As is written in
previous chapters, the Lying Strongman rules all
spirits of religion, guile, etc.

Israel, Zion's children, God's people, the righteous, the man that trusts God and delights to do
His will, those in the pit and the miry clay, the
kindreds of the peoples, all the earth, King David,
those that go down to the sea, the inhabitants of the
isles, the inhabitants of the rock, the four beasts,
the twenty-four elders, and the hundred forty-four
thousand who have the Father's name on their fore-
heads sing a new song unto God. I'm sure you qualify
and fit in there somewhere if you have put away all
systems of religion.

Again, it is important to note that we, ourselves,
are not all there is. God is the Living God. Our worship is to Him not to our own self. Although we are
in Him and One with Him we are not Him. Confusion on
this point is a sure path to destruction.

The Apostle Paul wrote that unbelievers were to
be ministered to with the "tongues of the Spirit" as
a sign and the Church was to be ministered to with
prophecy for their understanding. What does it mean
to be a worshipping people? Why did the Holy Spirit
inspire the Apostle Paul to write in three different
letters to worship God with spiritual songs?

*Ephesians 5:18-21 And be not drunk with wine,
wherein is excess; but be filled with the Spirit;*
speaking to yourselves *in psalms and hymns and spiritual songs, singing and making melody in your heart
to the Lord; giving thanks always for all things unto
God and the Father in the name of our Lord Jesus*

327

Christ; submitting yourselves one to another in the fear of God. KJV

*Colossians 3:16-17 Let the word of Christ dwell in you richly in all wisdom; **teaching and admonishing one another** in psalms and hymns and spiritual songs, singing with grace in your hearts to the Lord. And whatsoever ye do in word or deed, do all in the name of the Lord Jesus, giving thanks to God and the Father by him. KJV*

1 Corinthians 14:15 Then what am I to do? I will pray with my spirit [by the Holy Spirit that is within me], but I will also pray [intelligently] with my mind and understanding; I will sing with my spirit [by the Holy Spirit that is within me], but I will sing [intelligently] with my mind and understanding also. AMP

"For worship is to be truly holy and profound and of Me, saith the Lord, it must be initiated, directed, led and consummated by My Holy Spirit. For, My daughter, can true worship of a God Who is Spirit be performed by the natural man? Could I walk in the Garden of Eden with Adam and Eve after the Fall? No. I could only walk with them and fellowship with them when they were indwelt by My Holy Spirit. So it is today. Those who worship Me must worship Me in spirit and in truth. But so many of My children worship Me in their flesh. Shall I show you what it is like? It is like a mother whose small child has yet to learn to walk or to talk and that child tries to communicate its love verbally. There is no fellowship. There is no communication. There is only the compassion, the mercy, the grace of the mother upon

the child. The child is unable to effectively communicate its love to its mother. But when that child grows up, when that child becomes a man and takes a wife then that man is fully able to communicate his love for his wife—to come in to her and become one with her—to fellowship totally with her on every level. That is how it will be with My Bride. I will come in to her by My Holy Spirit and I shall become One with her and fellowship on every level.

First, however, I must purify My Body. First, before it is ready to love I must cause it to be fully mature and I must cleanse it of every fleshly impurity of every demonic infection and all else that causes a stain. Then, My daughter, I must cause her to be so filled with My Spirit that she will allow My Spirit to worship Me through her. For it is only My Holy Spirit that can worship Me. Only the holy can fellowship with an Holy God. Only the Holy Spirit can fellowship with an Holy Father. Only an holy, sanctified "Man" can approach an Holy God and live. "Man" = the collective consummation of all mankind. That is what I am about. That is My purpose in this earth. That is My goal. To have Man that I might truly love and that might love Me in spirit and in truth throughout eternity."

Therefore, let us, as God's true children, rise up and walk in the truths that have been lost from the beginning that our generation may know God as the first generation of Christians knew Him. Let us sing Him a **new song** of love from our heart. Whether in private worship or in public worship, let us be free in His freedom. Let us allow His Free Spirit (*ruwach*) to move through us. *Psalms 51:12 Restore unto me the joy of thy salvation; and uphold me with thy free spirit. KJV* As we grow in the grace and the knowledge of Jesus Christ with regard to this truly spiritual worship, signs and wonders and miracles shall occur. I believe this is one avenue that God can use that ALL shall be healed. With all my heart I believe this will lead us, as a worshipping people, into realms of glory where many shall experience true Oneness with the Trinity of God!!!

Many ministers have prophesied of the last, great revival to come forth before the return of the Lord, the second Coming of the Lord Jesus Christ to this earth. I believe God has spoken to me that this shall be a revival of Love—God's Love—upon this earth through the Body of Christ that will bring forth His Glory. This shall be the mightiest outpouring of the Holy Spirit that has ever been on earth. To facilitate this revival there must be true worship of God. Worship of God in spirit and in truth shall be accomplished by the Holy Spirit through sanctified, purified vessels of honor as they lift up to the Father God the **New Song** of the Holy Spirit. *Isaiah 30:29 Ye shall have a song, as in the night when a holy solemnity is kept; and gladness of heart, as when one goeth with a pipe to come into the mountain of the LORD, to the mighty One of Israel. KJV*

God's glory shall cover the earth as the waters cover the sea. God shall be glorified. Will He be glorified through you?

FOR A SHARE IN THE WORK OF REDEMPTION

Walter Rauschenbusch
1910

O God, thou great Redeemer of mankind, our hearts are tender in the thought of thee, for in all the afflictions of our race thou hast been afflicted, and in the sufferings of thy people it was thy body that was crucified. Thou hast been wounded by our transgressions and bruised by our iniquities, and all our sins are laid at last on thee. Amid the groaning of creation we behold thy spirit in travail till the sons of God shall be born in freedom and holiness.

We pray thee, O Lord, for the graces of a pure and holy life that we may no longer add to the dark weight of the world's sin that is laid upon thee, but may share with thee in thy redemptive work. As we have thirsted with evil passions to the destruction of men, do thou fill us now with hunger and thirst for justice that we may bear glad tidings to the poor and set at liberty all who are in the prison-house of want and sin.

Lay thy Spirit upon us and inspire us with a passion of Christlike love that we may join our lives to the weak and oppressed and may strengthen their cause by bearing their sorrows. And if the evil that is threatened turns to smite us and if we must learn the dark malignity of sinful power, comfort us by the thought that thus we are bearing in our body to marks of Jesus, and that only those who share in his free sacrifice shall feel the plentitude of thy life. Help us in patience to carry forward the eternal cross of thy Christ, counting it joy if we, too, are sown as grains of wheat in the furrows of the world, for only by the agony of the righteous comes redemption.

THE PRAYER OF INTERCESSION FOR THE LOST

Dear Heavenly Father,

The Lord Jesus Christ and the Holy Spirit live to intercede for Your people and I ask You that You would draw me into this intercession by the leading of the Holy Spirit. I ask You for a vision of hell and a revelation of eternity. I ask You to birth within me a spirit of intercession. I ask You to give me Your gift of compassion and a humble and contrite spirit. Please, Heavenly Father, open to me the hearts for whom I intercede.

It is my earnest prayer that Your kingdom would destroy the kingdom of satan in _____'s life by Your working through me to intercept the strategy of the enemy and exchanging it with Your will for his/her life. I release the angels of God to cover and protect _____ and I plead the shed blood of Jesus Christ over _____. In faith I place a hedge of protection around him/her and I claim him/her for the kingdom of God in Jesus Christ's Name.

I pray the powers of darkness would be removed from _____'s life. I command the Hand of the Lord Jesus Christ to remove the power of the spirit of Antichrist, the power systems of Behemoth and Leviathan and the spirit of the Queen of heaven from

blinding _____'s life and mind and ensnaring
him/her with the enemy's hierarchy of religious,
social, economic and political deception. I come
against and bind the power of satan without or outside of _____'s life and I put the blood of Jesus
Christ between satan and _____. I break the
power of the enemy to bring accusations, insinuations and temptations against _____.

_____ is loosed into the light of the gospel
of the glory of Christ Jesus, my Lord. I pray that
he/she will come from the darkness to the light in
every area of his/her life. I present _____ to
You today.

Heavenly Father, please grant unto me revelation knowledge and insight with understanding into
any strongmen spirits at work in _____'s life.
Thank You that out of the abundance of the heart
the mouth speaks. Enable me to stand in the gap and
to identify all generational sins and iniquities of
_____'s forefathers and them, themselves, in
order that he/she would be cleansed and set free of
all sins from his/her past.

I pray that _____ would be drawn by Your
Love, Heavenly Father, and I present him/her to
You right now. I command the Hand of the Lord Jesus
Christ to send laborers into his/her path today. Send
laborers that are born again, filled with Your Holy
Spirit and on fire with the love of God. Surround
him/her with these laborers on a daily basis so that
wherever he/she may go he/she will be confronted with
Your Love and Your power. Cause him/her to know that
this is a supernatural experience. I pray that Jesus
Christ will be lifted up for _____ to see Him.
I pray that _____ will experience miracles, signs
and wonders to confirm Your Word and that he/she will
have dreams and visions that originate in You.

O Father, I ask You to separate water from water
in _____'s heart, that he/she will be separated
and set apart from evil influences and associations
unto that which is of You. I pray that You will cause
_____ to be hungry and thirsty for the Holy Spirit

and the Word of God and all things genuine in God; that the gospel, the Word, which is preached, will be planted deep into the soil of _____'s heart.

Holy Spirit I ask You to convict _____ of sin, righteousness and the judgment to come. Please lead _____ into repentance from dead works and grant him/her faith toward God. I pray that _____ would believe in Jesus Christ and that he/she would give an outward public confession of faith that results in his/her salvation. I pray that when _____ accepts Jesus Christ as his/her Savior that he/she will utterly surrender to Him as Leader and Lord and Master of every portion of his/her being. I pray that having received Christ _____ will also receive strong assurance of his/her salvation resulting in great confidence against the wiles and strategies of the evil one.

Please draw _____ into the exact local church where You desire him/her to attend and plant him/her deep into the house of God. Grant _____ favor with his/her fellow heirs of salvation and with Your servants, the ministry gifts You would use to perfect him/her. Raise up a standard of righteousness within _____, a plumb line of the truth that will enable him/her to make decisions and give him/her direction. Give _____ a deep and abiding love of Your truth that will never leave him/her. Cause him/her to be a worker within the Body of Christ that will bring You glory. I command the Hand of the Lord Jesus Christ to loose life, vitality and the activity of God into the spirit of _____ and to drive back death, stagnation and corruption from him/her.

Heavenly Father, I pray that _____ will daily hunger and thirst for righteousness—for Your Word and Your Holy Spirit. Grant unto him/her a strong desire to obey You and to receive the sacrament of baptism in water. Cause _____ to enter into the kingdom of God in the realm of the Spirit. I pray that he/she is filled with the Holy Spirit with the evidence of speaking in tongues and that he/she would be baptized with the presence of the Father and into Your Love.

With the Holy Spirit's gifts enable me to identify and bind all evil spirits to be removed from within _____'s life. I pray for the application of Your anointing that would remove the yoke of bondage in every area of _____'s life. Seal _____ with the Holy Spirit unto all Your fullness authorizing _____ to act in Your divine power in all the acts and duties of the office You have called him/her to. Cause the evidence of Your acceptance of _____ to themselves and to others. I pray _____ would be preserved by the Holy Spirit unto eternal life. Praise You, Father God that you have provided for _____'s health and life by the stripes that Jesus bore on His back, the nails in His hands and feet, the spear in His side and the crown of thorns upon his brow at Calvary—the law of the spirit of life in Christ Jesus. Give _____ a revelation of Your principles of tithing, offerings, alms and vows and set him/her free of the world's system of economics. I pray that _____ would come into the ways of Your kingdom and Your true prosperity. I pray that _____ will be fruitful and that he/she will increase. Heavenly Father, give _____ Your blessing. Grant that he/she will hear Your Voice and obey You.

Cause _____ to increase in the knowledge of You, Father God, the Lord Jesus Christ and the Holy Spirit and Your righteousness. I pray that You would bless _____. Increase and loose Your knowledge and the power of the Holy Spirit over all that are seeking You. I pray for _____'s stability that he/she may avoid error and its inevitable destruction. I ask You to grant him/her understanding of Your ways, truths, laws and the principles of Your Word. I pray that he/she will hear Your Voice and that with intelligent, thoughtful, strategic planning he/she will build Your kingdom and will fulfill Your will, plans and purposes.

Open the eyes of _____'s understanding with insight and enlightenment. Grant _____ the revelation of who he/she is in Christ Jesus. Give him/her understanding with insight into the Mystery of Godliness, Christ in him/her the hope of glory. You are the Most High God. Grant that Your commanding spirits will rest upon _____. I pray that he/she will come into the fullness of both the gifts and the fruit of the Holy Spirit. I pray that _____ will receive Your vision for his/her life and the hope of Your calling upon him/her—that You would grant unto him/her the faith to receive his/her full inheritance in Christ Jesus, as a joint-heir who walks as Your son/daughter. Raise him/her up in Your image to fulfill Your purposes and to bring Your kingdom to pass in the earth. Work Your character, righteousness and the mind of Christ in _____'s life. Just as You chose _____ before the beginning of the foundation of the world as _____ in the Body of Christ, so let him/her come into the fullness of Your calling.

Heavenly Father, I thank You for causing _____ to be sanctified, justified, and full of Your grace and truth. Grant _____ an holy character, that he/she would live a life of unreserved heart-union with Christ enthroned within, through whose power working through the Holy Spirit, he/she would be enabled to "put off the old man" and "put on the new man", which is the holiness You wish him/her to have. I ask that You would work in _____ the holiness of character being the life of Christ reproduced in him/her by the mighty inworking of the Holy Trinity. Let Your holiness or sanctification, the Christ-life or "new man" be built upon the ruins of the "old man" in _____'s life.

Thank You Father, for giving _____ the power to overcome all the power of the enemy. I pray that _____ will learn Your techniques of spiritual warfare. Enable him/her to assume Your authority over satan and his hierarchy that the blood of Christ provides. I pray that he/she would be counted worthy to attain to the Bride of Christ, possessing all the jewels You have provided.

Enable _____ to give himself/herself wholly to You, to learn to live the Spirit-filled life, to make Christ the King of his/her heart; to live the crucified life, until he/she is conformed to the death of Christ (utterly denying self), and thus have every element in his/her nature that is opposed to You entirely removed from him/her, so that he/she may be habitually "filled unto all the fullness of God". Give him/her the victory in every area of his/her life. Enable him/her to receive Your best. Help _____ to live the Christ-filled life, to perpetuate it to its close and lead him/her to grow up into Christ in all things and reach the measure of the stature of Your fullness.

As the student is no greater than the teacher so _____ must come to the knowledge of the Most High by following in the footsteps of Jesus Christ. Just as He walked in the supernatural realm of the Holy Spirit and Your Glory, behind the veil while yet in the flesh so may _____ follow Christ's leading. Holy Spirit teach _____ to be thankful, grateful and full of praises to the Father. Create the fruit of his/her lips. Lead _____ to praise with upraised arms, words of rejoicing, and shouts of victory, dancing and leaping before You in the spirit of Liberty, while wearing Your garments of praise. Bring _____ into true worship and adoration before Your throne and the cross of Christ.

Father, give _____ insight with understanding of some of the eternal things which You have prepared for him/her. Grant him/her visions of Your heavenly rewards and Your heavenly kingdom and give him/her dreams of eternal things. Help him/her to press on towards the mark of the high calling which You have for him/her in Christ Jesus!

IN THE NAME OF JESUS CHRIST I PRAY

THE PRAYER OF SALVATION

*F*ather God, I come to you in the Name of the Lord Jesus Christ. I believe You are the Living God. You are Love. You are a Jealous God. I repent of sin. I ask You to forgive me of my transgressions and my iniquities. You are God. I am not. I surrender and submit to Your will.

Lord Jesus Christ, I believe You were born of a virgin, You suffered under Pontius Pilate, You were crucified, You died and were buried. You descended into hell. I believe that You, Lord Jesus Christ, were raised from the dead on the third day and that You are alive right now. You are seated at the right hand of the Father. I ask You to come into my heart, Jesus. Save me from sin. I receive by faith Your work on the Cross of Calvary. You are my substitutionary Lamb. Please cover me with Your shed blood. Deliver me of my selfish flesh nature and conform me to Your image. If You can do anything with my life, take it and use it for the Father's glory and the Kingdom of God. Put me where You have created me to be in the Body of Christ.

Father God and Lord Jesus Christ, fill me with the Holy Spirit with the evidence of speaking in tongues. Holy Spirit fill me with Your fruit and conform me to the character of the Lord Jesus Christ. Lord Jesus Christ and Holy Spirit baptize me with the Presence and the Love of the Father God. I give my life to You. Save me spirit, soul and body that I may also obtain the salvation which is in Christ Jesus with eternal glory.

Holy Spirit, please pray through me the will of the Father as I don't know what or how to pray as I ought to. As my Teacher, instruct me in the Word and the ways of God.

IN THE NAME OF JESUS CHRIST I PRAY. AMEN.

(Please pray this OUT LOUD in faith.)